Achieving Human Rights

D0222696

Richard Falk once again captures our attention with a nuanced analysis of what we need to do—at the personal level as well as state actions—to refocus our pursuit of human rights in a post-9/11 world. From democratic global governance to the costs of the Iraq War, the preeminent role of the United States in the world order to the role of individual citizens of a globalized world, Falk stresses the moral urgency of achieving human rights. In elegant simplicity, this book places the priority of such an ethos in the personal decisions we make in our human interactions, not just the activities of government institutions and non-governmental organizations. Falk masterly weaves together such topics as the Iraq War, U.S. human rights practices and abuses, humanitarian intervention, the rule of law, responses to terrorism, genocide, the Pinochet trial, information technology, and many other topics to create a moral tapestry of world order with human rights at the center.

Richard Falk is Albert G. Milbank Professor Emeritus of International Law at Princeton University. He is currently Visiting Distinguished Professor of Global and International Studies at the University of California, Santa Barbara.

Achieving
Human Rights

Richard Falk

Routledge
Taylor & Francis Group

NEW YORK AND LONDON

First published 2009
by Routledge
270 Madison Ave, New York, NY 10016

Simultaneously published in the UK
by Routledge
2 Park Square, Milton Park, Abingdon, Oxon OX14 4RN

Routledge is an imprint of the Taylor & Francis Group, an informa business

© 2009 Taylor & Francis

Typeset in Goudy by
Swales & Willis Ltd, Exeter, Devon
Printed and bound in the United States of America on acid-free paper by
Sheridan Books, Inc

Library of Congress Cataloging in Publication Data
Falk, Richard
Achieving human rights/Richard Falk.
p. cm.
Includes bibliographical references and index.
1. Human rights. I. Title.
JC585.F34 2008
323–dc22   2008018558

ISBN10: 0–415–99015–7 (hbk)
ISBN10: 0–415–99016–5 (pbk)
ISBN10: 0–203–88910–X (ebk)

ISBN13: 978–0–415–99015–8 (hbk)
ISBN13: 978–0–415–99016–5 (pbk)
ISBN13: 978–0–203–88910–7 (ebk)

For Zeynep, Huyen, and Juliet,
a Private Global Village!

Contents

Contents

Preface

In important respects this volume is a sequel to *Human Rights Horizons*, published by Routledge in the year 2000. The present volume attempts to provide a coherent account of the struggles to achieve human rights in the early years of the twenty-first century. It is written from the perspective of an American living in the United States who is critical of many of the overseas policies pursued by the U.S. government, especially in response to the 9/11 attacks. These policies have tended to divert some positive tendencies with respect to human rights that had been emerging during the 1990s, hopefully not permanently.

As is always the case, I have been influenced and helped by the work of friends and colleagues, as well as by the challenges associated with teaching courses on international human rights. Among many colleagues and friends whose influence has been most notable in my immediate environment of Santa Barbara I would mention Elisabeth Weber, Lisa Hajjar, Vicki Riskin, David Rintels, Rich Appelbaum, David Krieger, and, of course, Hilal Elver.

In this period I have continued to collaborate with Burns Weston, Hilary Charlesworth, and Andrew Strauss on a significantly revised fourth edition of *International Law and World Order*, a law course book that adopts a normative outlook and is heavily influenced by the expanding agenda of human rights. Perhaps my most important collaborative experience in recent years has been with Andrew Strauss, who has emerged as a world leader in the campaign to establish a world parliament, an important step in the struggle to democratize the norms, procedures, and institutions of global governance.

In recent years, my main teaching has been as a visiting professor in the Global and International Studies Program of the University of California at Santa Barbara. I have enjoyed the friendship and support of those who run this academic program that is so popular with UCSB students, especially Giles Gunn, its current director. I also had the experience in 2007 of teaching a course at the Law School of UCLA, where I had the benefit of impressive students and a most stimulating faculty.

An influential dimension of my life since 1995 has been summers spent in Turkey each year. The extraordinary political developments in Turkey have been fascinating to experience directly, but disturbing because of the extent to which they have been misconstrued from within and without. I have felt challenged to interpret this evolving Turkish political reality as best I could, and have enjoyed a supportive relationship with the important Turkish daily newspaper *Zaman*. Perhaps more than any other country in the Middle East, Turkey has been a crucible for contending visions of constitutionalism, especially for exposing the deep tensions that exist as between different versions of secularism and the proper scope of religious freedom.

It has again been a pleasure to publish with Routledge, and I am grateful for their consistent support of my work in recent years, as well as their professional efficiency during the production process. I have particularly enjoyed my relationship with Michael Kerns, who has acted as the principal editorial presence in relation to this book, and to Felisa Salvago-Keyes who has been as pleasant as she is skillful in managing the editorial process. And my warm thanks to Sophie Richmond, who has been a skillful copy editor, and heroic in the face of my logistical difficulties.

Most of the chapters are based on lectures, conference presentations, and previously published articles or chapters in edited books. The content has been extensively revised, reflecting my self-critical temperament, but also further consideration of the topics, as well as some effort to take account of events in a rapidly changing world.

As always, those who share the daily routine of my life are most deserving of my deepest thanks. In particular, my wife, Hilal Elver, has been my constant companion and deepest collaborator as we have shaped our life together in Santa Barbara and Istanbul—two contrasting and exhilarating urban experiences. We have struggled together, with the help and affection of friends in both places, to understand and interpret these two engagingly complex countries. I also want to say how much the love and companionship of my children, Chris, Dimitri, Noah, and Zeynep, and their wonderful partners, has meant to me. And finally, our special splendid Vietnamese 'daughter,' Huyen Ngoc Giap, who unfailingly charms and impresses, has already brought us much joy in this new century.

Introduction

The contours of human rights change to reflect the moral urgencies of the human condition. In the last decade or so this has meant, above all, a turn toward what the French philosopher, Jacques Derrida, referred to as "living together well." Such a refocusing of human rights concerns away from state/society/individual relations as specified by legal texts and governmental procedures is not meant to eclipse earlier efforts. Rather it seeks to reflect the psycho-political impact of globalization on all forms of social interaction, as well as the shrinking of time and space, the experience of interrelatedness, and the search for personal meaning and fulfillment in a period of growing societal anguish and tension.

More concrete is the pervasive experience of human vulnerability arising from a growing awareness, still mainly evaded by the powerful and ignored by the weak, of the adverse effects of climate change and a realization that humans, as a species, are living precariously. We are living individually and collectively with an array of risks and fears we only dimly appreciate and lack the tools to assess if we were to acknowledge their existence. We feel at a loss as soon as we try to decide what adjustments to make in view of these cascading dangers to wellbeing and survival.

In essence, increasingly, we are faced with conditions of radical uncertainty as the defining feature of human existence in the early twenty-first century. The anguish that results may partially explain the unanticipated rise of religion, which offers certainty, guidance, and consolation. It also reflects a widespread loss of confidence in the capacity of technology to improve the material circumstances of our individual and collective lives, which in turn undermines the Western belief in progress as characteristic of social, political, and cultural evolution. Without this belief in progress, especially given this heightened sense of risk, despair and resentment emerge, encouraging the more privileged to safeguard their security by walls, gates, alarms, and armed guards. For the less privileged multitudes, there is increasing hostility toward the stranger, and demands for governmental protection of national sovereignty by way of walls, barriers, deportation, and racial profiling. It is not surprising that a security-driven hyper-patriotism emerges, and targets illegal immigrants. This

1

foreground that impinges on governmental and societal behavior challenges us all to be more than ever attentive to human rights, especially at home, in our daily lives, but also abroad. These discouraging conditions are particularly manifest here in post-9/11 America, and have been abetted in the early twenty-first century by neoconservative political leadership, and by a steep economic downturn that always makes society receptive to demagoguery and scapegoating. Somewhat similar conditions pertain in other parts of the world, particularly Western Europe and Japan, where hope and prosperity are giving way to despair, hardship, and worries about global warming.

Of course, the conscious experience of daily life is infrequently *directly* affected by this onset of a nascent community of despair. Most persons on the planet remain preoccupied with traditional challenges associated with sustaining life itself, finding the food, housing, clothing, education, and health care needed to eke out a tolerable existence under conditions of impoverishment. In this sense, effective advocates of human rights need to be concerned with distributive justice, sustainable development, and a variety of public and private sector policies designed to enhance human security. Secondarily, there exist a variety of issues associated with the formal genesis of human rights by way of the great national revolutions in late eighteenth-century France and America. These historic happenings proclaimed that individuals possess inalienable rights. It was of enduring significance that these two revolutions established a moral foundation underpinning the core claim that all persons on earth deserved a life of human dignity. They also established both goals and norms to regulate the relations of governmental institutions to the members of society. Unfortunately, the abstract nature of these "rights" facilitated new forms of hypocrisy: proud proclamations of adherence to upholding rights, even as sanctified by law, yet forcefully maintaining the crudest and cruelest forms of *exclusion*: of slaves, of indigenous peoples, of women, and in most respects, of the poor and downtrodden. This birthing of human rights within the boundaries of sovereign states had little to do in these first manifestations with the *human*, and was mostly to do with endowing societal male elites with protection against tyrannical rule. The whole idea of rights arose in Europe to protect first, the nobility from abuse by autocratic monarchs, and later, to insulate a rising bourgeoisie from predatory governments on the one side and a rampant populism on the other. The affirmation of abstract rights managed to endow the modern state with a façade of legitimacy that successfully concealed its deep structures of injustice, abuse, and exploitation.

The achievement of human rights by shrinking circles of exclusion nationally and globally occurred not mainly because of ethical clarification and moral reflection, but as a result of stones thrown by critics and initiatives by and on behalf of victims. The spread of rights has depended almost completely on the dedicated work of nonviolent social and political movements that have challenged the established orders of power and privilege all over the world before their demands were finally translated into legally protected rights. The remarkable forward global momentum of the last half century is mostly due to the success of the anti-colonial and anti-apartheid struggles that liberated millions from oppressive conditions, but also to those developmental success stories that have lifted hundreds of millions more from the crushing burdens of extreme poverty. These achievements should not be romanticized. Post-colonial, post-apartheid political arrangements have been generally disappointing if judged from the perspective of human rights.

The idea of *international* human rights was initially a distinctly Western liberal project launched after World War II, although it was preceded by the group approach taken after World War I in the form of treaties designed to protect ethnic minorities in European countries. This emphasis on the protection of minorities was deemed a failure as it provided Germany with a pretext for military intervention. In reaction to this experience the human rights effort after 1945 emphasized the protection of the individual and discouragement of any encroachment on the sovereign rights of states. This reformulated international affirmation of human rights represented mostly a belated gesture of official respect for the hapless victims of the Nazi experience. Governmental engagement with this affirmation of human rights was understood from the beginning as never intended to be more than a gesture, and was carefully phrased so as not to challenge the sanctity of the sovereign state. The impulse to acknowledge the *universal* scope of the rights of men and women directly contradicted the operational and doctrinal primacy accorded sovereignty, nationalism, and territorial supremacy. This supposed gift to humanity of international human rights seemed almost worthless in a world order that was based more than ever on the guiding principle of "sovereignty first." Of course, it was not sovereignty as such that presented difficulties, but the prevalence of authoritarianism and colonialism, as well as the persistence of illiberal elements in even the most democratic of states. The Universal Declaration of Human Rights adopted by the United Nations (UN) General Assembly in 1948 avoided any reference to a right of self-determination so as not to challenge, even obliquely, the legitimacy of colonial rule.

What enabled the gift to be made at all were the accompanying dispiriting assurances that the norms of human rights would never be implemented by force. This promise of non-enforcement was signaled in many ways, but most clearly, by placing the norms, standards, and principles constituting the substance of human rights in a text named the Universal *Declaration* of Human Rights. By modestly labeling the framework document establishing the content of international human rights as a "declaration" it was acknowledged that these norms were never meant to be obligatory, but were intended only to express aspirational goals the fulfillment of which depended on voluntary political reforms undertaken *within* individual states.

What followed disclosed the cunning of history. A variety of individuals in Western countries were impressed with the promise and potential of international human rights, and with the opportunity that existed for civil society initiatives. Human rights NGOs began taking shape initially in liberal democracies within a Cold War climate. Such organizations as Freedom House, Amnesty International, and Human Rights Watch emerged with initial agendas mainly directed outward, associating human rights abuses only with the ideological enemy. Then came the presidency of Jimmy Carter in the immediate aftermath of the Vietnam experience. The Carter presidency was emphatic about its determination to make human rights a central feature of American foreign policy, and no longer to use it just for bashing Communist regimes in propaganda exercises or as an instrument of foreign policy that must be used in a manner compatible with strategic alignments, that is, never against allies and friends, only against hostile governments. Such an apparent shift in the American way of relating human rights to foreign policy was taken seriously by opposition groups around the world, undoubtedly more seriously than expected by Washington. This American governmental enthusiasm for human rights ebbed after 1979 as it had seemed to contribute to an upsurge of militancy in several countries, none more dramatically than Iran. The outcome of the Iranian Revolution, which replaced a valuable strategic ally with an intensely anti-American leadership, produced a barrage of angry criticism from political realists and conservatives. This led the Carter presidency to mute its human rights policy, especially after the American Embassy in Tehran was seized by Islamic militants and its occupants held hostage until Carter was replaced by Ronald Reagan as president. This experience with Iran reminded the political leadership in the United States that strategic and ideological alignments in world politics should be given precedence over normative considerations of law and justice. It should not be overlooked that Carter, and even more so Zbigniew Brzezinski, his chief foreign policy advisor, were members of the realist school of thought, and had simply miscalculated the strategic costs to the United States of seeming to give priority to human rights. Intriguingly, a different miscalculation has dogged the neoconservative promotion of democracy in the Middle East during the presidency of George W. Bush, bringing to positions of governmental authority in the region leaders whose views contradicted the hopes and interests of Washington policymakers. Similarly to the Carter experience, disappointments with the outcome of several key elections (Iraq; Palestine) led to a muting of the pro-democracy advocacy that had been so prominent in the early years of Bush's presidency.

Despite this experience, a certain contradictory bureaucratic momentum in support of international human rights had been established and persists to this day. It exists in the form of the influential reports on the human rights record of every country in the world that are prepared annually by the U.S. Department of State. Among the high officials in the Department is an Under Secretary for Democracy and Global Affairs whose writ includes human rights, and ensures some sort of constituency within the government, although its weight and outlook varies with the political leadership in the country, as well as with the perceived effects of pushing human rights, given the strategic interests at stake.

Human rights flourished in the final decades of the prior century, and it may be that the 1990s, despite some painful contradictions, will be remembered as "the golden age of human rights." Even earlier, the Cold War rivalry was transcended in the course of organizing a worldwide anti-apartheid campaign that received some of the credit for the generally peaceful transition in South Africa to a non-racist constitutional democracy. In the 1980s, especially, protest movements in Eastern Europe emboldened by the human rights provisions of the 1975 Helsinki Accords weakened the hold of oppressive Communist regimes on their citizenries, and when the more accommodationist Gorbachev leadership took over in Moscow in the mid-1980s, the stage was set for the unraveling of the Soviet empire. Human rights played an important part both in providing opposition groups with a sense of legitimacy, undermining the authority of oppressive regimes, and establishing supportive solidarity links between domestic activists and the robust Western peace movement. Also, in this period there were a variety of challenges to political authoritarianism in Asia that stemmed from mass support for human rights and democracy claims, producing mixed results in countries such as the Philippines, Thailand, Myanmar, and China. Such developments often led to authoritarian backlashes, including the bloody massacre in Tiananmen Square in 1989, but the popular demand for forms of governance that respected fundamental human rights had spread around the world. This meant lip service from elites, often reinforced by some reform measures, and expectations of more humane governance from the peoples of the world.

When the Cold War ended there existed a brief interval of a decade in which security concerns were moved to the background of world politics. The 1990s saw public relief that the Cold War had ended. It also was a time when most attention by political leaders was devoted to the world economy, which was being organized according to the precepts of market capitalism under the ideological banner of neoliberalism. Neoliberalism, without the challenge of socialism, dispensed with pretensions that economic policy should take explicit account of the needs of people to the extent politically possible, and world capitalism showed its cruel face. Despite sustained economic growth, and some national success stories in Asia, income inequalities within and between countries greatly increased, and mass poverty persisted.

This global setting of reduced concern about traditional war/peace issues and the rise of predatory globalization created a normative vacuum on the world stage. This was filled to some extent by moves to engage in peacekeeping operations under UN auspices whenever agreement could be reached among the permanent members of the Security Council as in the cases of Haiti, Bosnia, and Somalia. Far more controversial, but still relevant, were occasions when humanitarian interventions outside the UN were undertaken, most significantly by NATO in the Kosovo War of 1999.

The whole atmosphere changed as a result of the 9/11 attacks on the United States. There was a renewed emphasis on violent conflict and global security, although now the main actors were not normal sovereign states: the United States was a global state (or empire) that deployed and projected its power on land, sea, and air throughout the world; its adversary, Al Qaeda, was a shadowy transnational network, without a fixed territorial base, with a virtual presence everywhere, but with a verifiable actuality almost nowhere. In this inflamed setting of an international conflict unlike any in the past, yet framed by both sides as "war" of global scope, the cause and substance of human rights has suffered. The importance of the United States to the international protection and stature of human rights has been confirmed, although since 9/11 in a negative sense, casting a dark shadow over the human rights enterprise by its own "legalization" of torture as exhibited for the world to see as a result of the lurid portrayals and reports of widespread abuse associated with the detention of suspects at Guantanamo, Abu Ghraib, and elsewhere.

When George W. Bush confirmed that he intends to attend the Olympics in Beijing no matter what China does to repress Tibetan resistance it comes across as an arrogant gesture of moral assessment by a government that has itself lost credibility to complain about others. When Bush explains his position by saying that the Olympics are about "sport" he ignores the ugly memories of Hitler hosting the 1936 Olympics in a manner than brought legitimacy to a murderous regime at the time, and cast a long shadow of shame on attending foreign dignitaries who spread goodwill. There is no intention here to equate China with Germany during the Nazi era, which would be a moral and political absurdity, but rather to expose the current lack of American moral credibility in the field of human rights. It would be entirely appropriate to proceed with the sport aspects of the Olympics but deny China the prestige benefits of the game, which would be the case if leaders of prominent countries refused to attend, at least the symbolic opening ceremonies.

It is also important to notice that the weakening of this leadership by the United States represents a serious loss of political and diplomatic leverage in the global struggle to achieve the nonviolent implementation of human rights in foreign societies. Prospects for implementation depend heavily on what states are willing to do voluntarily *within* their own territorial space. But to the extent that external pressures can be brought to bear, the United States has unparalleled diplomatic and economic leverage, and thus its moral rehabilitation is essential if the forward momentum of the human rights movement on a world scale is to be soon resumed.

Of course, the United States' role, although crucial in a variety of settings around the world, is not the only source of external pressure for implementation. The European Union (EU) has notably protected human rights in Europe by developing a most impressive institutional framework of law for the implementation of human rights on a regional basis. The European Court of Human Rights is a respected and effective judicial body that overrides national sovereignty in the realm of human rights, and even allows citizens to be protected against abuses perpetrated by their own government. What is more, by tying membership in the EU with a record of adherence to human rights norms, Europe has coupled the enlargement of its organizational reach with non-coercive pressures to promote human rights. A strong example in the early years of the twenty-first century was the process of reform within Turkey undertaken to qualify for membership in the EU. This process has been slowed, if not altogether disrupted, by the evident reluctance of several leading European states to admit a large Muslim state to the EU, no matter what Turkey might do to improve its human rights record. It has also been disrupted by recurrent political turmoil in Turkey that has centered recently upon the militant resistance of the anti-religious minority to any moves to liberalize the old exclusionary approach of self-proclaimed secularists that has heretofore severely penalized religiously observant Islamic women in Turkey, denying them access to higher education and closing off many employment options.

This dynamic of victimization and humiliation is misleadingly justified as a defense of Turkish secularism, whereas it is more accurately understood as a struggle between exclusionary and inclusionary interpretations of secularism. This is a struggle involving the *rights* of *people*, although it is usually presented in the media and elsewhere as an encounter of *ideas*, or of *social* and *political forces* contending for primacy in Turkey. The real importance of the issue, at least in Turkey, is that the 60 percent of Turkish women who cover their heads for religious reasons are denied the full constitutional rights of citizenship, and besides, are beset in their daily lives with various forms of discrimination. This conflict is expressed ideologically in ways that hide many of its adverse impacts on individuals and communities. The treatment of religious women in Turkey has serious gender, class, and ethnic dimensions that are rarely acknowledged. Religious men in Turkey experience no comparable problems, the great majority of religious women come from lower-class backgrounds, many belong to ethnic minorities, and most do not connect the headscarf with politics.

In approaching the frontiers of human rights in this new century, there are many issues that will test the old human rights template based essentially on upholding human dignity of individuals in a world of sovereign states. Perhaps the most subversive force arises from the Internet, and the manner in which it constitutes borderless communities, and facilitates intrusions on privacy and identity theft as well as participation in both territorial and transnational political life. At stake is the appropriate nexus of regulatory authority, as well as the location of appropriate limits to patterns of resistance that violate applicable laws. It will also be necessary to grapple increasingly with the outer boundaries of "the human," especially if cloning occurs and robots are developed—as has been predicted—that exhibit increasingly human behavior. Upendra Baxi has written about human rights in post-human civilizational space as expressing this range of concerns arising from radical developments in science and technology that are narrowing the gap between the human and the non-human in a variety of contexts. As we investigate the normative implications of these still barely visible horizons, we are becoming more and more aware that traditional boundaries and distinctions are fuzzier than in earlier times. In part it is this fuzziness that explains the defensive reflex associated with building walls to keep unwanted immigrants out, reaffirming the traditional image of marriage as only between a man and a woman, resisting the extension of rights to animals or conceiving of collective rights as extending to future generations and indigenous peoples.

It has always been important to distinguish the discourse of law from complementary discourses of politics, culture, ethics, and religion. The legal architecture of international human rights has been established by formal legal texts negotiated and ratified by governments of sovereign states, as well as by the institutions and procedures for implementation that have been given an intergovernmental role either within the United Nations or elsewhere. Politics and culture plays a large part in exerting pressures for and against implementing particular norms contained in these texts, as do ethical standards and religious attitudes. In liberal democracies societal activism has been crucial in building support for human rights, but even in many authoritarian societies there has been enough political space to enable a variety of civil society initiatives seeking human rights goals.

Human rights, as much as any domain of societal endeavor, is always in motion as values change and social movements emerge. The global media and the Internet greatly accelerate this motion, and disseminate human rights concerns beyond their territorial locus. Whether it is a matter of protests in Tibet, challenges to Kosovo independence by Serbia, Palestinian or Kurdish claims of self-determination, or doctored elections in Kenya or Florida, the arena of controversy is immediately broadened beyond the national community, but not symmetrically. This remains a Eurocentric or West-centric world dialogue, with much more Western and international engagement in resolving post-election controversies in African countries than in Florida, despite the fact that the world has a much more direct stake in who governs in the United States than it does in who runs Kenya. In effect, the globalization of human rights resembles military intervention in its bifocal vision of abuses in the North and the South.

The most drastic claim being made in these pages is support for personalizing the practice and protection of human rights by locating freedom and responsibility in the countless daily decisions each of us makes about the treatment of others. This existential level of implementation for human rights also implies a refusal to treat otherness as a set of alien abstractions. Whether we talk of immigrants, transsexuals, or terrorist suspects we are talking about human beings unconditionally entitled to humane treatment. Such an ethos is not just an affair of governmental institutions or NGOs, and indeed institutions and civil society actors are reflections of social behavior. Given challenges as diverse as climate change, massive illegal immigration, and genetic engineering, learning to live together well in all arenas of social interaction will go a long way in determining whether human rights are effectively shaping the destinies of individuals, societies, and the human species in the difficult decades ahead. The role of the moral and social imagination should not be neglected. It is only by transforming the abstraction of undocumented worker in the United States into the sobering realities of someone escaping by desperate means lifelong impoverishment in Mexico that enables us to participate personally and politically in the immigration debate that has been both ugly and divisive in this country.

The chapters that comprise this book proceed against such a background of engagements and understandings of the human rights agenda. This background realizes that the struggles for human rights begin at home, not just in the home country, that is, within our own family and immediate neighborhood. Of course, our future as a species also depends on our farsightedness and sense of human solidarity when it comes to human rights. We need to feel the pain and urgency of abuse whether in Tibet or Gaza, as well as within our inner cities or in relation to lost farms and homes within our supposedly wealthy country. We need to be mindful of the wellbeing of future generations so that their life circumstances are not afflicted with disease, hardship, and authoritarian rule. Unavoidably, the vocation of human rights advocacy cannot be separated from the pursuit of justice in all domains of human existence. Human rights is ultimately about the quality of world order as was acknowledged, but ignored, in Article 28 of the Universal Declaration of Human Rights:

> Everyone is entitled to a social and international order in which the rights and freedoms set forth in this Declaration can be fully realized.

It is late, but not too late, to take this unnoticed promise seriously.

Part I

Overview

1

Toward a *Necessary* Utopianism
Democratic Global Governance

Imperatives

Unless the emergence of an effective form of global governance is adequately democratized it will not only reproduce existing acute inequities and exploitative patterns of the present world order, but will almost certainly intensify these malevolent features. Such forebodings are based on the assessment of present global trends that document increasing disparities among peoples, races, and classes, but also call to our attention the growing struggle over dwindling oil supplies and the overall harmful effects of global warming and various associated forms of environmental deterioration.[1] Without drastic normative adjustments in the interaction of states and regions, as well as an accompanying social regulation of the world economy, global governance is almost certain to adopt highly coercive methods of stifling resistance from disadvantaged societies and social forces.

The Bush presidency in the United States, while bringing to the fore an extremist leadership that is likely to be repudiated by the American electorate in the short run, may still be a crude forerunner of future hegemonic efforts by the United States to stabilize the unjust global status quo to the extent possible.[2] There are no indications that any plausible new political leader in the United States will draw down the American militarization of the planet under its sovereign control, including oceans, space, world network of military bases, global intelligence, and special forces presence.[3] Global governance under any such auspices, even if less manifestly dysfunctional than this currently failing neoconservative experiment to provide security for the world as administered from Washington, is almost certain to falter without ambitious moves to establish an inclusive consensual, cooperative, multilateral, and constitutional framework built around a truly operational global rule of law.[4] At present, there seems to be grossly insufficient political agency available to support mounting a credible challenge along such transformative lines to existing world order arrangements. That is, the neoconservative American vision of global governance has been defeated by resistance, but as matters now stand there is no alternative and it is likely that this vision will be altered to accommodate a more liberal style of promotion. It is due to this

13

inability to depict a plausible path leading from the here of dysfunctional Westphalianism to a more democratically constituted and institutionally centralized global governance that makes any current call appear "utopian," that is, not attainable except imaginatively.

Against such a background the advocacy of world government seems constructive and responsive, yet I would argue that to push for world government at this time is dangerously premature. Such a post-Westphalian governmental restructuring of global authority, particularly in relation to war-making, in the unlikely event that it were to become capable of enactment, would almost certainly produce a tyrannical world polity. Such a result seems almost certain unless the realization of world government was preceded by economic, social, and cultural developments that reduced dramatically current levels of material unevenness, poverty, and inter-civilizational antagonisms. So long as this unevenness persists any centralization of political authority is certain to be coercive, exploitative, and oppressive. Perhaps, in the decades ahead, the raw struggle for human survival may yield this kind of outcome misleadingly described as "world government," and may make it seem an acceptable or even the best attainable world order solution for the peoples of the world. This survival scenario is a rather realistic expectation, given the likelihood that pressures in relation global warming and energy supplies and prices will soon reach emergency levels. What is politically possible in a circumstance of imminent catastrophe or at the early stages of an unfolding catastrophe cannot be foretold, but given our best understanding of present political realities, the present advocacy of world government is both utopian (unattainable) and dystopian (undesirable). If this is correct, then the contemplation of a benevolent world government is an idle daydream that we as humans concerned for the future can currently ill afford.

An alternative approach, suggested by a similar understanding of the same set of planetary circumstances involves a focus upon the preconditions for achieving a *humane* form of global governance.[5] From this perspective the major premise of analysis is that without the emergence and eventual flourishing of global democracy the world seems assuredly heading for dystopia, if not irreversible catastrophe. Any reasonable approach to the future must exhibit an awareness of the probable relevance of crucial unanticipated developments.[6] Given this outlook, it seems useful to distinguish among several horizons of possibility when contemplating the shape and viability of global governance in the relatively near-term future. Current policy debate, including mainstream reformist proposals and projections, takes place in a political space that seems consistent with horizons of *feasibility* (that is, policy goals attainable without substantial modification of structures of power, privilege, authority, and societal belief patterns); such horizons can shift abruptly during moments of crisis and emergency. In a negative manner, horizons of feasibility receded dramatically after the 9/11 attacks making recourse to aggressive wars by the U.S. government much easier to justify, generating strong political backing at home. A more positive illustration involved the establishment of the International Criminal Court in the aftermath of the Cold War despite the opposition of several leading governments, but with impressively organized and intensely motivated support from civil society forces. If such a project had been launched in the 1970s or 1980s it would have been quickly dismissed as utopian, yet in the late 1990s it became a realized goal of a group of moderate governments working in tandem with a coalition of transnational civil society actors. Horizons of feasibility shift and evolve, and not necessarily in a linear and incremental rhythm, but by jumps, discontinuities replete with contradictions.[7] It is not enough to ponder the future through calculations and assessments made by reference to horizons of feasibility. We also require some sense of preferred alternative ways of sustaining life on the planet along lines that accord with scientific and professional judgments as to how to improve the material and social quality of human life for all persons. To do this is not just a technical matter. It is also ethical, calling for special efforts on behalf of those now poor, excluded, subordinated, and otherwise disadvantaged. It also presupposes that far longer-term perspectives inform public policy at levels of social integration than are now associated with domestic electoral cycles. As well, the shaping of a democratic form of global governance cannot be effectively or beneficially managed on the basis of either a world constituted almost exclusively by territorial political communities enjoying sovereign rights or a world that is controlled by either single or multiple hegemonic centers of territorial power of global and regional scope or by market-based global business and banking elites.[8] To devise what will work to ensure a sustainable human future that does not rest on naked force and entail grossly exploitative distributions of wealth and income requires a scientifically and ethically informed vision of what is needed, treated here as horizons of *necessity*. It is the gap between feasibility and necessity, as well as the fragility and complexity of current world order, which largely explains what is appropriately described as the deepening crisis of global governance. In this regard, the petroleum-based technologies of the twenty-first century, military and otherwise, make the consequences of failure and breakdown so much more consequential than earlier. This observation is particularly obvious with regard to any assessment of the destructive impacts of major wars fought with nuclear weapons as distinct from wars fought with bows and arrows or machetes. But the same condition exists in many other domains of international life, including of course, the use of the global commons as a dump for greenhouse gas emissions, as for various other kinds of waste disposal.

By itself this polarization of perspectives may not do more than help us understand the gathering gloom about the future of humanity by focusing our attention on what is needed, yet seemingly unattainable, rather than to be content with what is feasible. With this consideration in mind, it seems useful to look closely at what is desired and desirable with respect to the multi-dimensional challenge of global governance. In this respect, reflecting on horizons of *desire* is not entirely impractical, but rather provides an inspirational foundation for the mobilizing energy that will be required if horizons of necessity are to motivate action without adding to human suffering. The emphasis on democracy as the ground upon which global governance must unfold, if it is to be successful and benevolent, is an acknowledgment, with risks attached, of the political significance of desire and the desirable.[9] As suggested, tyrannical forms of global governance might, although at great human cost, more easily satisfy the imperatives of necessity, at least for some decades, but dystopicly. The preferred alternative is to embrace the utopian possibility of conflating horizons of necessity and horizons of desire, which seems only imaginable if global governance is radically democratized in the near future. Whether that conflation would help fashion the political agency required to establish a credible political project of global democratic governance cannot be foretold. There is also some support, especially in American neoliberal and neoconservative circles, for embracing benevolent hegemony, even empire, as the most attainable form of effective global governance.[10] As with world government, hegemonic or imperial solutions, even if arguably responsive to horizons of necessity should be rejected because they do not appear on the horizons of desire.[11] Global democracy seems necessary and desirable, although its realization, assuming obstacles can be overcome, may turn out to be not altogether positive. Much can go wrong by way of implementation: corruption, militarism, even repression and exploitation, could easily occur along the way, if the mechanisms of governance are not constrained by a robust regime of law that is itself responsive to the values and implementing procedures of a human rights culture and to demands for global justice. This regime of global law is particularly needed to offset to some extent the effects of gross inequality and disparity that currently exists, and seems built into the operational workings of the world economy.[12] The final test of social justice globally conceived, recalling Gandhi's criterion of "the last man" and John Rawls' emphasis on the most disadvantaged elements in society, will be how those at the margins of human vulnerability are treated, including the impoverished, the unborn, the indigenous, and the deviant. Procedural benchmarks will also be indicative of a more inclusive democracy that is not yet: progress toward accountability for wrongdoing by political actors, regulation of economic regimes to ensure the material and human wellbeing of all persons and groups, implementation of prohibitions on recourse to war as a political option, a dynamic of demilitarization, and, behind everything, a rule of law as administered by an independent and available judiciary so that there is a growing impression that legal equals (for example, governments of sovereign states) are being treated equally. In contrast, the present world order shocks the moral conscience by the extent to which powerful political actors are being given an exemption from criminal accountability while weaker figures are increasingly prosecuted and punished. Saddam Hussein or Slobodan Milosevic are prosecuted but George W. Bush, Tony Blair, and Vladimir Putin are de facto exempt from even indictment. More broadly, hegemonic actors are enjoying an informal, yet fully effective, right of exception with respect to adherence to international law, expressed both by the veto given to permanent members of the United Nations (UN) Security Council and by the operational freedom of maneuver enjoyed by major states.

This chapter will not attempt to look at this entire global canvas of democratizing initiatives but limits itself to an inquiry that highlights the place of the individual as "citizen" of this unborn global polity and the creation of an institutional arena that can give meaningful expression to democratizing sentiments and express grievances that come from below. In this rendering, the spirit of democracy is derived from respect for the authority of the grassroots, giving some sort of preliminary outlet for legitimizing processes of popular sovereignty.[13] More concretely attention will be given to a futuristic conception of citizenship—the citizen pilgrim—and to the establishment of means for collective political deliberation—a global peoples assembly or global peoples parliament.[14]

It needs to be understood that both structural aspects of Westphalian world order: the horizontal juridical order encompassing the interplay of formally *equal* sovereign states and the vertical order exhibiting the geopolitical structure of grossly *unequal* states now exhibits almost none of the characteristics of democratic governance. The clearest embodiment of the horizontal juridical order may be seen in the functioning of the UN General Assembly. Governments are somewhat equal with respect to one another, but this body is denied the authority to decide or the power to enforce of and there are no opportunities given for meaningful and direct participation by representatives of global civil society. The clearest expression of the vertical geopolitical order can be observed in the UN Security Council where many sessions on crucial issues of peace and security are held in secret, so that even transparency is absent in the context of debate. The UN is a quintessential Westphalian institution with respect to membership and operational responsibilities, although these realities are to some extent hidden behind the normative architecture of the UN Charter, which at least purports to impose major behavioral constraints on all states, including geopolitical actors. A slightly deeper scrutiny discloses a veto power that almost completely nullifies the Charter constraints, and looking still deeper reveals an operational code in which the main hegemonic actor(s) overrides in almost all circumstances the autonomy of ordinary sovereign states, despite their formal rights of equality based on membership.

This presentation of current world order does not take account of the rise of non-state actors both as participants and challengers.[15] These post-Westphalian elements of world order are arrayed around market forces, humanitarian voluntary associations, and mobilized social forces. Characteristic arenas of activity for such actors include the World Economic Forum, conflict zones, and the World Social Forum. These actors, although outside the formal framework of interacting governments representing sovereign states, are also not subject to any consistent criteria of democratic governance. Their current main roles as gadflies or adjuncts to states, makes their absence of democratic practices of less present concern, but if their future contribution to the shaping of democratic global governance is to retain credibility then appropriate forms of democratization of civil society actors need to be established.

Citizenship

Discussions of citizenship in the modern era focused mainly on the evolving relations of citizen and state in liberal democracies.[16] This concept of citizenship in the last half of the twentieth century became increasingly associated with a normative model of legitimate national governance, incorporating both the rise of international human rights and reliance upon private sector economic growth. The authoritative character of this model was universalized, at least rhetorically, after the collapse of the Soviet Union, the entry of China into the World Trade Organization, and the emergence of a consensus among governments in support of neoliberalism as the foundation of national economic policy. George W. Bush endorsed such an understanding of governance when he started his cover letter introducing the important document, National Security Strategy 2002 of the United States of America, with the following sentence: "The great struggles of the twentieth century between liberty and totalitarianism ended with a decisive victory for the forces of freedom—and a single sustainable model for national success: freedom, democracy, and free enterprise."[17] What is striking here is the regressive and revealing failure to mention any duty to protect those materially deprived by providing for basic human needs, as well as the arrogance associated with claiming to be the embodiment of the single model of societal success. Showing respect for social and economic rights of individuals and groups was deliberately avoided in the Bush approach, presumably because it would be regarded as an acceptance of the welfare state, and might attract conservative criticism as a backdoor acceptance of socialism.[18] Although this American retreat from a conception of citizenship that includes the responsibility of the state for the material wellbeing of its citizenry has taken an extreme form, it does reflect a wider trend that is partly responsive to the supposed imperative of a neoliberal global economy, partly a reaction to the failures of state socialism as embodied in the Soviet Union, partly a consequence of a weakening labor movement in post-industrial societies, and partly reflective of a rightward swing throughout the industrial world in relation to state responsibility for the welfare of their citizenry.

Traditional forms of citizenship, then, at their best involved meaningful participation (rights and duties) within national political space, especially, the enjoyment of civil and political rights (freedom), the opportunity to participate in an open political process that is framed by a constitutional document (rule of law), subsidized opportunities for education and health, the assured protection of private property and national and transnational entrepreneurial rights (trade and investment), and some measure of support in circumstances of material need. Such a view of what might be called Westphalian citizenship included a reciprocal series of duties; the most onerous involved obligations of loyalty and service to the state. The crime of treason continues to be punished everywhere with great severity. This legalizes a radical denial of a globalized moral conscience, presupposing that even if the state acts in defiance of international law, universal standards of morality, and with self-destructive imprudence, it is a crime to lend aid and comfort to its enemy. In this respect, there exists an unresolved tension between accountability of even government officials to international criminal law and the continuing claims made by governments to the unwavering, and essentially unchallengeable, allegiance of citizens. From the perspective of moral and legal globalization it seems like an opportune moment to advocate the abolition of "treason" as a crime. A serious debate on treason and conscience would serve the purpose of rethinking the proper vector of citizenship with respect to changing values, beliefs, and conditions, as well as acknowledging the global and species context of human action. As matters now stand, the absolutizing of allegiance to the state that confers nationality and citizenship undermines both human solidarity and respect for norms claiming global applicability. Such an allegiance inculcates a tribalist ethos that anachronistically privileges the part over the whole at a historic moment when the parts that make up the whole increasingly depend on the wellbeing of the latter. The Nuremberg ethos that held German, and later Japanese leaders legally responsible for their official crimes, almost obligates citizens of a state embarked on a course of international criminality to advocate treason, and certainly requires a rejection of blind obedience to the orders and policies of a state. Of course, this Nuremberg legacy is ambiguous, starting out as victors' justice and persisting as a normative framework that effectively exempts geopolitical actors and their servants from all efforts to impose criminal responsibility upon those who act on behalf of the state. The unsuccessful pursuit in national criminal courts of the former American Secretary of Defense, Donald Rumsfeld, for his role in authorizing torture illustrates the de facto immunity of those who act on behalf of hegemonic states.

Beyond this, there is the question of citizenship that is not tied to the national space of the sovereign state. To some extent this has been formally recognized by the conferral of a secondary layer of European citizenship on persons living permanently within the countries belonging to the European Union (EU).[19] This formal acknowledgment has a rudimentary corresponding structure of regional governance as especially embodied in such institutions as the European Court of Human Rights and the European Parliament. More challenging, however, is the failure to take account of the partial disenfranchisement that has occurred globally both by the operations of the world economy and by the emergence of the United States as a global state, that is, exercising its authority as an override of both the sovereign rights of other states and through a self-decreed exemption from either the authority of the United Nations or of international law, especially in the areas of war and peace. This disenfranchisement has the effect of precluding the meaningful exercise of democracy on the level of the state for many countries, particularly in the ex-colonial countries. If we could imagine an adjustment by way of allowing persons outside the United States to challenge policy affecting their wellbeing by way of binding referenda, or even by casting votes in national elections held within the United States, the leadership role of the United States in shaping global governance would likely be altered for the better (as measured by the principles of the UN Charter or by most accounts of global justice) in fundamental respects, and there would be a far better fit between the ideals of democracy and the benefits of citizenship. The Westphalian territorial grip on the political imagination remains so tight that such a recasting of electoral arrangements is almost unthinkable, conveying sentiments that have the ring of ultra-utopianism.

The aging of the Westphalian structure of world order is exhibited by the emergence of new arenas of global policy formation that are more responsive to the influence of non-state actors.[20] For instance, the World Economic Forum (WEF), especially during the 1990s, provided global market forces and their most important representatives with an influential arena. The WEF was established after the Trilateral Commission, which was an elite-oriented private sector initiative that was supposed to offset the inter-governmental influence on world economic policy attributed to the Non-Aligned Movement, and its efforts in the early 1970s to achieve a new international economic order. In many respects, the WEF shaped a policy climate that conditioned the behavior of governments and international financial institutions. In reaction to this post-colonial West-centric non-governmental continuing effort to steer the world economy in a manner that widened disparities between rich and poor within and among countries, civil society actors in the South formed the World Social Forum (WSF). The respective ideological and geographical centers of gravity of these opposing initiatives was expressed by the WEF meeting annually in Davos, Switzerland, and the WSF meeting initially for several years in Porto Alegre, Brazil. In a certain sense, these opposed initiatives represented forms of self-created "global citizenship," established without the formal blessings of states or international institutions, and yet producing meaningful forms of participation by non-state global actors. Such participation is quite likely more meaningful than what was possible through either individual and group participation in many national political processes. Of course, these two types of arena are not necessarily contradictory when it comes to policy, and could be partially understood as complementary undertakings to overcome the limitations of a purely statist world order. Kofi Annan, while serving as UN Secretary General, told the WEF at one of its annual gathering that the UN would only remain relevant in the new century if it found ways to incorporate both market forces and civil society actors significantly into its activities.

Whether intended or not, the former UN Secretary General was signaling the somewhat subversive opinion that the Westphalian era was over, or at least coming to an end, unless the purely statist structure of authority was modified at the UN, and presumably elsewhere in global policy arenas, to make room for certain non-state actors to take part in meaningful ways. Of course, these demands for access are not symmetrical. It is far easier for statist structures, including the UN, to accommodate private sector market forces, which already exert a huge influence through their strong representation in the upper echelons of officialdom in many governments. To varying degrees, national governments have been significantly constrained by domestic and global market forces that have narrowed the space available to leaders for political maneuver. This reality is accentuated by the fact that civil society actors are unrepresented in governmental circles. It remains a rarity for activist representatives of civil society to exert any direct influence on governmental policy formation or operations. Such a generalization is particularly true with respect to peace, security, and foreign economic policy. In the humanitarian domain of conflict management, civil society actors often collaborate with governments.

This structural challenge to Westphalian conceptions of world order remains unmet, and has unleashed a statist backlash.[21] Annan's rather mild efforts to implement his views on the future of the UN, especially with regard to the role of civil society representatives were effectively rebuffed by statist forces, a story largely untold. For instance, Annan proposed having an assembly of representatives of NGOs hold a meeting, intended as perhaps the first of an annual event, at the UN as part of the millennium celebrations in the year 2000. Even this largely symbolic gesture to civil society was opposed to such an extent behind the scenes by leading governments that the gathering had to be held in a diluted form outside UN premises and on the assurance that this meeting was a one-off event. This same Westphalian backlash has led the UN to abandon the format of highly visible world meetings on global policy issues, which became in the 1990s important opportunities for transnational social forces to organize and network globally, gain access to the world media, and to help shape the policy outcomes by influencing Third World governments.[22] The rise of non-state actors and the formation of non-state arenas seem to be reshaping the nature of citizenship in the twenty-first century as concept, as behavior, and as aspiration.[23] If modes of participation and psycho-political identities are shifting to take account of the realities of globalization, it is misleading to continue to reduce citizenship to a formal status granted by territorial governments of sovereign states, or even by such inter-governmental entities as the European Union. Such an opinion is not meant to deny that citizenship of the traditional variety continues to provide most individuals with their most vibrant and useful sense of connection to a political community, especially in determining entitlements and rights and duties, as

21

well as accounting for dominant political identities. What is being claimed, however, is that additionally *informal* modes of belonging and participating should begin to be acknowledged, encouraged, and evaluated as integral aspects of "citizenship."

There is also emerging a new outlook on citizenship, identity, and community. It reflects a growing preoccupation with the unsustainability of present civilizational lifestyles and petroleum-based modernities. Putting this preoccupation more positively emphasizes the relevance of *time* to an adequate contemporary conception of citizenship. This acknowledges that discourses on citizenship, even if visionary, have been essentially related to *space*, including those that articulated the ideal of "citizen of the world." If concerns about unsustainability and responsibilities to the unborn are added to the desirable, and possibly necessary, adoption of a pacifist geopolitics, it would be useful to signal this enlargement of outlook by adopting the terminology of "citizen pilgrim."[24] The pilgrim, although it has some misleading religious connotations associated with holy journeys, conveys the overriding sense that normative citizenship in the early twenty-first century involves a pilgrimage to a sustainable, equitable, humane, and peaceable future. The citizen pilgrim is on a journey through time, dedicated to what is being called here "a necessary utopianism." In contrast, the traditional citizen is bound to their territorial space, and at most can call on their government to be sensitive to long-range considerations.

The calling of the citizen pilgrim is to act without regard to territorial boundaries or the priorities of national interest when these conflict with the human interest in a sustainable future. As well, the citizen pilgrim is engaged in the project of global democratization in any of a multitude of ways, including establishing positive connections of affection and appreciation based on human solidarity and shared destiny. Sustained by an ecumenical spirit, the citizen pilgrim rejects the secular/religious binary that supposedly separates the modern from the traditional, and finds spiritual as well as mundane wisdom and visionary hope embodied in all of the great world religions.[25]

Global Parliament

Democratizing global governance raises a variety of issues, including greater degrees of accountability, transparency, and equity throughout the United Nations system, as well as establishing spaces for non-state participation. The most promising and practical way to acknowledge the challenge and organize a response is to establish *in some form* a global parliament with the mandate to incorporate transnational and futurist non-state civil societal priorities. I have collaborated for some years with Andrew Strauss in the development of support for this initiative.[26] Such an innovative step has been prefigured by the existence for several decades of the European Parliament, as well as the far newer African Parliament. Although a bold challenge to Westphalian notions of world order based on exclusive international representation by the governments of sovereign states, a global parliament is a flexible format that can be initiated modestly. In conception, the establishment of such an institution is a less radical innovation than was the International Criminal Court, which proposes a capacity to hold leaders of sovereign states accountable for certain enumerated crimes. Whether this mission will be fulfilled, especially with respect to leading states, seems doubtful at present, but the existence of the institution is a recognition of a principled approach to the uniform imposition of a global rule of law on all who act in the name of the state. A global parliament is capable of evolving into a lawmaking institution, but its initial phase of operations would be primarily to give the peoples of the world a direct "voice" at the global level, with a strong networking potential of benefit to the strengthening of global civil society and an institutional embodiment of populist concerns.

There are many organizational mechanisms that could be used to establish such a global parliament. Undoubtedly, the easiest approach would be to rely on national parliaments to designate a given number of representatives proportionate to the size of their population or reflective of some formula for civilizational distribution. But such a starting-point, although likely the most manageable, would seem likely to reproduce Westphalian attitudes in such a way as to defeat the main purposes of the global parliament. More promising, although potentially cumbersome, would be the voluntary decision by a given number of governments, say 30, to agree by treaty to the establishment of a global parliament via direct elections arranged either nationally or regionally.

It has been encouraging to experience reactions of growing receptivity around the world to the whole project of establishing a global parliament. I believe this represents both a gradual globalization of political consciousness and the spread of the idea that global governance needs to avoid hegemonic solutions, which requires a variety of moves in the direction of global democracy. The disappointing and alienating results of the American use of its unipolar geopolitical position has also contributed to this receptive atmosphere, as has the halting, yet cumulative progress toward the establishment of a European polity based on consent and an ethos of democracy. These developments suggest a slow merger of horizons of necessity and desire, as well as less remoteness from the horizon of feasibility. As a thought experiment, the emergence of a global parliament seems in 2008 less unlikely than did the establishment of an International Criminal Court a decade before its establishment in 2002. Of course, what happens to such an institution to make it live up to the hopes of its sponsors involves an equally difficult struggle.

There now exists much support for the global parliament idea throughout global civil society whenever world order reform is at issue. What is needed is a campaign, perhaps modeled on the collaborative efforts between coalitions of moderate governments and civil society actors that were so successful in relation to the treaties banning anti-personnel landmines and establishing the

International Criminal Court. The campaign for a global parliament could initially aim to achieve support for convening a treaty-making negotiating session that might itself break ground by combining governments of states with transnational civil society actors as negotiating partners. What would hopefully emerge from such a process would be a treaty that would not come into force until ratified by national constitutional processes and by referenda in participating societies, which need not necessarily be configured as "states."

As with the idea of citizen pilgrim so with the global parliament, much of the benefit would flow from the process itself. This process would shape a consensus as to organizational format, including membership, funding, constitutional status. A big issue is whether the global parliament would be formed as a subsidiary organ of the UN General Assembly or take some more autonomous character within the UN system. It might also turn out to be impossible to gain agreement for situating the global parliament within the UN, in which case it might be established for a trial period as a free-standing international institution, which is the case, for instance, for World Trade Organization.

Conclusion

This chapter, and its recommendations, proceed from the belief that politics as the art of the possible cannot hope to cope with the multi-dimensional, intensifying crisis of global governance. At the same time, it seeks to root its analysis and prescriptions as coherently and responsively as the imagination allows with respect to what have been called horizons of desire and necessity. Its main utopian element is to encourage a radical revisioning of citizenship that currently continues to serve mainly nationalist and even tribalist values. To be a citizen pilgrim in such a global setting is to be a lonely voice in the wilderness, yet representing an ethically driven commitment to truthfulness, human and natural wellbeing, and an overall quest for sustainability and equity. Similarly, to advocate a global parliament, given the structure of the United Nations and the resilience of statist geopolitics, is to whistle in the wind, but yet the wind can shift allowing the impossible to become abruptly feasible. Again, the rationale for establishing a global parliament rests on desire and necessity, not feasibility.

This leaves the question as to whether such a framework for advocacy can ground the struggle for global democracy, and ultimately hope in the human future, under present world conditions of denial, strife, oppression, exploitation, and alienation.

2

The Power of Rights and
the Rights of Power

What Future for Human Rights?

Ever since the end of World War II human rights have been a controversial and complex topic. Realists have been disappointed because of their central conviction that foreign policy should be governed exclusively by the pursuit of material interests. Liberal internationalists, believers in soft power, have been disappointed because political leaders often failed to take seriously human rights concerns in their dealings overseas. These opposing outlooks are further confused by the extent to which there are multiple roles for a human rights diplomacy. Even the most cynical realist appreciates a selective emphasis on the failures to respect human rights that can be attributed to hostile states. And most liberal internationalists are deferential to strategic relationships, and tend to overlook the violations of aligned states.

This chapter explores this tension between rights and power under the headings of the power of rights and the rights of power. The main argument is that rights of power prevail over the power of rights almost always when strategic interests of major state actors are at stake, and this is true whether the orientation toward world politics reflects a realist or a liberal internationalist persuasion. There is a second line of argument that insists that a critical perspective is adopted toward the relationship between the advocacy of human rights (rights talk) and the dynamics of implementation (rights work). A major contention here is that the United States has in recent years been particularly manipulative in these respects, championing rights talk as a key tenet of the neoconservative worldview while actively obstructing rights work whenever it obstructs its grand strategy, and worse, officially pursuing policies that involve flagrant rights abuse, especially in the aftermath of the 9/11 attacks.

The power of rights, although a much more potent reality than would have seemed likely a century ago, is still no match for the rights of power in a variety of settings. Part of this mismatch arises from the militarist forms of global hegemony that continue to be practiced by dominant sovereign states, despite some contradictory developments in international law, in defiance of the Charter of the United Nations. A more Gramscian turn in global hegemony could create incentives for the more powerful political actors to enhance their legitimacy by encouraging respect for human rights as the foundation of effective leadership on the world stage. There are no indications that such a turn is likely, but all is not lost.

Another set of possibilities will be explored. These are associated with a counter-hegemonic approach to human rights based on mounting challenges to the rights of power at the grassroots and in the development of post-colonial diplomacy. The anti-globalization movement, as mounted by governments in the South and by an array of civil society actors, is illustrative of efforts to augment the power of rights with respect to polices bearing on economic and social justice. This counter-hegemonic option is both establishing an appropriate discourse (rights talk on behalf of global justice goals) and a supportive practice (rights work by way of resistance and demonstrations, politics from below, as well as through coalitions between anti-geopolitical governments and transnational civil society movements). The global process that led to the establishment of the International Criminal Court is illustrative of counter-hegemonic diplomacy. This project as a juridical undertaking seemed unattainable from a realist perspective given the opposition of leading states, and yet it happened; but happening is only a symbolic victory for counter-hegemonic forces. A substantive victory would require that rights of power give way to the claims of international criminal accountability, and this seems unlikely in the foreseeable future, that is, so long as the structures of global authority sustain existing geopolitical hierarchies, politics from above. It should be observed that the concept of hegemony that has been adopted by the advocates of "counter-hegemonic" politics and law assumes an established order of inequality and exploitation managed through coercion and manipulation, and reinforced by a highly corporatized media. This is not the "benevolent hegemony" or "empire lite" so beloved by neoconservatives and liberal hawks, but rather a violent geopolitics that continues even in this post-colonial era to victimize most of humanity.

It follows that human rights is conceived of as a terrain of struggle in an ongoing battle between the disciplinary use of norms and rights to stabilize existing oppressive, exploitative, and humiliating power structures as distinguished from their emancipatory role when used by social forces aligned with the oppressed, the poor and weak, the forgotten, and the victimized margins of various societal and governmental arrangements.[1] That is, the rights of power include the appropriation of rights and norms to promote current geopolitical objectives, while the power of rights confers a normative edge with a still under-utilized potential for moral and legal mobilization in the struggle to achieve global justice and a humane global political order.

The first section of the chapter looks at top-down modalities that concentrate on the complex ways in which dominant political actors manipulate language, and use their geopolitical muscle, so as impose their will. The role of rights is especially important in this era as a way of legitimating, or at least rationalizing, the use of naked force in world politics in ways that violate international law and the United Nations (UN) Charter. The second principal section looks at bottom-up antidotes to the rights of power, exploring the capacity of grassroots forces in global civil society and their governmental allies to work toward global justice in a variety of settings. In these contexts the language and pursuit of rights provides a moral motivation for initiatives that aim both to resist oppressive moves emanating from the established order and to transform the status quo in accord with goals associated with equity, equality, and human solidarity.

The Rights of Power

There are many past and present human ordeals that could be chosen to illustrate the multi-faceted connections between "rights talk" and "rights work," as well as to clarify the closely linked appropriation of the "the power of rights" by "the rights of power." My overall intention is to work toward the construction of a normative language and praxis for human rights as discourse and behavior that is more consistently responsive to individuals and groups, including entire peoples, entrapped in highly oppressive, exploitative, and humiliating circumstances.

To select the Palestinian situation to illustrate the essential character of the rights of power is deliberatively provocative as it challenges Israel's main pattern of justification based on its defensive right to uphold the security of its territory and protect its population. To insist that these Israeli policies are unlawful is controversial in many liberal democracies, as is the contention that the Palestinian plight is both concealed and distorted in most mainstream formats of public communication, especially in the United States. From the perspective of normative expectations derived from international humanitarian law, objectively assessed, the Palestinians are victims of multiple abuses associated with prolonged Israeli occupation and harsh security tactics that defy the rules of conduct contained in the Geneva Conventions. The scale and severity of abuse approaches, if not attains, genocidal proportions as a consequence of the unremitting siege imposed by Israel on the people of Gaza in recent months. This siege has raised well-documented risks of imminent massive famine and disease, as well as causing many daily forms of psychological and material types of suffering.[2] It qualifies, politically and morally, as a continuing crime against humanity, and by its deliberateness in the face of information as to its impacts on the civilian population of Gaza, also as genocide.[3]

Yet that part of the world that stakes its claim to the post-colonial moral high ground on its adherence to the norms of liberal democracy and its advocacy of human rights seems hypocritical, considering the pronounced selectivity of what it fails to see and what it sees.[4] The main claimants to this high ground are the countries of Europe and North America.[5] As could be expected given this analysis, the zealously self-righteous leadership of the United States refuses to treat the unfolding Gazan catastrophe as a human rights challenge. On the contrary, official Washington actively supports the Israeli policies that seem directly responsible for the massive suffering that is befalling the 1.5 million people of Gaza.[6]

By their silence, and beyond this, by their diplomatic and material support of these repressive policies, these states that talk so much about human rights, and lecture the non-Western world about their duty to uphold these norms, never even reach the stage of admitting that there exists a challenge of rights work in relation to the Palestinians. These rights talkers, reinforced by the rights of power, intensified their punishment of the Palestinian people after the outcome of internationally monitored free elections brought Hamas to power in January 2006. For daring to vote as they did for Hamas candidates, the entire citizenry of Gaza have been severely punished by the imposition of a comprehensive siege and through withholding international economic assistance from a people that had already been mired in deep poverty, widespread unemployment, and the multiple dangers and hardships of a long and violent occupation, as well as enduring a series of lethal insecurities arising from frequent Israeli military incursions using advanced weapons technology and adopting menacing, humiliating, and arbitrary forms of border control.

On the level of rights talk, the Palestinian case is more deeply revealing of the extent to which the supposed global promise of human rights is broken whenever it seriously collides with geopolitical priorities, what I am calling with deliberate irony, "the *rights* of power." If the underlying conflict between Israel and Palestine were to be assigned to an independent third-party mechanism to assess from the perspective of law and morality the respective claims of the two sides, there is little doubt that the outcome would favor the Palestinians on every key disputed issue:[7] that is, ending the occupation by requiring an immediate Israeli withdrawal from Palestinian territory; by resolving territorial claims and reestablishing borders that existed before the 1967 War; by determining the legal status of Israeli settlements in accordance with the Fourth Geneva Convention;[8] by carrying out the mandate of the World Court in its Advisory Opinion relating to the legality of Israel's security fence constructed on occupied Palestinian territory;[9] by restoring the demographics and boundaries of Jerusalem, and by invalidating the assignment of sovereign rights over the city to Israel; by upholding the legal entitlements of Palestinian refugees claiming a right of return; and by determining the use rights of access to ground water aquifers located beneath Palestinian territory. A central aspect of the rights of power has been Israel's capacity, reinforced by the United States, to exclude such assessments of the legal merits and moral force of the respective claims of the two sides from the actuality of any unfolding so-called "peace process."[10] Instead of rights talk, which is excluded, what is offered up for discussion by Israel are "facts on the ground," the security concerns of the Israeli people, and the allegedly dysfunctional refusal of Palestinian leaders to accept whatever one-sided solution to the conflict an Israeli government puts forward at a particular time.[11]

Conceptually, what is exhibited is the displacement of rights talk, even talk, by the rhetoric and exercise of power, and in the process it should be noticed that rights work is erased altogether from the active political agenda. Resisting this erasure, often derided as irresponsible, meant opposing conventional wisdom at the time. This lonely work of resistance explained why Edward Said, and other principled and stalwart Palestinians, were so distressed by the Oslo Peace Process of the 1990s and by the grandstanding attempt of the Clinton presidency at Camp David II.[12] These diplomatic initiatives were at the time widely hailed as constructive breakthroughs for peace by the self-appointed moral guardians of the geopolitical order, and their structural bias against Palestinians was mostly overlooked at the time. The most telling indication of this bias was reliance on the United States as the "honest broker" of this peace process despite its consistently self-proclaimed identity as the unconditional ally of Israel. This should have been discrediting enough to invalidate the whole undertaking. There were other signs as well that the framework established for the peace process was itself too reflective of the unequal power relations to have any realistic hope of producing a fair outcome that should have been acceptable to the two sides, given their respective rights under international law and their reasonable expectations. In the Oslo framework agreement that initiated the negotiations there was an absence of any reference to a Palestinian right of self-determination or sovereign status, nor was there any indication that the imbalances in power and diplomatic leverage would be mediated by way of deference to the determination of rights via international law.

It is arguable that the weaker side deserves an intermediary biased in its favor to offset its bargaining disadvantages, but it would be unprecedented for the stronger side to agree to such an arrangement. The most, but also the least, that the weaker side could hope for is a neutral diplomatic setting, with an intermediary that was a credible interlocutor, bringing as much balance, reasonableness, and fairness to the negotiations as possible. As suggested, an intermediary biased toward the stronger side merely underscores the absence of any leverage on the weaker side, and with such weakness has almost no prospect of receiving any satisfaction for its contested claims and goals even if it is willing to engage in compromise and eager for a reconciliation. It was not surprising that the United States made little existential attempt to be an "honest broker" at Camp David, but rather crudely played the part of "power broker" and Israeli advocate, adding its formidable support to the proposals of Israel and blaming the Palestinians for their refusal to accept what Israel has offered with a display of gratitude.[13] It is disturbing that the mainstream media uncritically reported Washington's one-sided version of why the negotiations failed.

Such an erasure of the rights of the weak as a proper concern of inter-governmental negotiations has the unintended effect of relegating *genuine* "rights talk" and "rights work" to civil society militants, moderate governments, and the margins of world public opinion. This relegation process is uneven, being far worse in the United States with respect to the Palestinians than elsewhere in the world, including even Europe. The attention of almost all "reasonable" people in the West is thereby shifted by a manipulative mind game to the prudent exercise of the "rights of power." This becomes the inevitable result of an unequal bargaining relationship in which the rights of the weak side are disregarded altogether by being deliberately placed outside the domain of diplomacy. Adding to public confusion, the mainstream media, especially in the United States, disarmingly claiming objectivity, portrayed the proposals of Ehud Barak at Camp David II as "generous" and "courageous." Yasir Arafat, representing the Palestinians, was cast in the role of "spoiler" whose opposition to the Israeli proposals was treated as convincing evidence that he had never been truly interested in achieving "peace," was intent on resolving the conflict through violence, and came to Camp David lacking the good faith needed to negotiate a peace agreement. This false rendering of the failed diplomacy later was relied upon by Israel to vindicate its use of excessive force to subdue the Second Intifada. This angry challenge to the status quo emerged in late September 2000 directly from Palestinian frustrations and Israeli provocations (especially Ariel Sharon's notorious September 28, 2000 visit to the al Aqsa mosque on the Temple Mount/Harim-al Sharif).

Against this background it was hardly surprising, yet inflammatory and inaccurate, for President Clinton and other notables to declare in public that Arafat was responsible for the breakdown of the peace negotiations. This background set the stage for positing the unilateralist claims of Ariel Sharon to the effect that since the Israelis had no "partner" in their search for peace, they were entitled to proceed unilaterally, imposing their own solution to the conflict and calling that "peace." As argued, the geopolitically compliant media played a decisive part in producing such a distorted view of these realities, inverting the equities in a manner that would make even George Orwell blush: the strong side, while being insistent on retaining most of its unlawful advantages resulting from military and diplomatic dominance, as well as its successful reliance as occupier on state terror and political violence, is applauded for its peace initiatives and its reasonableness, whereas the weak side is scorned for its imprudent and defiant rejectionism and its supposedly addictive reliance on terrorism.

In this manner the rights of power consistently overwhelmed the power of rights in public space. At the same time existential conditions of acute injustice are almost totally exempt from mainstream scrutiny and criticism. Of course, this perception and discourse relating to Israel/Palestine is largely inverted, with comparable imbalance, throughout the Middle East and South Asia. This pro-Palestinian rights talk has little impact on the dynamics of the frozen conflict: the problem-solving matrix for this conflict, despite its geographic location, remains as firmly anchored in the Eurocentric West as was the case during the colonial era.

This argument can be generalized far beyond the particular tragedies of the Palestinian narrative, which is admittedly an unusual situation due to the degree and unconditionality of American support for Israel that partly reflects domestic political pressures that is arguably often at odds with United States national interests.[14] Rights talk is excluded from public consciousness, or artfully manipulated, whenever it gets seriously in the way of the rights of power. For this reason the very possibility of rights work is occluded from consciousness. This structure sustaining oppression and obscuring various forms of cruelty was explicit in the relations between Europe and the Middle East and South Asia during the colonial period, but it persists in many, but not all, post-colonial settings, although in often disguised and inconsistent forms. The root causes of different contexts of human suffering as it appears in many political spaces continues to exist because the rights of power usually have the will and capacity to prevent even a critical awareness from emerging.

This pattern is definitely descriptive of many intergovernmental and inter-regional realities, but also in more complicated ways it affects a variety of intra-governmental settings. For instance, the issue of Indian untouchability, dalits, and caste subordination is almost as occluded from international rights talk as is the ordeal of the Palestinians in Gaza, not because of any self-conscious strategy by outside political actors, but because the plight of culturally and politically victimized Indians is not nearly so geopolitically resonant as is the plight of Tibetans or the Chechens. Whatever the governmental context, by achieving this subordination, the question of rights work never even gets onto official political agendas. Arguably, and in a range of circumstances, oppressive economic, political, and cultural structures *within* sovereign states are responsible for the most persistent and severe denials of fundamental rights in the world that affect by far the greatest number of lives. These human wrongs are mainly indigenous, and can often be only indirectly, if at all, linked to the colonial legacy. This fundamental distribution of authority to shape human behavior continues almost exclusively under the control of leaders situated behind the high, and virtually unbreachable, walls of sovereign states. This deference to sovereignty is reinforced by continuing to accord legitimacy to a world order composed of sovereign states.[15] These states have long served as sanctuaries of impunity in which the commission of "human wrongs" often goes unnoticed, and almost always goes unpunished.[16]

A spectacular exception occurred in 1998 when the former Chilean dictator, Auguste Pinochet, was detained in Britain in response to an extradition request to face charges in Spain for crimes against humanity and other abuses of power during his tenure as president of Chile. The drama surrounding the detention of Chile's former dictator suggested that it might be possible in certain rare circumstances to overcome impunity. After a long litigating process in Britain Pinochet was sent home to Chile because he was found unfit to stand trial by the British Foreign Secretary in what many observers felt to be a political decision dictated by a concern about the treatment of political leaders by foreign legal systems. Pinochet died some years later in Chile before any punitive initiatives were consummated in his home country. German courts in the last few years have, for thinly disguised but presumably similar political reasons, been unwilling to exercise the jurisdictional authority contained in their criminal laws to hold Donald Rumsfeld accountable for torture at Abu Ghraib, despite the submission to the prosecutor of a strong dossier of incriminating evidence. The promise of "universal jurisdiction" has titillated the imagination of liberal legalists, but it currently lacks the capacity to overcome the insulation of international crimes of state from procedures of legal accountability except in some rare special instances.[17]

This dynamic is actually given explicit recognition in some conceptualizations of international law that accord hegemonic status power *within* the law, creating a tension between the political/juridical myth that international relations and world order are based on norms of "sovereign equality" and assertions that inequalities of status and power deserve to be acknowledged as having a "desirable" lawmaking effect.[18] The most symbolically significant example of such an acknowledgment of hegemonic international law is written into the Charter of the United Nations, which makes the five states that prevailed in World War II (and were the first five to acquire nuclear weapons) permanent members of the Security Council and alone entitled to exercise a veto over its decisions. This two-tier UN hierarchy is actually less overtly deferential to geopolitical claims in some respects than was the League of Nations Covenant's juridically inexplicable statement of deference to the Monroe Doctrine. But the UN approach to power and law has far more operational significance given the centrality of the Security Council on matters of peace and security, and considering the use of the veto, and its threatened use, by permanent members whenever controversial decisions are being made, thereby often gridlocking the UN at times of greatest urgency. In effect, this veto power institutionalizes "hegemonic international law" by formalizing sovereign *inequality* as a basic ordering principle of pervasive operational significance.

It was also reinforced in judicial settings at the outset of the UN's existence by the reservation attached to the US acceptance of the compulsory jurisdiction of the World Court, which allowed the US government to prevent the submission of any legal dispute within the domestic jurisdiction of the United States as determined by the United States government. When the World Court established its legal competence over vigorous objections from Washington to decide the Nicaragua case back in the 1980s, a dispute involving various hostile actions of the U.S. directed at undermining the legitimate Sandinista government in Managua, the U.S. government rescinded its acceptance of compulsory jurisdiction altogether, typifying its unwillingness to risk an impartial application of law and rights reaching an adverse outcome.[19] The rights of power also control the interminable yet frustrating discourse on UN reform, with most attention by governments being devoted to the rather superficial challenge of taking account of shifts in the geopolitical landscape that have taken place since the UN was established in 1945. In effect, at issue is whether India, Japan, Brazil, and others should be elevated to this status of permanent members, with or without a veto power, but without any more general consideration of whether a right of veto can ever be reconciled with the supposed commitment of the UN to a law-governed world.[20]

The docility of the United Nations with respect to its central mandate of war prevention is a further demonstration of the rights of power overwhelming the power of rights. The UN was widely acclaimed when the UN Security Council resisted in 2003 U.S. geopolitical pressures to authorize the initiation of an aggressive war against Iraq, but this was an extremely modest gesture of resistance. If more dispassionately considered, the UN role would itself confirm the distortion of rights that is achieved by the claims of power. From the perspective of legal rights, Iraq should have been protected by UN collective security mechanisms against unlawful threats and uses of force that had been made and carried out for many years prior to 2003 by the United States and Great Britain, as well as from sanctions that were a form of collective punishment victimizing the civilian population of Iraq.[21] It is widely remembered that when Madeleine Albright, the American Secretary of State during Clinton's second term, was asked by a TV newscaster in 1996 whether she thought the several hundred thousand civilian casualties attributable to sanctions were worth this price in lives, she replied chillingly: "Yes, we think the price is worth it."[22] In relations to the imposition of sanctions, the UN was so effectively manipulated that it had endorsed a geopolitical stance of the U.S. government that was completely oblivious to the rights of the people of Iraq, and again, expectations were so low, that it was considered a victory for "compassionate liberalism" to soften the cruelty being experienced by the Iraqi people during the 1990s to allow some food to be sent to Iraq in exchange for a small portion of Iraqi oil revenues. The point here is that if we look at the manner with which rights and power are configured internationally, it becomes clear that even rights talk at the UN and in other arenas where the participants are governments, is often reduced to formalistic verbal communications that lack any pretension of substantive seriousness in the sense of seeking behavioral results.

Or another example, the U.S. government, after proclaiming in many ways, especially since 9/11, that it will never be constrained by international law in the pursuit of its security interests, in mid-February 2008 indignantly invoked international law to protest the failure of the Serbian government to protect its embassy in Belgrade after Kosovo's controversial secessionist declaration of political independence.[23] What this illustrates, then, is the opportunistic use of international law, a variant of "rights talk," by a hegemonic actor such as the United States whenever the political leadership finds it convenient to do so. Because of the rights of power, such opportunism rarely attracts adverse comment. The American claim is evaluated by the UN membership as if the United States is itself a model adherent of international law rather than being one of the worst offenders.

The dark side of this schizophrenic relationship to international law and human rights is vividly disclosed by the approach taken to crimes of state committed by political leaders. The extension of the Nuremberg Principles to the circumstances of the 1990s helped create the profoundly misleading appearance that "a golden age of human rights" was emerging out of the leftover debris of the Cold War. More accurate perceptions might have discerned the dawn of a new dark age for international law and human rights: first came the legally dubious Kosovo War of 1999 under NATO auspices with its plausible human rights rationale, then came the American response to 9/11 that included an array of encroachments on individual rights, and then came the Iraq War with its flagrant disregard for international law and the authority of the United Nations. On the glossy surface of world politics this darkness was effectively ignored. With a variety of maneuvers behind the scenes, the International Criminal Tribunal for Former Yugoslavia, was induced to indict Slobodan Milosevic while the NATO bombs were raining down on Serbia in a non-defensive war never endorsed by the UN Security Council.[24] Worse still, despite the US launching an aggressive war against Iraq, the captured leader, Saddam Hussein was subjected to political trial, managed behind the scenes by the aggressor state, and summarily executed in a disgracefully discrediting manner. In both instances, the enthusiasm for criminalizing the behavior of political leaders was undertaken to provide an aura of legitimacy for the lawlessness of the hegemonic instigators, an almost perfect instance of "empire's law," as there was a virtual guarantee of an absence of symmetry in this revival of the Nuremberg ethos of accountability. Of course, at Nuremberg itself this guarantee of impunity was formally part of the structure of judicial assessment, which was somewhat later derided as victors' justice.[25]

Despite such contradictions of usage, the geopolitical status of the United States makes power of rights appear formidable on those occasions when such a hegemonic actor manifests the political will to implement rights claims. The rather dispiriting point here is that the "rights of power" are indispensable for achieving the "power of rights" in many specific situations given the way the world continues to be organized. This pattern strengthens the impression that the most vulnerable are either erased from view altogether (as had been the case until rather recently for indigenous peoples, or currently, the people of Gaza) or their grievances are entirely ignored as any corrective response is generally perceived as existing in a realm beyond the reach of practical politics (as is the case for many abused minorities in larger states). Such an assessment would be even more depressing from a humanistic perspective if it were not the case that power itself is undergoing a variety of transformations that enhance the leverage of the dispossessed and vulnerable.

The Power of Rights

No recent voice has been clearer than that of Balakrishnan Rajagopal in exposing the hegemonic orientation of the liberal human rights movement, including that associated with such leading human rights NGOs as Amnesty International and Human Rights Watch. By hegemonic orientation Rajagopal has in mind the selectivity in the way rights talk and rights work are implemented, highlighting some instances, ignoring others. This critical task is necessary to undercut, especially, arguments favoring "humanitarian intervention" so as to circumvent the prohibitions of law and morality associated with recourse to non-defensive force that does not elicit approval from the UN Security Council. In the period of strategic unipolarity since the end of the Cold War, the United States has been the predominant hegemon, and has consistently fused controversial claims to use force with various humanitarian rationales. This practice has been particularly pronounced during the Bush II presidency, and especially so since 9/11. And it has encouraged the perception that rights talk obfuscates both the rights of power and lawlessness.[26]

Rajagopal is equally insightful in contemplating a counter-hegemonic potential for a reoriented human rights movement. His words are worth quoting at some length because they identify so clearly the uncertain fault line that separates hegemony from emancipation when it comes to human rights:

> Current human rights discourse and practice has a choice, a fork in the road … it can either insinuate itself within hegemonic international law or it can serve as an important tool in developing and strengthening a counter-hegemonic international law. By ignoring the history of imperialism, by endorsing wars while opposing their consequences, and by failing to link itself with social movements of resistance, the main protagonists of the Western human rights discourse are undermining the future of human rights itself.[27]

It is crucial for those world citizens with a progressive agenda not to bow down before this hegemonic appropriation of human rights discourse, and limit a negative response to exposé and criticism, however deserved.[28] There exists an important corpus of counter-hegemonic practice and discourse that can take political advantage of the intergovernmental normative architecture of international human rights law. This structure incorporates norms that are ethically helpful in challenging prevailing forms of oppression and exploitation. This corpus of norms provides tools for struggle and resistance, as well as critique, and offers a conception of engagement that re-situates human rights on the emancipatory side of the geopolitical ledger of accounts.

In this spirit of sincere dedication to the values that give rise to the norms, progressive activists should pay close attention to Upendra Baxi's broad injunction, made several decades ago, "to take human suffering seriously," or as he more recently formulated his outlook, to bridge:

the immeasurable distance between what we call "human rights" and the right of all to be human . . . this distance can begin to be traversed only if we claim the audacity to look at the human rights models from the standpoint of the historically oppressed groups . . .

This is the foundational imperative of a counter-hegemonic human rights movement.[29] To similar effect, with an eye toward not confining popular struggles to the formal arenas of law and international institutions, Smitu Kothari and Harsh Sheth write of the importance of evolving "a social praxis, rooted in the need of the most oppressed communities, that seeks to create norms of civilized existence. In any final instance, it is only this—a shared vision of how we want to live as a collectivity—that can provide us the moral basis for evolving our own conduct."[30]From these perspectives, the power of rights has had several instructive historic successes within the broad framing of world order issues, including the discrediting of colonial claims and the upgrading of the right of self-determination; the affirmation of national sovereignty over natural resources; the anti-apartheid, anti-racism struggle; the liberation of Eastern Europe by nonviolent means; the pursuit of "another globalization" oriented toward human wellbeing rather than the efficiency of capital; and the continued elaboration of a human rights architecture (norms and procedures) that provides legitimation for a variety of emancipatory struggles (while admittedly also simultaneous providing tools to validate an array of hegemonic projects). Reverting to Rajagopal's reference to the fork in the road confronting the human rights movement, reminds us of the closing lines of Robert Frost's familiar poem "The Road Not Taken":

Two roads diverged in a wood, and I—
I took the one less traveled by,
And that has made all the difference.

I think that there exists a better way to contemplate the contextual realities of the counter-hegemonic approach to rights than to contemplate what to do at a fork in the road. It is to recognize that the choice has actually been made quite a long time ago by both sides: the mainstream human rights movement in the North generally, yet not invariably, has chosen to work within the frame of hegemonic international law. This is in line with the precepts of liberal internationalism (the "empire lite" of Michael Ignatieff) and moves along on the well-travelled road with positive results achieved in those sectors of international life where the strategic motivations of the hegemonic actor are either minimal or absent.

The other, less traveled road has been best articulated by post-colonial thought, made manifest through civil society initiatives, and given a loose institutional identity by the World Social Forum. It links perceptions and activities directly to the plight of the vulnerable, the marginal, the oppressed, exploited, and abused. This emancipatory undertaking finds itself moving in spurts and stops on this less traveled road, sometimes effectively and at other times futilely, but its steadfastness and courage is what, in Frost's words, makes "all the difference." Thus the historic moment is characterized, not by a choice between alternatives but by two opposed sets of priorities, one guided by grand strategy, the other by compassion and human solidarity, that only rarely converge in thought or action. One instance of convergence occurred during the latter stages of the anti-apartheid campaign, when dominant governments were induced to empower claims for racial justice in South Africa, achieving dramatic results.

This less traveled road, as it pertains to human rights, is synonymous with the imperatives of counter-hegemonic discourse. Its heritage is most easily traced to the efforts of Latin American jurists early in the twentieth century to use international law with some success as a defensive strategy to mitigate, and eventually invalidate, U.S. interventionary diplomacy, and the accompanying unequal economic arrangements that had been forcibly imposed and maintained. More globally, and in the setting of the Middle East and Asia, it can be traced through the anti-colonial movement based on a creative adaptation of the highly constrained self-determination ethos as disseminated by Woodrow Wilson at the close of World War I, as well as the more faithful borrowing by nationalist figures in Asia and Africa from a comparable endorsement of self-determination made after World War I by Lenin.

What rights work has been done in recent years on the less traveled road of counter-hegemonic creativity has been mainly due to the efforts of civil society actors with a transnational agenda. There are many examples, but among the most poignant, was "the tribunal movement" prompted by the Iraq War (and a natural sequel to the pre-war global demonstrations on February 15, 2003) and by the silences of governments and the United Nations. This movement consisted of trials in some 20 countries around the world. It was financed and organized by representative of civil society to assess the legality of the invasion and occupation of Iraq and the criminal accountability of those leaders (and supportive actors, including corporate officers, journalists). These efforts culminated in an elaborate proceeding, enjoying wide coverage on the Internet and alternate media, in Istanbul in 2005 that examined all facets of the legal and ethical case against the U.S./UK policies in Iraq.[31] This kind of initiative is the mirror image of the hegemonic prosecutions of Milosevic and Saddam Hussein referred to above, but lacking the backing of the power of rights, and resting its claims on the authority of the rights of power. This counter-tradition associated with international legality and criminality was organized during the Vietnam War on the initiative of Bertrand Russell, who was able to enlist the participation of leading intellectuals of the day, including Jean-Paul Sartre, and was followed by the establishment in Rome of the Permanent Peoples Tribunal dedicated to the same goals of exposure and truth-telling. From the perspective of my understanding, a significant development over the years is reflected by the geographic move away from Europe to Istanbul, which can claim a location that is at least as much Asian and Middle Eastern as it is European.

A Trajectory for the Power of Rights

The rights of power are well financed and motivated by the material sensibilities that control almost every modern society. The power of rights needs to motivate its varied constituencies by both the urgencies of its cause and the genuine, although not assured, possibilities of producing improvements in the human condition. Without motivation there will be no struggle, and without struggle there will be no progress. A few lines from a poem by the German poet, Günther Eich, express the promise and responsibility associated with the power of rights:

> No, don't sleep while the arrangers of the world are busy!
>
> Be suspicious of the power they claim
>
> to have to acquire on your behalf!
>
> Stay awake to be sure that your hearts are not empty, when
>
> others calculate on the emptiness of your hearts!
>
> Do what is unhelpful, sing songs from out of your mouths
>
> that go against expectation!
>
> Be ornery, be as sand, not oil in the thirsty machinery
>
> of the world!

3

Orientalism and International Law

This chapter contends that mitigating an American-led Orientalism is a matter of urgency. Conveniently for pedagogic purposes, and dangerously with regard to its political and human effects, this Orientalism is presently configured in the crucible of Middle Eastern turmoil. This is not a marginal matter but a core issue if there are to be positive responses to the threats to world order of the early twenty-first century this side of severe catastrophe. Part of the challenge is to redeem the role of international law as a foundation for constructive, inter-civilizational, normative discourse and mutually beneficial international behavior by purging it, as far as possible, of the taint of Orientalism, or at the very least, alerting observers to the Orientalist twists and turns of international law doctrine and practice.[1]

There is a preliminary definitional point. "International law" is used here as a shorthand to designate the legal conception of a global normative order and is not to be understood in its strict Westphalian sense of a regulative framework primarily associated with norms regulating the interaction of sovereign states. At the same time, those portions of international law that transcend Orientalist manipulation most successfully—for instance, the Universal Declaration of Human Rights and the Geneva Conventions on International Humanitarian Law—continue to serve mainly as guidelines for the behavior of sovereign states. Of course, this transcendence is constantly in jeopardy, due to the dynamics of geopolitical manipulation by way of interpretation and practice on the part of leading political actors, a manipulation reinforced by a generally subservient global media. As has so often been observed, but from varying ethical and political angles, we live in a time of transition in which the state system is being superseded in many respects, and yet it is this statist conception of world order that continues to provide the most authoritative bases for restricting the abuse of state power within states and in relation to contested uses of international force.[2]

General Considerations

In any approach to this topic, it is neither possible nor desirable to avoid the centrality of Edward Said's inspirational influence. In his 2003 Preface to the 25th Anniversary Edition of *Orientalism*, Edward Said highlights a perspective that I adopt as my own: "Above all, critical thought does not submit to state power or to commands to join in the ranks marching against one or another approved enemy."[3] A little further on in this important reflection on the Orientalist discourse as it has evolved, Said observes, "And lastly, most important, humanism is the only, and I would go so far as to say, the final resistance we have against the inhuman practices and injustices that disfigure human history"[4] I would insist, perhaps paradoxically, that despite the pervasive Orientalism of the main traditions of international law scholarship and doctrine, it is from international law that we derive the most geopolitically relevant framing of humanist resistance to the criminalization of world politics over the course of recent decades. My standpoint, then, is to emphasize a creative tension between international law as an instrument for Orientalist domination and exploitation of the non-Western peoples of the world, on the one hand, and international law as a fragile, yet indispensable, humanist enclave embedded in realist and imperialist geopolitical behavior, which has provided the normative foundations for resistance against and emancipation from contemporary forms of imperialism, on the other.

A further framing observation is to realize that the critical task of exposing the Orientalist features of international law cannot be entirely disentangled from the humanist achievement of supporting the contributions of international law to the establishment of a humane normative order for all forms of political interaction. Expressed differently, the authority of international law rests, in part, upon its overt affirmation of the ethical premises of human solidarity and a positive engagement with the promotion of peace, equity, sustainability, and human rights. Of course, such legitimating claims also function to disguise the historic role of international law as an invaluable instrument contrived by the powerful to pursue their destructive and exploitative goals in the world, giving an aura of legitimacy to the domination and oppression of the weak.

A distinguishing feature of Orientalism, narrowly conceived, is to associate influence and the case for forcible intervention in non-Western societies with the pretensions of Western civilizational superiority. Indeed, the more forcible the intervention, the more strident the claims to civilizing—as was the case during the period of European colonialism—and the more detrimental the human effects. This ideological posture of civilizational superiority was endorsed by the most enlightened intellectual figures of the colonial era (e.g., John Stuart Mill) and even such revolutionary thinkers within the Western tradition as Karl Marx. The current pretensions of American normative superiority are a recurrent theme of the Bush presidency, as Washington

continues to assert that America's gift to the world is its exemplary democratizing reality, despite the sordid revelations of torture and crimes against
humanity that have been emerging from the entrails of U.S. behavior in
Afghanistan, Iraq, and Guantanamo.[5] In essence, the Orientalist presupposition
of American grand strategy is that the United States is entitled to an exemption
from the legal prohibition on "aggression" because its motives are to implant
universally valid values in the political soil of non-Western foreign countries
governed in accordance with regressive political traditions. Of course,
American leaders present this pattern of aggression and abuse in more benign
guises, as "humanitarian intervention" and anti-terrorism, but the essential
undertaking involves the non-defensive use of force against a sovereign state,
a use of force that is best understood as constituting aggression of a criminal
character. And furthermore, the ideological spin-masters in Washington
contend that America, due to its normative achievements at home and in the
world, deserves the benefit of the doubt when it acts unilaterally on the global
stage. In criticizing the Bush articulation of this Orientalist perspective, I do
not want to suggest that this recent phase of American foreign policy represents
an ideological rupture from that of Bush's predecessors. Bill Clinton's combined
advocacy of the enlargement of democracy and promotion of human rights
by force of arms as goals of American foreign policy, especially in the context
of economic globalization, was different in text and context, but not with
regard to the goal of normative domination of the entire globe. And the deeper
roots of American claims to moral, political, and legal exceptionalism,
expressed in the biblical imagery of "the new Jerusalem" and the "city upon
the hill" stretch back to its colonial period.[6] Thomas Jefferson spoke of an
American mission to establish "an empire of liberty," and there was an insistence on moral exceptionalism to the effect that, unlike the states of Europe,
the United States based its policy on admirable "values" of general benefit
and not on selfish "interests." We are still yoked to this delusionary mythic
portrayal of America in the world, precluding, so far, a national process of
self-corrective disavowal of Orientalist arrogance. In this increasingly outrageous and essentially absurd defense of American innocence, the demoniza-
tion of the Arab world is centrally required to avoid provoking a critical account
of the American role in the world. Such academic figures as Bernard Lewis
and Fouad Ajami have become the main ideological mercenaries, especially
since the 9/11 attacks, supplying the power-wielders in the White House and
Pentagon with propagandistic support for their claims to geopolitical destiny.[7]
The present historical circumstances of "transition" need also to be taken into
conceptual account. It not enough to lament how, throughout the history of
the Westphalian world order, powerful states have relied on subtle forms of
Orientalism to validate the use of international law in smoothing some of the
rough edges of hegemonic geopolitics, using a variety of "legal" encroachments
on the supposed guiding principle of the sovereign equality of states. These
encroachments reached their climax during the colonial period and were

somewhat eroded by the gradual legitimization of the anti-colonial struggle, especially by the validation of the right of a people to self-determination and by the contributions to norm creation by the United Nations (UN) General Assembly during the 1960s and 1970s.[8] It remains to write this history from the perspective of international law, although a promising start has been made by Balakrishnan Rajagopal, which appropriately acknowledges the influence of Said on the undertaking.[9] This re-writing of the history of international law needs to be correlated with wider shifts in patterns of dominance in international relations.[10]

The emergence of a post-Westphalian world order complicates our inquiry. It is one of the salient features of our time, arising from many factors converging on contradictory trends toward globalization and geo-governance and altering the earlier modernist preoccupation with abridgements of the supposed *juridical* equality of states.[11] The most responsive post-Westphalian inquiry is one on the multiple roles of international law in validating the American project of global domination and in contesting that outcome from the perspective of international human rights, international humanitarian law, and a revisiting of sovereign equality. We must also take into account the constructive and essential role of international law in validating resistance to anti-Orientalist political violence by non-state actors that threatens orderly and consensual political life throughout the planet, especially in light of the 9/11 attacks and subsequent violent assaults on civilian targets.[12] This imperative becomes part of the normative puzzle that needs solving in the aftermath of 9/11. There are alternative, yet overlapping, paths of response: the United States' war framing offers a contrast to Spain's law-enforcement framing in reaction to the March 11, 2004 train bombings in Madrid. It remains fair to accentuate the Orientalist features of the transition because its central drama involves the struggle to re-establish world order on asymmetrical terms favorable to the West, specifically to the United States, but without neglecting concern about those forms of anti-Orientalism that are morally and legally unacceptable. And also without overlooking the transnational movement of progressive popular forces to establish a rights-based, universal normative order, based on democratic principles of participation, accountability, transparency, the rule of law, and above all, human rights comprehensively conceived.[13] International law is a project of global civil society, as well as an instrument useful to state actors that project their power beyond their borders.

There is an additional preliminary point that is well articulated by Said; namely, the degree to which our own understanding of a subject matter is itself infused with Orientalist influences. As Said puts it, "In many ways my study of Orientalism has been an attempt to inventory the traces upon me, the Oriental subject, of the culture whose domination has been such a powerful factor in the life of all Orientals."[14] Speaking as an Occidental, there is no doubt that being an educational and cultural product of the dominating political actor, participating in the discourse from such a social and political location, has shaped the tone and substance of my response, however radically critical my approach to international law may purport to be. And in a fuller investigation of the topic, I would be bound to investigate the traces that condition my approach and make it unsatisfactory to varying degrees from subaltern perspectives.[15] While insisting on a progressive undertaking, I still cannot pretend to adopt a subaltern voice but rely on others for an enactment of subalternity.[16] I am indebted to the Orientalist appropriation of international law in my attempt to depict beneficial normative horizons.[17] This may seem foolishly utopian, if evaluated according to realist canons of feasibility, but strikes me as desirable and necessary if our goal is to achieve equity, peace, dignity, and sustainability for the peoples of the world. I draw some comfort from Jacques Derrida's important assessment along similar lines.[18]

Matters of method help frame an inquiry to accord with the goals pursued. Any proper investigation of the Orientalist traditions embedded in international law would include a careful reading of the main texts produced by the most influential Euro-American jurists from classical times to the present, as well as a close reading of the work of non-Western jurists, both critical and apologetic, to discern the extent to which hegemonic normative presuppositions have been assimilated by the dominated and exploited. This more ambitious investigation will have to be consigned to the future. Some partial and ambiguous moves in that direction have been made by Third World legal scholars and by "critical legal studies," especially David Kennedy and several of his students.[19] Kennedy makes the pertinent observation that international law can only be appreciated in relation to "a distinction between the West and the rest of the world, and the role of that distinction in the generation of doctrines, institutions and state practice."[20] My undertaking here is rather limited: to illustrate the hegemonic role of international legal discourse and doctrine in specific behavioral contexts that show the extent to which international law is embedded in the geopolitics of domination by the West. Although some historical examples will be given in summary form, the greater effort will be to exhibit some of the ways in which the United States, as the self-anointed imperial epicenter of world order, uses and abuses international law in pursuit of its grand strategic design. It is important, at this point, to distinguish between the deep structure of this normative Orientalism that has been the underpinning of American foreign policy since 1945 and its current crude and especially militarist enactment during the presidency of George W. Bush. In the deep structure, the creative tension mentioned earlier generates subtler forms of domination and exploitation and makes international law available, on occasion, as an instrument for the weak to resist the predatory policies of the strong. In the crude enactment, the creative tension disappears and is replaced by a rather more naked struggle of domination and resistance, as is on grim display in occupied Iraq and occupied Palestine at this time. Even here, international law, although largely generated as a Eurocentric artifact, provides markers that identify impermissible behavior and mobilize political opposition against the excesses of the United States and of its acolytes, principally Great Britain and Israel. Indeed, the neoconservative hard line on American grand strategy emphasizes this bonding of weakness with an insistence on the relevance of international law. For instance, Robert Kagan's account of the European/American cleavage points to this correlation of weakness and law as indicative of Europe's weakness, as America's power-driven approach to global policy is seen as confirmation of its strength.[21] And Richard Perle, with far less artifice, insists that it was a geopolitical virtue to ignore the obstacle of international law, including the absence of a UN mandate, in undertaking the Iraq War.[22]

My standpoint is, then, shaped by three somewhat divergent objectives:

- to give some content to an Orientalist critique of international law as an adequate foundation for a universal normative order;
- to affirm the actual and potential role of international law as oppositional to both Western hegemony and the American imperial project; and
- to recognize that international law, if revitalized in certain respects to take account of legitimate subaltern grievances, does provide a series of stepping stones across the transitional divide to a post-Westphalian normative order, resting on a balance between universal constraints and rights, on the one hand, and deference to a wide range of cultural diversities, on the other.

This move toward establishing a sustainable, normative (legal/ethical) order on a global scale is advocated as a matter of urgency, given the precariousness of existing arrangements associated with "world order."

The next section of the chapter examines a few of the ways in which the Westphalian juridical ethos of equality has been encroached upon during the period of "modernity" associated with the rise of the sovereign state in the 17th century as the constitutive political actor in world affairs. The final section considers *contradictory* attempts to invoke international law as the normative foundation for a post-Westphalian world order.

Orientalist Fixes in the Westphalian Era

My idea here is not to survey the range of Orientalist practices but to give some examples that illuminate the flavor of a process by which international law becomes a vehicle for infusing Westphalian statecraft with a distinct Western bias. As suggested, the bias consisted of carving out "exceptions" to the rules and generating rules that were mainly of benefit to the dominant actors. But there was also a dialectic at work, allowing the normative veneer given to domination to be creatively adapted to tactics and strategies for subaltern resistance.

Legitimizing Colonialism

This is a large subject in itself. International law fully recognized colonial arrangements, denying representation to colonized peoples. It also endorsed rights of conquest that reinforced Western military superiority, and peace treaties and international concession agreements were treated as legally valid even if ratifying wars of aggression and military interventions. International law grotesquely disregarded the rights of native (or indigenous) peoples, and in some instances denied their personhood. International law, for a considerable period, validated the international slave trade and the institution of slavery. It both violated the sovereignty of non-Western countries with reckless abandon and insisted on unconditional sovereignty for Western countries, allowing the commission of a horrendous array of what Ken Booth has memorably named "human wrongs."[23] A benchmark of the colonialist era was the Berlin Conference of 1884, where European statesmen arrogantly divided up African nations among themselves, fixing boundaries and establishing political entities that were often unnatural political communities. The process was repeated for the Middle East after World War I, under the guise of producing a sustainable peace in the region, and disguised colonial administration with the establishment of the mandatory system, which purported to require some minimal accountability by the administering power vis-à-vis the organized international community (the League of Nations). These countries did eventually achieve independence and full membership in international society, illustrating the rise of anti-colonial self-determination norms supported by some geopolitical developments, including the anti-colonial diplomacy of the Soviet Union, the ambivalent attitude of the United States, the rapidly declining power of colonial Europe, and the rise of an ethos of national liberation.

That is, international law has been both a *managerial* tool in the hands of aggressors, oppressors, and exploiters and a site of *struggle* and *resistance* by those victimized seeking to vindicate individual and collective rights. The law of war is a graphic tableau for these contradictory tendencies. On the one side, the most savage tactics are exempted from legal accountability by claims of "military necessity." On the other side, those subjected to abuse by occupying powers, lacking the capabilities to challenge the existing situation by political or military means, rely on the norms of the law of war, especially the Fourth Geneva Convention, to express their claims and validate their resistance.

Israel's failure to uphold its obligations under international law has lent weight to Palestinian claims to self-determination and to affect the contours of a peace process. The fact that Israel's reliance on collective punishment violates Article 33 of the Geneva Convention, and its establishment of Israeli settlements on the West Bank and Gaza violates Article 49(6), is certainly relevant to identifying a fair solution to the conflict for both peoples, but whether these unlawful practice will be taken into account remains very doubtful at this point. International law is being used opportunistically by the West-centric world order, which itself is expressive of "orientalization," international law being relied upon when helpful to the West, cast aside when not. It is this double reality that exhibits the essential character of international law, a Western self-interested construct and a Frankenstein creation that cannot be consistently controlled by its inventors.

Diplomatic Protection of Nationals Abroad

There emerged, as a doctrine of legal right, the authorization to override sovereignty to protect nationals abroad whose security, interests, and rights were being jeopardized by the territorial government. This involved the legalization of intervention, especially by the United States and particularly in relation to Latin America, as so-called "gunboat diplomacy" evolved out of applications of the Monroe Doctrine. The Monroe Doctrine was initially proclaimed in 1823 to prevent any further European colonization in the Western hemisphere, but was later invoked as a tool entitling the United States to engage in repeated armed interventions, often followed by prolonged occupation. This practice was particularly flagrant in Central America and the Caribbean. In a remarkable exhibition of manifest Orientalism, the Monroe Doctrine was explicitly acknowledged as a valid part of world order in Article 21 of the Covenant of the League of Nations, despite its radical inconsistency with the foundational principle of the sovereign equality of states. Article 21 uses quaint language that disguises the interventionist prerogatives and imperial characteristics of practice relating to the Monroe Doctrine by referring to it as a "regional understanding" that serves the purpose of "securing the maintenance of peace."

The Standard of "Civilization"

The implicit and explicit Orientalist claim was to locate "civilization" in Europe and to suggest a contrast with the otherness of inferior cultures that were lacking in civilization and the ethical and aesthetic refinement of the West. The contrast was even drawn between civilization and barbarism to heighten the sense of difference. It was the civilized world that claimed for itself an exclusive norm-generating role. Even as late as 1945 the Statute of the International Court of Justice reflected this Orientalist trope in its famous Article 38 on the sources of law to be consulted in a dispute between states. In Article 38(1)(c), after giving priority to treaty and the customary norms of international law established by consent of governments, a residual source of law is described as follows: "the general principles of law as recognized by civilized nations." This use of civilized also underlay the capitulary regimes and analogous arrangements that exempted nationals from Orientalist countries from the application of territorial

46

criminal law, presumed corrupt and inferior. The Status of Forces Agreements negotiated by the United States during the Cold War era also embodied an exemption from territorial accountability for military personnel and even for civilians if their crimes were committed on foreign military bases.

Subaltern Juridical Creativity

Again this is a big subject. The basic idea is that the non-Western objects of international law were able to become subjects and assert agency in certain settings. Latin American diplomats and jurists were especially adept at articulating subaltern approaches to international legal doctrine in the broad field of international economic relations.[24] Such ideas as the Calvo Doctrine, the Drago Doctrine, and the Estrada Doctrine were all designed to restore sovereign equality to relations between the dominant states and the weaker states of Latin America. In particular, these moves were an attempt to regain sovereignty over natural resources and to limit the remedies of foreign investors in the context of nationalization. The cumulative effect of these developments was to create a normative counter-momentum, leading the West to renounce the use of force to safeguard overseas economic interests. The United States responded by purporting to substitute, in the 1930s, "a good neighbour policy" for the discredited Monroe Doctrine. During the Cold War, the interventionist diplomacy associated with applications of the Monroe Doctrine was revived with a vengeance, disregarding Latin American sovereign rights and reversing moves toward democratization. Two of the many covert interventions during this period that proved especially disastrous for the peoples of a given country were those in Guatemala in 1954 and in Chile in 1973, bringing to power brutalizing dictatorships. The effort to destroy the regime of Fidel Castro in Cuba, including numerous attempts since 1961 at assassinating Castro, are a chronicle of defiance by the United States of the most fundamental international legal obligations, a defiance that continues unabated to this day.

Legalization of Geopolitics

International law is used by the dominant political actors to lend an aura of legitimacy to the geopolitical stratification of relations among sovereign states. Such stratification is in direct conflict with the norm of the juridical equality of states, which is affirmed in the United Nations Charter, Article 2(1): "The United Nations is based on the sovereign equality of all its members." Even within the United Nations, stratification emerges prominently in the form of a veto power given to the five permanent members of the Security Council. In effect, the veto assures the permanent members (United States, Russia, China, France, United Kingdom) an exemption from legal accountability with respect to the obligations of the Charter, including the core commitment to refrain from non-defensive uses of force to resolve international disputes.

It is revealing that the five original states to declare that they possessed nuclear weapons were the five permanent members of the Security Council. Stratification has been reproduced by the Orientalizing of the regulatory mechanism evolved by states with respect to nuclear weapons. By defining the regulatory issue as one of "non-proliferation" rather than "possession" and "use," the Treaty on Non-Proliferation of Nuclear Weapons implicitly legalized a dual structure that allows a few countries to base their security on nuclear weaponry while prohibiting other states from acquiring such weapons. Indeed, the Iraq War was undertaken on the basis of the legal claim by the United States and the United Kingdom that it was permissible to invade another country to prevent its acquisition of such weaponry. It is notable that the claim, as such, was not opposed but only the factual foundation relating to whether or not Iraq possessed such weaponry and, if so, whether it posed the sort of threat that could not be removed by relying on the UN inspection process. In relation to chemical and biological weapons, a consensus exists on regimes of unconditional prohibition because such categories of weaponry threaten rather than sustain geopolitical structures of stratification.

But there is a creative tension present even in relation to nuclear weapons and international law. To obtain the consent of non-nuclear states to give up their option to acquire nuclear weaponry, the nuclear weapons states agreed to pursue nuclear disarmament in good faith, as well as to transfer peaceful nuclear technology. In an advisory opinion, the International Court of Justice held that the nuclear weapons states had a legal obligation to pursue nuclear disarmament in good faith and that threats and uses of nuclear weapons would almost always be in violation of international law unless, possibly, under conditions where the survival of the state was genuinely at stake.[25]

Extreme Geopolitical Orientalism: After the Cold War and 9/11

While I will not attempt any detailed depiction of these developments, the outcome of the Cold War produced a surge of triumphalism that reinvigorated the American myth of exceptionalism and turned its attention to the Middle East. The most inflammatory expression of this climate of opinion was undoubtedly the shoddily argued thesis of Samuel Huntington, in his notorious article (and subsequent book) entitled "The Clash of Civilizations?"[26]

Orientalism re-emerged also in the 1990s in the discourse associated with economic globalization, especially the privileging of the modern, as identified with American technological mastery, market economics, and constitutional democracy. The Islamic world was faulted for its failures to mimic Western material achievements, as had been so impressively done by several Asian countries, and was warned by the pundits of globalization that it would experience disorienting consequences if it failed to meet the challenges of modernization.[27] This perspective also lent support to the rationale for the

Iraq War of 2003. Of course, Arab intellectuals responded in many ways to modernity, but recently the most influential response was to repudiate the West as hopelessly decadent, and especially America, on normative grounds, and call for renewed adherence to Islam as a source of guidance at all levels of social and political existence.[28]

This discourse was also given a geopolitical twist by branding some states as "rogue states," a unilateral American designation, mainly directed at countries in the Islamic world plus holdover Communist regimes and intended to convey a refusal to respect the sovereign rights of such countries. The United States as the sole surviving superpower, assumed the role in the Clinton presidency of setting the rules of inclusion and exclusion in the world order, seeking multilateral support to the extent possible, but willing to act alone if necessary to do so. The reliance on sanctions against rogue states was the prime example of imperial rule-making, most disastrously imposed on Iraq, causing hundreds of thousand civilian casualties, mainly women, children, the aged, and sick, during the twelve years of sanctions maintained between the Gulf War of 1991 and the Iraq War of 2003.[29] The ability of the United States to gain UN Security Council Support for these indiscriminate sanctions, despite numerous accounts of their impact on the Iraqi people, is indicative of the geopolitical leverage being exerted by Washington. In effect, the UN Security Council became, in this period, an arena amenable to Orientalist geopolitics.

The Bush presidency accentuated these tendencies by its emphasis on a global grand strategy that focused on control of the Middle East and a dependence on war and unilateralism to achieve U.S. goals. In these respects, statements such as that by Donald Rumsfeld, who reacted to 9/11 on September 12 by saying it provided an "opportunity" to attack Iraq, are revealing.[30] Such an assertion would seem to be a non sequitur to 9/11 and have little to do with the main geographic locus of the Al Qaeda threat, as well as to ignore the reality of a secular, stable, and weakened Iraq. On the second anniversary of 9/11, interviewed by Jim Lehrer on the TV program *News Hour*, Rumsfeld called the attacks on the World Trade Center and Pentagon "a blessing in disguise." Again, strange language, unless it is read back into the broader neoconservative vision of global domination. It then makes sense as pointing to a favorable political climate for the militarization of American geopolitical ambitions such as had not existed prior to 9/11. The justifying rhetoric of anti-terrorism is an Orientalizing smokescreen, in which actions that make the real threat much worse are undertaken as part of a broader strategy. The Iraq disaster is the prime example of a shell-game fraud that is usually confined to the sidewalk but now has become the lynchpin of geopolitics.

Portraying the other as associated in any way with "terrorism" enables the United States to free itself from normative constraints, even from those it acknowledges. On the one side, the United States claims the prerogative of "preemptive war" whenever it senses a threat emanating from an "axis of evil" country, thereby repudiating the core commitment of the UN Charter to refrain from wars of choice. But on the other side, it expressly indicts these countries that are so categorized because they exhibit no respect for international law. What is stunning about this double assertion is its insensitivity to such a blatant contradiction.

Along the same lines, the United States castigates enemy states because they are accused, often falsely, of seeking to acquire nuclear weapons. Indeed, the war against Iraq was mainly so justified, at least before it occurred. When such enemies are accused along these lines, the allegation is bolstered by pointing to their evidently criminal intention of acquiring what are described as "terrible weapons." In a dazzling display of cognitive dissonance, such statements seem oblivious to the U.S. possessing the world's largest arsenal of nuclear weapons, as well as to its recent steps to develop new kinds of nuclear weapons designed for battlefield use in future wars: specifically, nuclear weapons designed to penetrate the earth and to have yields that confine the scope of devastation to battlefield proportions.

In effect, this form of imperial Orientalism relies on its capacity to brand any force of resistance as outside the protective domain of law. It did this explicitly when it described those captured in Afghanistan as "enemy combatants," and hence not entitled to protection as prisoners of war under the Geneva Conventions, a claim described as "quaint" by Alberto Gonzales, the main lawyer of the Bush White House. Such a unilateral opting out of an internationally negotiated and widely endorsed framework of standards is emblematic. It is hardly surprising that the abuse of those held in Guantanamo became standard operating procedure for the United States in Iraq, where there was an announced unwillingness to treat detainees by Geneva standards. As the photos told the full story of torture in Abu Ghraib and elsewhere, the profound implications of declaring oneself exempt from international law became apparent to the world, even if minimized in the American setting by the "bad apples" analogy.[31]

The outer reach of this radical version of geopolitics is articulated by David Frum and Richard Perle, leading voices of the neoconservative presence within and around government. In their book, *An End to Evil: How to Win the War on Terror*, there is a telling assertion to the effect that "Iran defied the Monroe Doctrine and sponsored murder in our own hemisphere," a reference to a terrorist incident in Argentina that was attributed to Tehran without any show of evidence.[32] Of course, blowing up a Jewish Community Center in Buenos Aires was a crime and, if truly sponsored by Iran, was an international crime of grave magnitude, but it was a crime in Argentina. To invoke the discredited Monroe Doctrine, a relic of the colonial era, as a continuing pillar of American foreign policy that other countries were bound to respect is quite extraordinary.

But at the same time, it is not at all extraordinary and is rather suggestive of the full reach of Washington's project of global domination. One way to capture the grandiose pretension of this project is to understand it as a Monroe

Doctrine for the world. President Bush, from the outset, declared the whole world to be a battlefield in the war declared against global terror. He indicated that countries that "harbor" terrorists would be treated as equally responsible with terrorists themselves and, further, that those countries that did not join with us in the war against terrorism would be considered enemies ("If you are not with us, you are with the terrorists"). This kind of global reach is magnified when it is realized that anti-terrorism is fronting for an effort to achieve global domination. This is the enduring significance of the Iraq War, and possibly its failure, will refocus efforts to respond as Spain did to the genuine threat associated with transnational political extremism.

The Orientalist thrust of American leadership in the world is also revealed in relation to the efforts by most other countries to work toward individual criminal accountability for leaders who abuse their authority by practicing torture or committing genocide and other crimes against humanity. This revival of the Nuremberg Principles associated with the prosecution and punishment of Nazi leaders after World War II was widely viewed as one of the great achievements of the 1990s.[33] It took two main forms: the assertion of universal jurisdiction by domestic courts claiming the right to prosecute and punish international crimes regardless of where they occurred;[34] and the institutionalization of authority in tribunals, either of an ad hoc character to address particular situation, as was the case with respect to former Yugoslavia, or through the establishment by treaty of a new international institution, the International Criminal Court, that came into formal existence in July 2002. What is disturbing, although hardly surprising, is the effort made by the United States to curtail these initiatives, and especially to arrange exemptions for itself. It pressured Belgium successfully to revise downward its law authorizing universal jurisdiction so that it would only apply in instances where the victim or perpetrator was Belgian, thereby relieving Henry Kissinger, Ariel Sharon, and many others of the apprehension that they might be detained and charged, as happened in 1998 to Augusto Pinochet in London. It has also managed to negotiate agreements with 89 governments in which they have agreed not to surrender Americans accused of international crimes to the International Criminal Court but to turn them over to American authorities for appropriate action. An American official, connected with this approach, was quoted as saying, "It's never been our argument that Americans are angels. Our argument has been that if Americans commit war crimes or human rights violations, we will handle them."[35] Such a claim that American national procedures of accountability are sufficient for us but that international procedures are needed for others is an unvarnished expression of Orientalist pretension. In the wake of the Iraq War, and not only with respect to the torture of prisoners, this self-interested insistence on an exemption seems increasingly intolerable. At this point it seems doubtful that those most responsible for these international crimes, the blame certainly rising to the level of the Secretary of Defense and the chief military commanders, will be in any way held accountable.

Prospects for Geo-Governance: Orientalist
or Democratic?

The transition to a regulated structure of world order is underway and is assured unless a catastrophic breakdown occurs, due to ecological, economic, or political collapse. That is, the Westphalian form of world order, based on the state system, while resilient, is essentially being displaced from above and below. It is not only the case that the main struggle since 9/11 is being waged by a global state on the one side and a loosely linked headless network on the other side; the impact of multi-dimensional globalization is also making borders less important in most respects (although more important in some—for instance, restricting transnational migrants). And normative developments are now associated with *international* accountability for gross violations of human rights and for the commission of such crimes as genocide, torture, and ethnic cleansing.

Much of the literature that recognizes this emergent global governance stresses the inevitability of American leadership. The mainstream debate is whether this leadership will take a cooperative, economic form as it did in the 1990s or move in direction of the unilateralist, coercive form of the early years of the twenty-first century.[36] The outcome of the November 2004 American presidential elections, together with the impact of the purported transfer of sovereignty to Iraq on June 30, 2004, as well as the anti-war outcome of the 2006 congressional elections seemed to supply a short-term answer. The main argument being made seems likely to be unaffected by a change in the elected leadership of the United States, although the 2008 presidential elections might produce some tactical adjustments associated with the high costs of continuing the Iraq War. Either foreign policy path is essentially Orientalist in the sense of building a future world order on the basis of American interests, an American worldview, and an American model of constitutional democracy. Neither is sensitive, in the slightest, to the ordeal of the Palestinian people, and thus bitter resentments directed at the United States will be kept alive, especially in the Arab world. International law will continue to play a double role, facilitating the pretensions of the American model of "democracy" as an expression of a commitment to the realization of international human rights and offering opponents of this model legal standards and principles by which to validate their anti-imperial, anti-American resistance.

In my view, only a non-Orientalist reshaping of global governance can be beneficial for the peoples of the world and sustainable over time. In that process, the de-Orientalizing of the normative order is of paramount importance, providing positive images of accountability, participation, and justice that do not universalize the mythic or existential realities of the American experience and that draw fully upon the creative energies and cultural worldviews of the diverse civilizations that together constitute the world. Such expectations may presently seem utopian, but that is only because our horizons are now clouded by warmongering "realists" and global imperialists. To dream freely of a benevolent future is the only way to encourage the moral and political imagination of people throughout the world to take responsibility for their own future, thereby repudiating in the most decisive way the deforming impacts of Orientalism in all of its sinister forms.

Part II

Nurturing Global Democracy

4

Toward Global Democracy

Perspectives

There exists a disquieting disconnect between the almost universal advocacy of democracy as the sole legitimate way that domestic society can be organized and intense resistance from leading state actors to any steps taken to democratize the ways in which global governance in its present forms is constituted and administered.[1] The contrast is particularly striking as between the political language that has been used by the current American political leadership in the course of the Bush presidency, which has made its signature claim to moral leadership in the world depend on its supposed championship of democracy, while at the same time displaying an active hostility toward democracy as it might inform global governance. The neoconservative version of this disconnect is more explicit than a similar "democratic gap" that existed earlier, and was especially characteristic of the Clinton presidency, which also made support for the spread of democracy on the national level an essential element of its foreign policy (what it called "enlargement"). As with Bush, Clinton also was not supportive of civil society efforts to open up the United Nations (UN), or global governance more generally, to the impact of democratizing pressures. An inquiry into global democracy proceeds against this background of understanding.

The idea of global governance is itself elusive. It is a term of art that has come into being rather recently, at least most prominently, to consider the need for and form of governmental capabilities to establish and implement policy at the global level without implying the existence or desirability of world government.[2] There is considerable sensitivity on this matter of language as "world government" is associated with the movement for "world federalism" and radical abridgements of sovereignty, which in turn is derided as utopian or as likely to pave the way toward tyranny on a global scale.[3] The idea of global governance, in contrast, is firmly situated in most formulations at the interface between realism and liberalism, grounded in the resilience of the Westphalian world order based on the interplay of sovereign states and on the liberal effort to promote international cooperation and collective action as ways to promote humane values without requiring modifications in the structure of world order.[4] The interest in global governance reflects a growing sense that a stronger set of institutional procedures and practices is needed at the global level to address a series of challenges associated with protecting the global commons, addressing climate change, polar melting, deforestation, over-fishing, extreme weather. This interest also reflects regulatory concerns about a range of issues, including transnational crime, disease, and terrorism, as well as international business operations. Increasingly, there exists an acknowledged need for a normative framework for economic globalization that will ensure greater poverty reduction and a less unequal distribution of the benefits and burdens of growth on a global scale.[5] Such a preoccupation with global governance can also be thought about as an evolutionary stage in the unfolding of the Westphalian world order, in effect, a geopolitical successor to the simpler mechanisms of so-called "Great Power" management of international society that provided all societies with the benefits of global stability, which can be considered as a collective public good.[6]

Another way of conceiving of the present historical circumstances is to postulate a "Grotian Moment," that is, a transitional interlude that is signaling a tectonic shift in world order.[7] We are presently experiencing both the terminal phase of the Westphalian framework and the emergence of a different structure of world order that is sufficiently receptive to the emergence of supranational forms of regional and global governance, as well as exhibiting the agency of non-state actors, as to qualify as "post-Westphalian."[8] This assertion, in part, reflects the growing realization that states are incapable of adapting to mounting global-scale challenges without a significant recon-figuration of the world order. This assessment is not meant to suggest that states have lost their primacy in global political life, or are without adaptive capabilities, but rather to observe that a sustainable world order in the future depends on some major structural and ideational innovations to protect an otherwise severely endangered global public interest in the years ahead.[9] Institutional and normative expressions of regional and global solidarity will be needed to address such issues as climate change, regulation of the world economy, establishment of security, maintenance of human rights, and implementation of the ethos of a responsibility to protect peoples confronting an imminent humanitarian catastrophe. As well, sustainability will depend on taking into present account the needs of future generations, with respect to resources and the foundations of life supportive of individual and collective human dignity.[10]

More than the United Nations, the extraordinary regionalizing develop-ments in Europe over the course of the last half century prefigure a post-Westphalian world order that draws on a number of complemetary structural and attitudinal ideas to solve the deepening crisis of global governance. The European Union (EU) can be conceived as foreshadowing such modifications on the regional level in Europe, and potentially elsewhere, in a manner that seems fundamentally consistent with democratic values and procedures.[11]

Europe has achieved internal mobility, a common currency, economic progress, regional governance, limitations on internal sovereignty, and most impressively, a culture of peace that makes intra-regional arms races, inter-state uses of force, and extra-regional wars almost unthinkable. In current debates about the future of Kosovo it is being influentially claimed that the only serious hope for reconciling the strong Kosovar push for national independence with the Serbian insistence on the unity of its state boundaries is for both of these contending entities to be formally absorbed into the larger reality of Europe by a new cycle of EU enlargement, thereby making traditional zero-sum calculations about territorial sovereignty less salient.[12]

It is notable, although ironic, that it is Europe, which had invented and developed the Westphalian world order back in the seventeenth century that is taking the lead in shaping a radical post-Westphalian form of governance for its region. Of course, Europe manipulated the state system for as long as possible to serve its geopolitical ambitions, which led to the colonizing of much of the non-Western world, and subjugating most of the rest in an exploitative set of relationships. In this respect the EU should be understood as much as a belated response to a series of European geopolitical setbacks as it is an expression of European creativity, or even less so, European idealism. The anti-colonial movement, the debilitating impact of the two world wars, the challenge posed by Soviet expansionism during the Cold War, and the difficulties of competing in the world economy all played a part in moving European leaders to seek greater unity through mutually beneficial cooperative practices and procedures. As is well known, the growth of the EU from its outset was premised on an appeal to the self-interest of individual sovereign states, especially with respect to economic policy. It is only by stages that this European experiment in regional world order moved forward, with such steps mired in controversy. Building a regional political and cultural consciousness is a continuous process with setbacks as well as advances.

Such an understanding helps us realize that normally there are two major ways of stimulating significant world order reforms: the first, illustrated by the establishment of the League of Nations and the United Nations, is associated with efforts to reconstruct world order in the aftermath of a destructive war;[13] the second, best illustrated by the EU, is based on the evolutionary potential of building upon modest functional beginnings, where the benefits of institutional growth are weighed periodically by participating governments and their publics, leading to forward surges generally formalized by treaties negotiated and approved by the EU membership, but also by backsliding in periods of disenchantment with aspects of this momentous political experiment.[14] Since 2005 there has been serious debate about whether the EU has reached, or possibly even exceeded, prudent limits on its scope (the enlargement issue) and depth (the question of the European Constitution). European public opinion has been recently agitated by the costs of enlargement, the tensions associated with immigration, the controversy over possible

Turkish membership, and the interplay between Islamic extremism and Islamophobia. Such incidents as the assassination of Theo van Gogh, the Danish cartoon controversy, the French urban riots, and leftist views that the EU was anti-worker and a vehicle for neoliberal globalization, were instrumental in the French and Dutch rejection of a proposed European Constitution.[15]

Despite this recent cascade of discouraging developments that have certainly cooled some of the enthusiasm about the EU as a model of world order, there remain important reasons to expect a rebound in confidence, as well as to reaffirm this set of regional initiatives to be an extremely positive demonstration that post-Westphalian change and reform is possible to achieve by peaceful means: the European Parliament shows that electoral democracy can be made to work in multi-state, multinational political domains; environmentalist pressures to reduce carbon emissions are being most effectively articulated and organized under the auspices of the EU; and, along similar lines, the advocacy of a more moderate approach, relying on diplomacy and law rather than force in responding to such threats as are posed by political Islam and non-proliferation, is being led by European statesmen.[16] In 2003 opposition of such stalwart American allies as France and Germany to the proposed invasion of Iraq illustrated vividly a growing divergence in approach to world order as between Europe and the United States that especially related to attitudes toward force and war as policy options of governments.

That is, this apparent European submission to the rule of law promises a more successful accommodation to the demands and opportunities of a post-Westphalian world order. In contrast, the United States, especially during the presidency of George W. Bush, has been far more reliant on a militarist approach in fashioning its efforts to move beyond a Westphalian world order, including the seeming acceptance of the inevitability of a hard landing associated with lengthy foreign wars, financing a worldwide network of military bases, and relying on the militarization of space for control over the entire earth.[17] That is, Europe since the end of the Cold War, and especially since the Bush presidency in 2001 and the ascent to influence of a neoconservative entourage of political advisors, has developed a regional self-consciousness that is defined in part by seeking an alternative path to world order that is less likely to produce catastrophic results. Whether this regional experiment, which can be compared with far less evolved regional frameworks in Latin America, Africa, and Asia, will spread sufficiently to itself constitute a post-Westphalian alternative form of world order beyond Europe seems quite doubtful in the near future. Even so, the regionalization of the world is a possibility worthy of attention, even if only to illuminate "the Grotian moment" as associated with a struggle to provide the world with a post-Westphalian form of global governance.[18] Implicit here is the idea that the state-centric world order that evolved out of the Westphalian peace settlement was a form of global governance that generally seemed successful until the outbreak of the world wars of the prior century. Its approaching catastrophic dysfunctionality was initially dramatized by the development and use of atomic bombs in 1945. Of course, despite a certain success from the perspective of dominant elites, there was much to lament about Westphalian global governance aside from its vulnerability to technological innovations that subverted its stability. The larger sovereign states provided secure sanctuaries for the commission of "human wrongs" under the rubric of sovereign rights. The state system, despite some feeble efforts by international law during the last hundred years, more or less legitimated the war system and lent a certain kind of validity to colonialism.

There is little doubt that the combination of opportunity and danger created by the end of the Cold War and the collapse of the Soviet Union encouraged the neoconservative imaginary to formulate a grand strategy based on global dominance.[19] The 2000 election of George W. Bush as president and the 9/11 attacks enabled this neoconservative blueprint for grand strategy to morph into a political project that became the centerpiece of the "war on terror."[20] This ideological set of moves can be considered from the perspective of global governance as a means to overcome the anarchic character of world order given the globalization and transnationalization of security. It is within this historical and ideological setting that the neoconservative leadership of the United States has tried to solve the crisis of global governance by opting for an "empire" model of world order.[21] The form of empire pursued was definitely distinctive, and unlike all historical empires in important respects. This American way of empire combined a rhetoric of respect for the political independence and territorial integrity of foreign states with a set of security claims of global dimensions that circumvented foreign sovereign authority to limit American discretion to use force in times and places of its choosing. It has also given unprecedented emphasis to a call for democratic constitutionalism at the level of the state, even selectively justifying intervention and regime change to rid countries of dictatorial rule, particularly in the Middle East.[22] It has resorted to aggressive war and exercised extra-territorial authority to implement its counter-terrorist foreign policy. Aside from its militarism, it might be difficult to disentangle neoconservative visionary geopolitics as it has been enacted during the Bush presidency from other less provocative ways of establishing American control of world politics in a manner that was also arguably of an imperial character.[23]

An imperial geopolitics is perhaps most clearly expressed by the relationship of the United States government to international law and to the United Nations.[24] International law and the UN, because of their potential as well as their reality, are anti-imperial, clarifying thereby crucial aspects of what, in contrast to empire, a global democracy would entail. Global democracy would certainly entail some kind of respected institutional presence that effectively provided alternatives to war in addressing international disputes, particularly with regard to those issues that touched on vital interests of governments and their citizens. Global democracy would also engender a political culture of respect for the kinds of restraints on the behavior of states that arise from long diplomatic experience and are then encoded in agreements among governments and other international actors to establish obligatory standards of behavior. As such, it would override the insistence of American leaders on unilateral prerogatives with respect to the use of force, so vividly expressed by President Bush when he said in the 2004 State of the Union Address that the United States will never ask for a permission slip whenever its security is at stake. The intention as stated, which was greeted by thunderous bipartisan applause, amounted to a crude insistence that this country, and only this country, retained the discretion to wage war without reference to either the authority of the United Nations or the constraints of international law. This is expressive of a unilateralism that is the decisive repudiation, or the decisive sign of a repudiation, of a commitment to a law governed way of addressing international political behavior.

A repudiation of such unilateralism does not mean a commitment to a legalistic view of the role of international law in our present world. One can appreciate that there may be occasions where the tension between the survival and security of the state and the general prior understanding of international law appear to be in conflict and to pose difficult moral and legal and political choices for national leaders. Recognizing such a possibility of deviating from strict legal strictures still contrasts with the imperial mode that, in principle rather than under existential pressures, repudiates the very idea of constraints on war-making derived from standards and procedures external to the sovereign state.

As important as is adherence to the rule of law with respect to war and peace issues for the establishment of humane forms of global governance, it is not at all synonymous with what we mean when we talk about global democracy. It is my intention to try to provide some introductory understanding of what global democracy would entail, in terms of the organization of the world. In his pioneering work on "cosmopolitan democracy," Daniele Archibugi has argued persuasively that global democracy cannot be properly apprehended as the extension of democracy as it has functioned on the level of the territorial sovereign state to the global level.[25] If global democracy is guided by statist experience, the logical culmination of advocacy of global democracy would be support for a world state and a world government. It is important to understand that this kind of global statism is one possible way of actualizing a commitment to global democracy, but it is probably not the most plausible way and it is certainly, from the perspective of the present, not the most desirable way. It would pose great dangers of world tyranny and world anarchy that would be highly unlikely to produce a form of global governance that could be called "humane."[26] Also, transition to world government seems politically infeasible to such an extent that its endorsement is quickly dismissed as "utopian," that is, unattainable and generally undesired. Although we cannot peer into the future to discern what pathways to global governance will open up under a variety of circumstances, it does not seem useful at this time to give serious attention to world government whether proceeding from perspectives of global governance or global democracy.[27]

Accordingly, I would like to discuss in a preliminary way some of the developments during the last two decades that seem to be groping toward a set of political outcomes that could culminate over time in a type of global governance that it would be reasonable at some point to call global democracy. We remain very far removed from reaching such a goal at the present time, but this should not blind us to a series of important initiatives that point beyond Westphalia without reliance on imperial prerogatives.

The first of these initiatives that deserve mention are the global conferences on policy issues that were held under the auspices of the United Nations, particularly in the 1990s. I regard these public events as experiments in global democracy, and as the birthing of global civil society.[28] The conferences provided arenas within which non-governmental organizations, as representatives of civil society, had a number of opportunities. They were able to participate in dialogues that included governments and to develop transnational civil society networks. The strong media presence at these conferences, together with access to the Internet, enabled much greater visibility for civil society perspectives, so much so that the *New York Times* actually overstated the significance of this aggregation of influence by referring to global civil society as "the second superpower" active in the world after the Cold War. This form of democratic participation by the peoples of the world within global arenas was definitely something new, and certainly hopeful from the perspective of engendering democratic participation beyond the limits of sovereign states. I would argue that it was precisely the success of these experiments that led to a geopolitical backlash that closed off this pathway to global democracy and humane global governance. The major states were not at all ready to yield their primacy in the domain of global policymaking and problem-solving to populist forces expressive of what the peoples of the world demanded and desired.

A second area, which I think is extremely relevant and important, is the previously mentioned experience of the European Union, also a political experiment intent on moving the theory and practice of democracy beyond the nation-state and establishing a political community that is only *indirectly* based on state sovereignty. As with global democracy, the EU has paused in its evolution, with its future currently in limbo. Part of a hopeful scenario for the emergence of global democracy depends on the emergence of democratic forms of regional governance that moderate or even neutralize the turn in the early twenty-first century toward global and regional forms of hegemony and empire.

A third area that points toward global democracy, is what I would call "the new internationalism." This kind of post-Westphalian diplomacy was most clearly exhibited in the extraordinary movements during the 1990s resulting in the adoption of an Anti- Personnel Landmines Treaty and the establishment of the International Criminal Court (ICC). The defining novel feature of this new internationalism was active and very effective coalitions between clusters of non-governmental actors and governments of states. This innovative diplomacy was able to overcome the concerted geopolitical objections of the most powerful political actors, notably the United States itself, but also China and Russia, to produce new authoritative norms, procedures, and institutions for international society. Whether the refusal of leading states to participate will eventually doom these efforts by making them ineffectual remains to be seen. Already, in relation to the ICC, the United States, so determined to oppose, yielded somewhat to international pressures to encourage the indictment of Sudanese officials alleged to be responsible for crimes against humanity in the context of Darfur. As with the UN global conferences, this kind of new internationalism establishes a mode of democratic participation for the peoples of the world, independent of governmental representation, in shaping the realities of global governance.

A fourth initiative involves the activation of national judicial bodies to implement international legal standards. In the context of criminal account-ability this initiative is described beneath the rubric of "universal jurisdiction." This initiative is perhaps best illustrated by the Pinochet litigation that commenced during 1998 in Britain. The Chilean dictator was indicted by a Spanish court, later detained in Britain where extradition hearings were held, culminating in a historic judgment rendered by the highest British court, the Law Lords.[29] What is important here is that the weakness of the global institutional structure is complemented by a more active judicial role in giving substance to international standards by relying on national judicial institutions to implement universal legal norms. In other words, if courts, national courts, become enforcement agencies for international norms, particularly with respect to holding leaders of sovereign states responsible for the crimes against humanity and other crimes of state, there emerges a sense of global governance guided by potential accountability based on a set of minimum constraints on the highest officials governing sovereign states. Again the challenge to Westphalian modes of geopolitics has provoked a backlash. Belgian laws that were the most revolutionary with respect to universal jurisdiction led to a strong hostile reaction by the U.S. government, accompanied by threats to move NATO headquarters away from Brussels and take other steps to harm Belgian interests. Belgium relented by amending its laws, substantially renouncing its earlier embrace of universal jurisdiction. But all is far from lost. Leading political figures, including Henry Kissinger, have reportedly changed travel plans for fear of being indicted. Complaints filed with a German prosecutor against Donald Rumsfeld for his alleged role in the practice of torture at Abu Ghraib came to nothing, but signaled the possibility of detention for prosecution or extradition if Rumsfeld traveled to countries that have laws implementing international criminal law. As in the Rumsfeld case, geopolitics will prevail in the short run. The German legal system essentially ignored its own enacted law and the strong evidence against Rumsfeld when dismissing the complaints. At the same time, these laws exhibit a growing sense that global governance depends on establishing the accountability of leaders with respect to international criminal law. Those who act on behalf of powerful countries apply without hesitation such standards of accountability in relation to their adversaries, such as Slobodan Milosevic and Saddam Hussein. Such a show of "empire's law" underscores the existence of double standards that delegitimize the authority of law in general, which is costly for powerful actors in an era of globalization.[30]

A fifth initiative has been championed by Andy Strauss and me, namely the proposal, in its various forms, to establish a global peoples assembly.[31] Symbolically and substantively this initiative recognizes the crucial importance of people participating in a direct manner in the institutional operations of global governance. The initiative presupposes that governmental representation of people, as in the United Nations and global diplomacy, is insufficient. This democratizing demand has proved controversial, but has become accepted and successful in the European setting over time. The European Parliament has finally established itself, and been acknowledged, as an integral operating part of the European Union, and a fundamental element in moves toward European democracy. Much more could be said about the importance and feasibility of a global peoples parliament as contributing to a democratic form of global governance. As an undertaking it seems now far less utopian than the project to establish an international criminal court did in the early 1990s.[32]

A sixth initiative is the existence of tribunals formed by civil society itself. The World Tribunal (WTI) on Iraq was held in Istanbul in June 2005. It was a very powerful and comprehensive assessment of the status under international law of the American invasion and occupation of Iraq.[33] It included 54 presentations to a jury of conscience that drew on the expert knowledge of prominent international lawyers and international political experts, as well as receiving emotionally powerful testimony from notable Iraqi witnesses. The primary justification for the creation of such a tribunal was to fill the gap created by the unwillingness and inability of either governments in international society or the United Nations to act meaningfully to uphold the fundamental norms of international law prohibiting aggressive warfare and the unlawful occupation of sovereign states. The WTI was impressive for a number of reasons. It was the culmination of 20 earlier civil society tribunals held all over the world on the Iraq War, and represented the first time that civil society was mobilized on a global basis to oppose a war that was widely perceived throughout the world as illegal and an example of aggressive war of the sort prohibited by the UN Charter. It exhibited an entirely new phenomenon that might be called "moral globalization," a spontaneous expression of support for the implementation of agreed fundamental norms, the constitutional basis of humane global governance, and a corresponding repudiation of geopolitical claims of entitlement with respect to war as a political option.

The last initiative that I will mention is the dependence of a movement toward global democracy upon the education of citizens, especially here in the United States. More generally, it is a vital component of the educational responsibility of institutions of higher learning throughout the world to prepare young people for engaged citizenship in this young twenty-first century. Furthermore, I believe that the prospect of achieving global democracy depends on internalizing the sort of values and global outlook that would allow that kind of political development beyond the sovereign state to take place. I think that two areas of educational emphasis would be particularly valuable at this stage of history. One is the importance of making citizens of this country and of other countries much more familiar with the relevance of a culture of human rights as part of their own development as members of any political community entitled to all aspects of human dignity. It seems clear that, to the extent that human rights are internalized as part of legitimate governance at any level of societal organization, it will facilitate a popular acceptance of the need for the construction of global democracy by consensual means.

The second educational priority is currently more controversial, but at least as necessary. It involves making a pedagogy of peace and human security an important part of the learning experience of every young person. It is my view that available evidence suggests the increasing obsolescence of war as a rational instrument for the resolution of conflict. On this basis, it is a virtual imperative to explore alternatives to war and political violence. Our education should challenge the political and moral imagination of students by considering the benefits of reliance on nonviolent politics as the foundation of global security, reform, and justice in the world. The essence of global democracy involves a shift in expectations from a geopolitics of force to a geopolitics of dialogue, collaboration, and persuasion.

The goals of global democracy and humane global governance certainly seem remote from current patterns of behavior in all sectors of the world. The position taken here is that, without such normative horizons, we will be enveloped by the storm clouds now gathering so menacingly as to defy disbelief. Hope begins when we have the moral courage and intellectual energy to transcend what seems possible by considering carefully what seems necessary and desirable, and then having the daring to plan for the "impossible." I think the changing parameters of debate on climate change, facing that "inconvenient truth," is an encouraging sign of an emerging receptivity to an acceptance of constraints on all forms of political behavior for the sake of a humane future.

5

Citizenship and Globalization

Introductory Reflections

A surge of interest in the theory and parameters of citizenship reflects the impact of a series of recent trends: globalization, migration, identity politics, regionalism, humanitarian intervention, and human rights. The relative clarity of a statist framing of world order focused inquiries about citizenship mainly on the evolution of state/society relations within the Euro/American context of liberal democracy, and particularly on the gradual expansion of the identities and rights of individuals who could claim the status of citizen within a particular nation-state. In general terms, most influentially specified by T.H. Marshall, this evolutionary path led from the protection of elemental civil rights (in the sense of restraints on governmental abuse) to the provision of political rights (of a participatory character in the collective life of a society), and on to promotion of social rights (of a character that ensured basic human needs would be addressed by safety nets and state subsidies to the extent necessary).

What gives the question of citizenship its current salience results from the contradictory tensions generated by increased normativity of international life versus the strong neoliberal ideological climate. These tensions are aggravated by the widespread erosion of responsibility on the part of national governments for the material wellbeing of their citizenry, as well as a decline in creativity, capacity, and autonomy, which overall diminishes governmental contributions to the problem-solving mechanisms of world order. The forms that this erosion has taken have been strongly influenced by the general technological and economistic embrace of corporate or neoliberal globalization by the upper levels of most political bureaucracies. This latter point can also be made inversely. The state has become more accountable internally and externally for its undertakings, breaking down the inside/outside dichotomy between unconditional sovereignty within territorial space and the lesser capacity of managing realist power politics that is conducted in the political anarchy that prevails among states. That is, the expectation of individuals is for a multiple extension of rights that cannot be fulfilled as the state is gradually losing its actual grip upon the main arenas of decision bearing on identity, wellbeing, and security.

An aspect of this loss of control arises from the success of transnational market forces in inducing almost every national government in the world to adhere to a neoliberal policy framework that includes minimizing the social role of government and subordinating the provision of public goods, while endorsing policies leading to the liberalization and privatization of the economy as designed to enhance the efficiency of capital and global competitiveness. As a result, individuals cannot look as confidently to the state for the fulfillment of basic aspirations, making traditional forms of citizenship less organically connected to an individual's search for personal security and meaning in life. Put differently, to the extent that the state has been instrumentalized by a combination of global market forces and the rise of a general antipathy toward bureaucracies and regulation, the sphere of governmental autonomy with respect to promoting the wellbeing of the territorial citizenry is being diminished. Such trends, while not uniform or invariable, were temporarily cumulative, although recent developments suggest a certain leftward swing of the political pendulum, especially in Latin America.

This dynamic is intertwined with other influential developments, none more consequential than the rise of information technology (IT) as a basic restructuring and wealth-creating influence in business, politics, military affairs, human relations, and worldview. The shift from hierarchy to network as an organizational mode also has an overall psycho-political effect of de-centering authority, lessening the significance of territorial boundaries, and creating a multitude of systems of interaction seemingly beyond the control of the state.[1] The cyber-mentality associated with this technology parallels in certain respects the mindset embedded in market-driven ideologies. Both highlight the virtues of self-organizing modes of social action, and marginalize and demean the regulative role of the state; they also share a tendency to oppose relying on governmental solutions to alleviate unemployment and poverty, or even to handle the challenge of global warming. The overall impact of IT on political consciousness has not yet become clearly fixed, although it is certainly facilitating a quasi-libertarian ethos and even has endowed the cyber-community with a participatory form that resembles citizenship, being appropriately called "netizenship." This sense of belonging challenges the previously near exclusive claims on loyalty of a state-centric world, thereby rendering a traditional notion of the unitary citizen almost obsolete. So far this sort of non-territorial counter-identity is potential and partial, of relevance to that small minority who are pioneering on the various electronic frontiers and inhabiting "virtual communities" that have so far taken hold in cyberspace. Despite this limited size and uncertain effects, these developments inevitably lead to new configurations of belief and allegiance.

The behavioral patterns are diverse, even contradictory. Libertarian IT patterns are being countered in various ways. The state is fighting back, seeking to reestablish and retain the primacy of territorial control. IT also facilitates intrusions on privacy, especially justified by reference to counter-terrorist security goals that have been widely invoked since 9/11, especially in the United States.

These developments interact with others that complicate the picture still further. The partial and uneven breakdown of state authority, as well as migration patterns and increased labor mobility, contributes to multiculturalism within states, and to the embrace of intense forms of separatist politics by abused minorities that increasingly conceive of themselves as "captive nationalities," or alienated ethnic enclaves. These centrifugal tendencies are strengthened by the legal, moral, and political promise of a right of self-determination to all "peoples," a right initially subordinated to Westphalian categories of statist unity, but endorsed in state-shattering forms in relation to former Yugoslavia during the 1990s.[2] Precisely these concerns with migration and an altered ethnic identity within borders have led to widespread preoccupation with the policing of borders and the removal from territory of unwanted immigrants.

The claims of indigenous peoples to a right of self-determination, at the very least, further dilutes the notion of territorial sovereignty, threatening to establish zones of self-government and autonomy within the boundaries of existing states.[3] These developments subvert the modernist idea that the secular state incorporates ethnic and cultural differences into an integral whole that is administered by a governmental center on the basis of a single overarching legal framework. Even the federalist notion of the state was based on an ideal of nationalist solidarity based on a shared framework of socio-economic values premised on rationality and modernity, that is, negating the relevance of religious, ethnic, and cultural difference. To the extent that indigenous peoples win an exemption from such a normative consensus, rather than accepting offers of assimilation, there is an ideological crack in the traditional claims of unity made by a political authority that purports to enjoy the status of sovereign territorial state. It is not surprising under these circumstances that interpreters of world order write about a new medievalism.[4]

As significant, is the rise of normative claims based on international law that are binding on the state, and recognize that the rights and duties of individuals no longer begin and end with the discretion and authority of the state. Of course, conceptually the state can absorb these wider normative imperatives within its domestic legal structure by incorporating global norms through legislation. Yet such adjustments do not hide the remarkable trend toward the rise of various types of external accountability, along with moves toward procedures and institutions with a mandate to implement these global norms internally. These moves toward global normative governance seem like a dramatic encroachment on the sort of sovereignty that allowed the state to dominate the political and moral imagination of individuals, and lent such powerful credibility to the Westphalian architecture based on a statist system of world order.

One dimension of such accountability was illustrated by the Pinochet litigation, suggesting that individuals, including even heads of state, could be held criminally liable potentially anywhere in the world for conduct performed within their own country in accordance with the prevailing governmental structure, including for official actions.[5] A related dimension was the revival of the Nuremberg imposition of criminal responsibility through the establishment by the UN Security Council in 1993 of the International Criminal Tribunal for the former Yugoslavia located at The Hague and for Rwanda in Arusha. These initiatives led in turn to the 1998 Rome Treaty that led quickly to the establishment of a permanent international criminal tribunal available to handle credible accusations of extreme criminality against participating states at the level of the state that are not being addressed by national courts. Whatever else, the emergence of external criteria and procedures of accountability that are responding to demands for redress of grievances weakens the statist character of world order in a decisive way.[6] Or, alternatively, transnational redress radically reconfigures our conception of the state, as in Andrew Linklater's influential formulations arguing in favor of the emergence of "the post-Westphalian state."[7]

There are complications that must be noted. A hegemonic dimension of global politics gives particular influence to the actions, attitudes, and values professed by the United States. In this period, the United States seems embarked on a project to consolidate its global power by reliance on space-based weapons systems, a missile defense shield, and deployments of offensive weapons in space. Such an undertaking can be viewed either as a dimension of global governance that provides the best hope for global minimum order in the decades ahead, or an unacceptable move to achieve global dominance designed to freeze the inequities of the present world. In this regard, the war-making ethos and capability of a dominant state or states remains central to an interpretation of world order. Equally sobering is the insistence by the United States that it will not follow agreed international standards governing the emission of greenhouse gases, arguing that implementation would endanger American living standards and growth prospects, while ignoring the adverse impact of non-implementation on climate change. The extensions of citizenship beyond the state, and the impact of global norms, needs to be qualified to the extent that hegemonic structures of power and authority set limits on accountability. In effect, we need to assess the impact of the strong state or hegemon on the character of citizenship in this era of globalization, especially the disempowering effects of unilateralism on the rights and security of the peoples of the world. Also, at stake, is the way in which responses to world risks are organized given this hegemonic power/policy structure.[8]

Equally, it is important to take the measure of the weak state, unable to maintain order or minimal adherence to global norms within its territorial space. Sub-Saharan Africa has become the scene of the breakdown of Westphalian structures in the most devastating forms, producing genocide, massive atrocities, persistent warfare, lethal epidemics, and pervasive criminality and corruption.[9] This challenge of the pathologically weak state raises difficult issues about intervention, trusteeship, and human solidarity. Citizenship in such nominal states provides none of the Westphalian benefits aside from symbolic matters of status.

The question of what constitutes political community is drawn into question by these developments, and with it either the weakening of the bonds of traditional citizenship and territoriality as the foundation of community and identity or the refashioning of citizenship to take account of multiple identities, shifting centers of authority and responsibility, and diverse notions of community. As such, the capacity of the state to function as the center of loyalty and aspiration is thrown into doubt, particularly in advanced, affluent states where dying on behalf of one's country is being increasingly questioned.[10] Of course, the persisting unevenness of international society creates wildly different attitudes toward the linkage between state and identity. For peoples denied statehood, and enduring oppressive circumstances, the acquisition of a state of their own is likely to function as the highest political goal, the attainment of which is worth dying and killing for. Nevertheless, the leading states establish and bear witness to systemic trends toward a more complex ethos of citizenship than had prevailed prior to this advent of globalization and regionalization of authority structures and the civilizational and religious frames for cultural identity. These trends are accentuated by rising normative expectations relating to human rights and criminal accountability. Superimposing global standards of accountability renders uncertain under what conditions the state provides a safe haven for someone accused of criminality in relation to action that was permissible at its territorial point of origin.

There is an ambiguity in the way citizenship is used. It can refer to the formal linkages established by law, but it can also refer to the psycho-political linkages arising from patterns of aspiration and belief. In this respect it parallels the ambiguity associated with the idea of "nation-state," which is a technical recognition that the state confers nationality by its juridical authority, but also an ethical/political claim that the state embodies a specific national identity. This claim may be psycho-politically untrue to varying extents, depending on what minority inhabitants of the territorial community "feel" with respect to identity and community. Kurds in Turkey, Iran, and Iraq do not, by and large give their psychological and nationalist allegiance to the state, but rather to a particular ethnic community that defines their societal reality; often they feel resentment and fear with respect to the government, which is seen as a vehicle of oppression and exploitation acting on behalf of the dominant ethnic community. It is this duality that makes problematic the whole idea of nation-states, which tends to conceal the fact that within the borders of the state there often exist alienated and persecuted minority communities.

Against this background, it seems most useful to consider the new matrix of citizenship in relation to several crucial frames of reference: the resilience of the sovereign state and the persistence of Westphalian citizenship; regional citizenship; the idea of a citizen pilgrim. Such emphases pick up selected aspects of an overall assessment of a confused, confusing, and exceedingly complicated pattern of shifting, inconsistent, multiple and overlapping identities and loyalties that now inform the overall theme of citizenship, but ensure its incoherence so far as its applicability to diverse political realities is concerned.

Westphalian Citizenship: A Resilient Reality

Despite the various impacts of globalization, the individual overwhelmingly continues to be caught in a statist web of rights, duties, and identities. At one level, the right to travel across borders depends on passports issued by states to their citizens and to none others (with trivial exceptions); borders are exclusively managed by governmental authority and an abuse of rights in a foreign country is almost always dealt with by seeking help from one's country of citizenship. By controlling the conditions of legal access to sovereign territory, states control mobility in the world, including the possibility of entry into labor markets of foreign countries. Migration to the extent that it is "legal," rests on Westphalian notions of territorial sovereignty. To the extent that migration is "illegal," it exhibits strains on Westphalian patterns of control, but it also discloses their persistence, as the illegal migrant is a figure of acute vulnerability, exposed to risks of deportation, manipulation, and abuse, as well as often denied the opportunity to partake of the full benefits of legal residence and citizenship.

At another level, the duty to defend a country is related to the reciprocal privilege of being a citizen, although there are mercenaries and those impressed into military service whose service is not premised on citizenship. Citizenship also engages most individuals in their most meaningful form of political action, voting for political leaders, accepting the outcome of an electoral process as the expression of consent to be governed. Even in non-democratic states, where power is exercised without constitutional constraint and without respect for the rule of law, those who are treated as citizens are beneficiaries of certain rights of movement, travel, and eligibility for government and military service.

And, in contrast, those who cannot claim citizenship may be unable to cross borders freely unless they become recipients of a special status in recognition of their vulnerability. Refugees are supposed to be protected by the UN High Commissioner of Refugees that has some authority to issue travel documents, which may or may not be widely recognized and accepted by sovereign states. "Statelessness" remains a condition of severe deprivation, suggesting the persistence of statism—that is, without the certification of identity and status by a sovereign state, an individual has no assured right to enter or remain in a particular country.

Beyond this, those "citizens" who are victims of persecution or discrimination due to their specific ethnic or religious identity, remain vulnerable to state power. That is, to the extent that citizenship fails to secure basic human rights there does not exist a reliable means of asserting and upholding claims to proper treatment. The international community lacks the means and the political mandate to protect most instances of abuse that take place internal to sovereign states. The state remains empowered, especially larger states, to commit "human wrongs" that may severely victimize some of those present within a given territorial community, often including citizens.[11] In effect, despite a few examples of "humanitarian intervention," non-Westphalian modalities of citizenship have not demonstrated any efficacy in providing protection to those abused by the state or those suffering as a result of cultural or societal practices.[12] Ethnic cleansing and genocide, despite being criminalized on an international level, are not regularly or effectively challenged.[13] The only reliable protection for individuals and groups arises from the structures of constitutional authority operative at the level of the state, and in subordinate institutions under its control. The most important opportunities for reform bearing on human wellbeing also remain related to changes in domestic laws, administrative practices, political leadership, and cultural climate.

In this respect, the citizen who lives under the authority of a well-governed democratic state is generally secure, but not equally, whereas citizens who are subject to the vagaries of a gangster, corrupt, or inept state are daily confronted by dangerous and troublesome forms of insecurity. Even in democratic states with strong traditions of constitutionalism, there are important, even decisive, gaps in citizen protection. The circumstances of racial and religious minorities, the homeless, the sexual deviant, the cult member, the member of lower castes, and the political dissident are illustrative of categories of individuals that may find themselves targets of abuse even in those Westphalian states that receive the highest ratings in the annual reports from Freedom House and the Human Development Reports of the UN Development Programme.[14] In this regard, the key indicator of the quality of citizenship remains the internal governing process of the Westphalian state, which is itself subject only to the most minimal forms of global regulation, and these are not consistently implemented. And it is not only a matter of governmental policy. Education and culture are of fundamental importance in determining the extent to which global norms are internalized in societal patterns, especially in relation to tolerance and respect for difference. With the exception of Western Europe, the citizen cannot gain substantive relief from internal denials of rights by invoking external norms and procedures. Because such norms and procedures are accepted to varying degrees in different parts of the world, it is possible under some circumstances to obtain *symbolic* relief by way of media exposure, people's tribunals, censure moves in the UN, conditionalities imposed by international financial institutions, and pressures exerted by local, national, and international human rights NGOs.

In the end, it is impossible to deny the centrality of Westphalian citizenship, which means that the state is the core actor in determining its quality within the lifeworld of individuals and groups. It is true that globalization, the spread of electoral democracy and human rights, and a worldwide media can influence many states to uphold certain standards of behavior in dealing with their citizens (and with foreigners, especially from leading countries). But contradictory standards accentuate unevenness, including in the assessment of the post-colonial reality of the peoples of non-Western civilizations, making critical reference to such developments as the existence of failed states, the neoliberal antipathy to the implementation of economic and social rights, and the perceived failures of humanitarian intervention under UN auspices.[15]

Regional Citizenship

Regional citizenship is both competitive with and complementary to Westphalian citizenship. It is competitive in the fundamental sense of challenging the unitary, exclusivist, and primary ideal of citizenship associated with the juridical/political construct of the nation-state, the backbone of the modern system of world order. There is an inevitable zero-sum attribute to citizenship that arises as soon as what was once unquestionably situated, if at all, at the level of the state is transferred to other levels of authority and loyalty. In this respect, not surprisingly, ultra-nationalists are instinctively and intensely suspicious of and opposed to any deepening of regional attachments.

Viewed more constructively, regionalism complements Westphalian citizenship in a manner that is mutually beneficial. The emergence of regional community helps overcome attitudes of disillusionment with respect to the declining capacity of the territorial state to uphold the interests of its population. Also, the regional reality, to the extent that it is a functional success, helps to raise material standards, protect against environmental challenges, and cooperate against transnational criminality. Furthermore, regional levels of identity potentially allow micro-nationalisms to participate in larger collective frameworks without the bitterness arising from a long history of subordination to a dominant territorial nationalism. At the same time, common bonds of culture, religion, language, and history give psychological strength to regional identity, allowing it to be set off against "others" in either defensive or assertive modes. In this regard, it is possible to view some regional frameworks as counter-hegemonic projects, which in this historical period are designed to restrict the influence or dominance of the United States or the West. But it is also the case, especially with European regionalism, that it is partly counter-hegemonic, but that it is also assertive, facilitating the projection of European influence and interests in a manner that is more effective than their pursuit via the disaggregated activity of separate European states.

There is considerable regional variation with respect to function, purpose, and psycho-political role. Some regional frameworks, as is the case for such purely economic groupings as NAFTA or MERCOSUR, have no ambition to alter loyalty patterns in any way that bears significantly on citizenship. Others operate as vehicles for hegemonic domination on a regional level, and again serve mainly as instruments of policy within a Westphalian setting, as was the case for the Organization of American States (OAS), especially during the Cold War.

It could be contended that raising the issue of regional citizenship is premature, except possibly in the setting of the European Union (EU). Vague ideas of African or Latin American consciousness or assertions of "Asian values," although widely shared, fall far short of establishing the sort of bonds of loyalty and allegiance associated with Westphalian citizenship. In these post-colonial regions, even where state formation lags or is artificial, there is an attachment to political community defined by the boundaries of the sovereign state, if only as a contrast to the sort of subjugation that was characteristic of the colonial era. But patterns of ethnic nationalism in Asia and Africa are subverting the idea of citizenship altogether, except in the aspirational sense of a secessionist movement seeking to create a Westphalian state of its own, as has been the case in former Yugoslavia where the constituent republics broke off to form their own states, culminating in the 2008 declaration of independence by Kosovo, which was not even a republic, but only a province of the republic of Serbia..

Even EU regional citizenship has yet to be tested as a viable complement to Westphalian citizenship. The existence of the euro, labor mobility, borderless intra-European tourism, and the growing influence of the directly elected European Parliament provide strong foundational realities upon which to build a genuine European identity. There exist also the sort of continental bonds based on shared values and memories that might, over time, nurture the sort of collective identities that go far beyond the functional advantages and geopolitical benefits of regional cooperation. Part of the complexity of the European experiment arises from its double hegemonic dimension, as further complicated by security arrangements left over from the Cold War. European regionalism is widely interpreted as containing elements of U.S. (external) and German (internal) domination. Unlike colonial and imperial structures, the implementation of hegemonic influence in Europe is based on modalities that are made to appear and are generally accepted as "legitimate." The interplay of European security concerns with these hegemonic preoccupations is also rather convoluted, combining views that the peace of Europe depends on continuing American engagement with the idea that, with the collapse of the Soviet Union, there is no longer any need or justification for accepting the primacy of the United States in the European security sphere. Such factors, along with the dilution of European identity that has accompanied enlargement to incorporate the countries of Eastern Europe, works against the near-term construction of comparable sentiments of allegiance to those associated with robust instances of Westphalian citizenship.

To the extent that Europeans perceive European regionalism as a vehicle for American or German hegemony, it obstructs the formation of even weak attitudes of loyalty and allegiance, and encourages regressive forms of nationalism. At the same time it is impressive that in the EU setting there has been a juridical willingness by the constituent states in the Maastricht Treaty to agree formally to the conferral of European citizenship. Such a move expresses some willingness by sovereign governments to relinquish, at least symbolically, their exclusive claims of allegiance, and in this sense participate in the transformation of the Westphalian structure. Just how much of a relinquishment is unclear, and will not become evident for some decades. Formal acknowledgment of European citizenship does not necessarily produce changes in substantive behavior or psycho-political identity. The experience of federal states underlines the extent to which juridical statehood cannot itself establish Westphalian citizenship in a stable form. Where sub-nationalisms remain dissatisfied, or where the federal entity encompasses deep cleavages on values and identities, feelings of unity and of belonging to the whole will not be forthcoming. The parts generate stronger feelings of solidarity than the whole, and, when crises occur, the whole tends to fragment. The recent experiences of the Soviet Union, Indonesia, and especially the former Yugoslavia, illustrate some facets of weak citizenship within the Westphalian framework. In this regard, a European polity is likely, at most, to offer an exceedingly fragile form of regional federalism, where allegiance to the parts will continue to overshadow allegiance to the whole for the foreseeable future. Such a pattern means that the regional entity is mainly sustained by the perceived benefits of cooperation (as, unlike failed federal experiments, European institutions of governance are not likely to have the mandate or the capability to prevent withdrawal of discontented members). Many civil wars are fought as a result of secessionist claims, including the American Civil War. In this regard, the prospects for *robust* European citizenship need to viewed skeptically.

At the same time, the Westphalian prism may not determine the quality of European or regional citizenship. If functional and normative factors convince Europeans that their life is greatly enhanced by its regional character, and its cultural formations take hold, then there may arise a psycho-political process of confidence-building that is more comparable to what has occurred in strong and successful federal states. The United States since the American Civil War is exemplary. Canada, Australia, and India, despite strong sub-nationalisms, have each managed to produce durable Westphalian states where the whole dominates the parts. Europe has this possibility, initially due to an economistic rationale for regional nationalism that enabled a better response to the challenges of globalization than European countries could have made acting separately. There is also some realization that the European experiment has produced a culture of peace that has cut almost to zero the risk of a war within Europe, as well as encouraging a demilitarization of security policy toward extra-regional threats.

In any event, it is to be expected that other regions, especially Asia, will closely watch this European experiment with regionalism, including its conferral of citizenship, and will either be drawn toward or away from imitation. There is no question, as Jacques Delors made so clear some years ago, that economic integration cannot advance beyond a certain point without parallel political integration, and that the latter presupposes the formation of complementary allegiance patterns of the sort associated with at least weak or thin forms of citizenship. Whether this makes the emergent European polity stable and sustainable over time is a matter of conjecture at this point.

Visionary Perspectives: The Citizen Pilgrim

The contemporary predicament of citizenship is associated with the resilience of the Westphalian state in a global setting that bypasses and penetrates the state, but does not generate alternative political frameworks that can become new focal points of identity and loyalty. The European regional response is an experiment in supplemental citizenship, but it remains at such an early stage of identity formation that its impact cannot be assessed. Another approach to this diffusion of authority and the porousness of borders has been to invoke the image of the medieval precursor to the Westphalian era of states, arguing that the new reality can be best understood on the basis of multiple centers of authority and allegiance. This neo-medieval projection rests on the globality of the normative, human rights, the religious revival, and international law, and the functional, as associated with regulating the world economy and addressing global climate change. It also rests on a variety of developments that challenge the territorial primacy of the state, including the rise of ethnic politics, the claims of indigenous peoples, the emphasis on local sites of struggle. The combination of global, statist, transnational, regional, and local is what gives plausibility to this neo-medieval hypothesis of locality and non-territorial community. But the plausibility of this hypothesis is mainly a conceptual construct to explain the complexity of the postmodern circumstance of politics, and does not seem to be fashioning the sorts of identities that can be associated with "citizenship." True, social movements create strong gender, religious, civilizational identities that to some extent have displaced Westphalian identities. But the sense of belonging is not comparable to the idea of being a member of a comprehensive political community, which is the core meaning of "citizenship."

When world citizenship is claimed by idealists, who are usually proponents of world government as a desirable fix for world order, most eyes glaze over. The cosmopolitan governmental sentiment is detached from any viable political project or emergent political community. It is dismissed even by reform-minded students of world politics as a form of utopian foolishness. Similarly, when more recently members of the global corporate or banking elite fancy themselves to be world citizens, it exhibits confusion about the nature of citizenship, associating it more with a global lifestyle and transnational modes of business and finance that do not restrict their operations by reference to territorial boundaries. The extreme thinness of such "citizenship," if it even can be so denominated, is exhibited by the lack of commitment of such "world citizens" to global public goods, to the absence of concern about the wellbeing of all persons on the planet, and to the lack of support for effective forms of global governance.

My point here is that the only kind of visionary citizenship that can be taken seriously will be grounded in what is occurring on the level of fact, norm, and value as both trend and potentiality. It must be rooted in the future, the not-yet, rather than unconvincingly affirm as "real" such a spatial enlargement and reconfiguring of political allegiance. I have used the metaphor of "citizen pilgrim" to describe the spirit of a sojourner, committed to transformation that is spiritual as well as material, that is premised on the wholeness and equality of the human family, and that is not disposed to put much trust in prospects for a technical fix that might claim to enable global governance to succeed provided it is self-delineated as a functional project and nothing more.[16]

I believe that a sustainable world community can only result from a combination of secular and spiritual energies, and that from this perspective the religious resurgence is an indispensable source of hope, as well as a dangerous threat to undo the achievements of modernity.[17] The many initiatives associated with inter-civilizational dialogue are a crucial part of this world cultural preparation for the next stage in world order, centered on human solidarity, sustainable development, global civil society, human rights, the rule of law, global taxation, and multi-level arrangements of global governance. So comprehended, the negative energies of resistance to such transformative possibilities arouse intense emotions, as was evident in the global resonance to Samuel Huntington's depiction of the coming clash of civilizations. The clash hypothesis is the shadow side of post-Westphalian struggle, a darkness that lacks any impulse toward transcendence. The silver lining of dialogic interaction, and even conflict, is not merely an exchange of views to avoid perverse misunderstandings and recriminations. It must be also an endeavor to collaborate in unleashing the political and moral imagination of peoples throughout the world. Such an imaginative surge must occur on a global scale if a transformative outcome is to be eventually welcomed by the peoples of the world and their leaders, rather than feared and resisted.

The citizen pilgrim is engaged as a militant in this process. The religious factor need not be explicit or direct, and certainly may be quite independent from organized religion. Reliance on "human rights" as a universal political language is a secular alternative for engaging in dialogue, despite some serious drawbacks arising from perceived Western biases, the marginal role of non-Western civilizations in the norm-generating experience, and the hegemonic roles performed by the Western-dominated human rights discourse and practice.[18] By accepting the challenge of dialogue, as in the work of such seminal non-Western thinkers as Chandra Muzaffar, Tu Weiming, and Ahmet Davutoglu, there arises a real possibility that mutual trust will give rise to a shared understanding of what needs to be done to safeguard the human future can begin to take shape.

The moves in this direction remain at the margins of entrenched power, both the residual power of the state and the new constellation of forces associated with globalization (and regionalization). But there are signs on the horizons that such a dialogic civilizational/religious challenge will become stronger and more credible. As yet, little has been done to prepare humanity for the advent of radical technologies likely to emerge in the course of the next several decades. The ethical/political problems associated with biogenetics (including human cloning), advanced robotics (including sophisticated robot armies), and super-computers (with problem-solving and decision-making capabilities far exceeding what humans can achieve) present a series of challenges to the meaning and nature of life and the human condition that cannot be confined in space without risking catastrophic developments that could imperil human survival.[19] It is not relevant to pronounce upon the controversy as to whether these technological innovations on the horizon are as a big a menace as Bill Joy supposes or as large a boon as Ray Kurzweil believes.[20] What seems inevitable is that human consciousness will be profoundly challenged throughout the world to respond in a manner that will lend strong support to a global democratic process of assessment and regulation.

It is within such a future that the citizen pilgrim will have prefigured a community of believers in the collective destiny of the human species. When such attitudes intersect with tendencies toward transnational networking and institutional innovation, the foundations for new varieties of citizenship will quickly emerge, with appropriate patterns of allegiance, participation, and accountability. Such varieties presently remain over the horizon, beyond even our imagining capacities, but their preconditions are beginning to become clear, relating to an ethos of nonviolence, sustainability, compassion, and solidarity. Such an ethos is the clay out of which the citizen pilgrim is beginning to mold the sculptures of future life forms, including sustainable political communities that are bonded by a temporal commitment to the future as much as they are by a spatial commitment to the present.

Part III

International Criminal Law

6

The Holocaust and the Emergence
of International Human Rights

Situating the Inquiry

What seems, at first consideration, surprising is the rather muted character of any explicit acknowledgement of the relevance of the Holocaust to most accounts of the origins of the movement for the *international* protection of human rights. It is particularly surprising because the historical setting of the late 1940s was significantly shaped by the shocked awareness of the systematic extent, ferocity, and forethought of Nazi genocidal atrocities. This awareness was an essential aspect of the moral consciousness that dominated the period during and immediately after World War II. It was in these years that any kind of political and legal commitment to international human rights was *initially* clearly articulated. The inspiration for this development was most prominently provided by Franklin Delano Roosevelt's "Four Freedoms." This description of the war aims of the victors in World War II paved the way for the insertion of several hortatory provisions in the United Nations (UN) Charter, which in turn led to the first comprehensive formulation of international human rights in a text that was to achieve enduring influence and admiration, the Universal Declaration of Human Rights (1948).

It is necessary to admit that this commitment to uphold international human rights at these points of origins was so feeble from the perspective of implementation that it is even questionable to attribute the word "commitment" to what had been carefully set forth to avoid any implication of legal obligation constraining the policies of sovereign states. The assertion of international human rights standards at this stage, although notable, should be understood in the spirit of articulating widely shared "moral sentiments" or "aspirations." No claims were being made to set forth binding juridical commitments of even a declaratory character, much less was there any political will to push toward international or domestic implementation in the future. Such an extremely modest understanding of what *international* human rights was intended to mean at this initial stage is disturbing if it is meant to offer humanity a solemn promise by governments that future genocides would not be tolerated. It was more acceptable if interpreted as an unpretentious, and more accurate, expression of what could be done given the realities of a world order that was based on the territorial supremacy of sovereign states.

It should be noted that even these mere gestures acknowledging international human rights had "revolutionary" implications because they conceptually did challenge prevailing ideas of unconditional sovereignty of the state with respect to governance within its boundaries.[1] It should be understood, of course, that "human rights" as such had a much longer lineage, deriving from natural law thinking, and later "legalized" as essential elements in the American and, especially, the French Revolutions. The international status of such obligations associated with human rights was conceived within the framework of a state-centric world order as essentially voluntary orientations *internal* to the state. Prior to the mid-twentieth century, it should be noted that a great majority of states were authoritarian or totalitarian, imposing structures of governance that were abusive of basic human rights. The doctrinal innovation brought about after World War II was to extend this idea of rights *externally* and *universally*, and by their status, give to them a potential domestic applicability independent of the outlook of a particular sovereign domain. This claim of universality, although rather blandly endorsed in the years after 1945, came under a variety of pressures in later decades, especially due to the rise of non-Western civilizational consciousness and the religious resurgence. Especially in the period following the ending of the Cold War this alleged universality was challenged as an ill-fitting designation of what were essentially Western ideas. This post-colonial backlash prompted debates that are not yet fully resolved about "Asian values," "Islamic perspectives," and a variety of other civilizational standpoints, including those of indigenous peoples.[2]

It seems likely that part of the reluctance to link the Holocaust very directly to these early moves to establish human rights on an international level may have to do with precisely this disjunction between the magnitude of the evil and the weakness of the proposed response by way of this establishment of international human rights as non-obligatory. Clearly, this early phase of the human rights movement gave no indication that the leading governments of the world were politically or psychologically prepared to act effectively in the face of future holocausts, or, even more manifestly, were in any way willing to accept international accountability for themselves. And indeed, the historical record since World War II confirms this resistance, despite the evolution of a far more robust human rights tradition than could have been reasonably imagined in 1945 and despite a temporary upsurge of humanitarian diplomacy in the 1990s that included several claims to act under the rubric of "humanitarian intervention." The efforts to alleviate a humanitarian crisis in Somalia in the early 1990s and the 1999 NATO intervention in Kosovo span the spectrum of efforts undertaken during this period, as well as illustrating the sorts of debates about whether such efforts were desirable and effective.[3]

I would like to reinforce this introductory point from a somewhat contrasting angle of analysis. If one compares the surge of claims around the world for monetary reparations and historical redress for past harms that has surfaced since the end of the Cold War a dramatically different reality is encountered. One is immediately struck by the reliance on the invocation of the memory of the Holocaust as an instance of primal injustice that, even after the passage of more than half a century, requires redress to diminish the pain of persisting wounds. This reliance is paramount in the sense that it was the acknowledgment of the wrongs done to Jewish survivors and victims of the Holocaust by the Swiss government, along with its formal establishment of a $5 billion fund, seems decisive. It seems to have ushered into being this remarkable phenomenon of an expanded willingness by governments, banks, corporations, and civil society to accept a series of moral and legal obligations to take material and symbolic steps designed to mitigate severe instances of past injustice. This line of thinking is persuasively analyzed and depicted by Elazar Barkan in his important book *The Guilt of Nations*, which investigates the grounds for positing what he suggestively calls "a potentially new international morality."[4] There are two points worth noting: first, there was a pragmatic silence after World War II on these issues because of tactical and doctrinal reluctance to embarrass implicated governments that had been acting opportunistically in relation to the Nazi phenomenon, but in an amoral manner that is normal for sovereign states; second that, contrary to Barkan's hopes for a more morally responsive world order, the new urgencies of the early twenty-first century have again marginalized the pursuit of global justice.

Of course, it is important to distinguish between the protection of international human rights and this belated global movement in the 1990s to seek restitution in various forms for what Ken Booth has characterized as "human wrongs."[5] In the former case, there are rights whose violation provides the foundation for corrective and protective action primarily on behalf of individuals, whereas in the latter instance there are "wrongs" or "injustices" that imply collective action, generally insulated from scrutiny by canons of territorial legality and geopolitical convenience prevailing at the time of their commission. The Nazi penchant for legality accentuated the degree to which virtually the entire program of persecution that eventuated in the Holocaust was provided with a morally incriminating gloss of statist legality.[6] The 1990s moves for redress, in contrast, led to a deliberate retroactive reassessment of injustice relying on a different moral and legal compass than had been used at the time the harm was inflicted. The promotion and support of these assorted claims for redress often arose in this period directly or indirectly from sustained pressure mounted by and behalf of Holocaust victims putting forth a series of monetary and symbolic demands directed at those who are regarded as the legatees of the earlier wrongdoing. It is only by invoking the Holocaust, or some parallel ordeal of an extreme nature, reinforced by civic mobilization, that such claims can be endowed with sufficient historical stature to engender a meaningful response. On such a basis it became possible for a limited period of time to exert leverage over the political and moral imagination of those who were *then* acting on behalf of society, including its private sector constituted by banks and corporations. Such receptivity evaporated almost as rapidly as it had emerged when the global climate was again preoccupied by global security concerns after the 9/11 attacks.

Of course, the Holocaust is not the only human wrong that has stimulated the urge for redress, but I would argue that its salience was crucial for the creation of a climate of opinion that lent plausibility and weight to *other*, parallel claims. Indeed, one technique relied upon for mobilization of support for a redress process was to contend that such and such an occurrence was "a forgotten Holocaust."[7] In other settings, as with the push in California and elsewhere to hold corporations accountable for employing slave labor during World War II, the political animus came from efforts by organizations associated with Holocaust survivors. The California statute seeking to validate such claims clearly expresses this primacy of Holocaust concerns. And with wrongs long ago done to indigenous peoples or via the institution of slavery, the impetus for claims of reparations or restitution of rights *implicitly* draws on the precedent of validating a variety of claims associated with the range of Holocaust injustices. My contention is that, without the Holocaust, many of these claims for redress arising from wrongs that appear remote in time and historical circumstance would have continued to be treated as frivolous, as had been the case prior to the 1990s. But in the atmosphere of receptivity created by Holocaust claimants there emerged an entirely new credibility for non-Holocaust claimants who had previously been entirely ignored.[8]

This introductory contrast between the muted acknowledgement of the Holocaust during the late 1940s and its salience in the redress era that commenced in the 1990s presents a puzzle. One would have expected the relevance of the Holocaust to diminish with time and yet the opposite is the case. Why? Why should the relevance of the Holocaust have grown greater with the passage of time and despite the increasing participation of non-Western societies in world politics, with less consciousness associated with European experiences? The short answer is a shift in the locus of geopolitics associated with the transition from the Cold War to a period of globalization, which itself was brought to a dramatic close by the 9/11 attacks. An aspect of this shift was the distinctive character of the U.S. leadership role in world affairs during the decade of the 1990s, and its particular responsiveness to Holocaust claimants that had been long delayed during the Cold War decades for geopolitical reasons. Part of this American responsiveness seemed associated with its need for normative stature in a global setting lacking strong ideological issues and dominated by global economic priorities set by an amoral market mentality.[9]

Returning to my assigned theme of linkage, two kinds of assessments will be offered about the connections between the Holocaust and international human rights. First, an effort will be made to explain why the establishment of a regime for international human rights got off to such a humble beginning, despite the prompting for a much more robust effort given the failure to challenge Nazi policies internal to Germany in the years leading up to World War II. Second, it will be shown that, despite the apparent modesty of this start, seeds were sown that, at least indirectly, resulted from the Holocaust, and have given rise to a series of initiatives that have produced a cumulative movement on behalf of an *international moral order*, backed by law and capable of limited implementation to the extent that a supportive geopolitical consensus emerges in the context of specific challenges.

Domestic and Geopolitical Obstacles

My assessment on the linkage is two-sided—the Holocaust definitely exerted an influence on the moves toward the establishment of an international human rights regime, but it was less pronounced than might have been expected given the enormity, immediacy, and shocking character of the Nazi phenomenon. Furthermore, the war aims of the United States, for reasons of political culture and its style of political leadership, were stated in a rhetoric that seemed to project universal human rights quite independently of the Holocaust, phrased as a matter of positive goals than as a reaction to a negative experience.

Beyond this, as earlier indicated, it is strange that the pressure of the Holocaust, given the heightened awareness brought about by disclosures at the end of World War II, and especially at the Nuremberg trials of German wartime leaders, did not lead to the establishment of a more robust and obligatory international human rights regime. Why were the first steps taken so tentative and behaviorally ambiguous?

I think the first line of response here is that the culture of human rights was not congenial to the practices and outlook of many political elites, even as a matter of shaping state/society relations, and much less so for state/state relations. Aside from North America and Western Europe there were few instances of national commitments to individual freedoms and rights securely implemented *internally* by the rule of law, reinforced by an independent judiciary and an accountable police. That is, to a significant degree the very concept of human rights was incompatible with the practice and theory of domestic governance throughout the world as of the mid-twentieth century. Such incompatibility is obvious with respect to the Communist bloc of countries aligned with the Soviet Union and in relation to the surviving Fascist regimes of Franco's Spain and Salazar's Portugal.

Yet to a degree it pertains even to the liberal democracies. The United States was a racist country in the 1940s, with the civil rights movement two decades away, and in its projection of overseas power in the Western hemisphere, its support tended to reinforce rather than challenge authoritarian rule. Such a pattern became even more pronounced in the Cold War era, during which U.S. interventionary diplomacy seemed skewed against the pursuit of human rights in Third World countries.[10]

As for Europe, Britain, France, Portugal, and the Netherlands, they did their utmost to sustain their overseas empires, including the ruthless suppression of individuals of conscience who peacefully challenged the legitimacy of colonial rule. As a matter of geopolitical priority, especially until the end of the 1950s, the United States as global leader and provider of economic reconstruction assistance, lent strong indirect support to the position of the colonial powers. Aside from alliance relations with the colonial powers in NATO, and elsewhere, U.S. policymakers tended generally to view Marxism, or at least radical forms of nationalism hostile to foreign investment, as the likely sequel to colonialism, and hence to regard anti-colonial victories as Cold War defeats.

In other words, neither the political culture nor the geopolitical outlook of the post-1945 period was favorably disposed toward the emergence of an effective international human rights regime. Putting this observation differently, but for the impact of the Holocaust on the political and moral imagination, it is unlikely that even the modest moves to promote international human rights would have been taken in the post-war period of 1945–50, when a variety of significant global reforms occurred.[11]

Rights and World Order: Westphalian Premises, the Realist Consensus, and Cold War Human Priorities

The most fundamental obstacles to the establishment of an international human rights regime after 1945 were *structural* and *ideological*. World order had evolved for several centuries on the basis of an essentially state-centric logic, or on the basis of Westphalian premises.[12] A major feature of this structure was a series of normative ideas associated with the territorial sovereignty of states, including norms of non-intervention and of the equality of states. The persistence of this normative order was strongly reaffirmed in the United Nations Charter, not only by several general references in Article 2, but even more persuasively, by the prohibition of Article 2(7) on any UN intervention in "matters essentially within the domestic jurisdiction of Member states." Article 2(7) can be understood, among other things, as a pledge against the implementation of human rights standards. As such, it put the commitment to human rights in the Charter, and elsewhere, on an essentially *aspirational* and *voluntary* basis.[13]

In essence, this normative endorsement of a state-centric system also reflected the long history of international relations, including most spectacularly the non-interventionary response of the liberal democracies to the humanitarian abuses of Nazism that led up to the Holocaust. Ken Booth's indictment of the Westphalian sanctuary for wrongdoing and criminality on these grounds is suggestive of the strong resistance by political elites to the emergence of anything more substantial than a nominal international human rights regime, despite the fresh memories of the Holocaust and the utter failure of a non-interventionary approach to the emergence of European fascism. It was, indeed, pressures from civil society that were mainly responsible for even the nominal regime. These pressures were reinforced by guilty consciences of governmental leaders about such notable official accommodations of the Hitler challenge as amicable participation in the Berlin Olympics of 1936, the diplomacy of appeasement, the rejection of refugees, and the failure to bomb even the railroad tracks leading to Auschwitz during the latter stages of the war despite realizing that doing so would disrupt the killing taking place in that principal death camp.

There was a second strand of this post-1945 global setting, which related to the role and outlook of the U.S. government, and its principal policymakers. Even Franklin Roosevelt conceived of global reform on anti-Wilsonian terms that relied on the primacy of geopolitics for the maintenance of international peace and security.[14] Roosevelt's vision of the future, which turned out to be optimistic (and naïve) in a manner quite different from that of Woodrow Wilson, conceived of an effective UN as resting on a high degree of continuing cooperation after World War II among the main members of the victorious anti-fascist alliance. Such a vision was shattered, not by the U.S. removal of itself from the process as had occurred after World War I, but by the outbreak of the Cold War almost as the guns used against Germany and Japan were falling silent. Had Roosevelt lived beyond 1944, it is possible that East/West cooperation would have lasted a bit longer, but it seems highly unlikely that a cooperative relationship between the two postwar superpowers could have been maintained, given their ideological differences and the extent to which international relations facilitate geopolitical rivalry.

Other more intellectual factors were also at work in shaping the outlook of post-1945 United States leadership. An important element here is perversely related to our theme—it is that the most glaring failure of U.S. foreign policy associated with its reluctance to get involved with European politics resulted from an ill-conceived embrace of moralism and legalism, part of the now repudiated Wilson legacy. The main architects of U.S. foreign policy after 1945, and the most influential academicians, were united in their embrace of a realist frame of reference as alone applicable to international relations. Such notables as Dean Acheson, George Kennan, Paul Nitze, and Hans Morgenthau led the realist charge. In its essence, realists were arguing that the United States should be guided by a rational calculation of its strategic interests whenever it acts in the world. Furthermore, its security policy should be built around unsentimental calculations of countervailing power, stable alliance relations, and the pursuit of military superiority without being diverted by hypocritical and diversionary undertakings to promote humane results in foreign societies or by unreliable restraints on the use of force embodied in legal instruments.

George Kennan's diatribe on these matters is most telling, and carried the day so far as debate was concerned. Kennan writes in his famous Walgren Lectures delivered in 1950 at the University of Chicago as follows:

I see the most serious fault of our past policy formulation to be in something that I might call the legalistic-moralistic approach to international problems. The approach runs like a red skein through our foreign policy of the last fifty years. It has in it something of the old emphasis on arbitration treaties, something of the Hague Conferences and schemes for universal disarmament, and something of the more ambitious American concepts of international law, something of the League of Nations and the United Nations, something of the Kellogg Pact, something of the idea of a universal "Article 51", something of the belief in World Law and World Government. But it is none of these entirely.

Although Kennan does not bother to include human rights in this litany of "normative wrongs," the intention to do so is clear. And it becomes even clearer in Kennan's policy pronouncements contained in "top secret" communications made while serving as director of the Policy Planning Staff in the U.S. State Department. For instance, in PPS 23, dated February 24, 1948, Kennan is openly dismissive of a human rights component of U.S. foreign policy in relations with Asian countries. Within the setting of a "Top Secret" communication there is no need to give lip service to idealistic concerns, and Kennan was among those who feared that such public rhetoric might be taken seriously enough to distort policy. In PPS 23 Kennan writes:

We need not deceive ourselves that we can afford today the luxury of altruism and world benefaction. We should cease to talk about vague and—for the Far East—unreal objectives such as human rights, the raising of living standards, and democratization. The day is not far off when we are going to have to deal in straight power concepts. The less we are hampered by idealistic slogans the better.[16]

It is significant that nowhere in this important collection of documents is there any favorable mention of human rights or reference to rethinking foreign policy in light of the Holocaust. The object lesson of the period was "Munich" and "appeasement," that is, German external policies of aggression. There was a resolve to learn from that perceived failure of policy, but not, so far as I can tell, from Nazi genocide. To be sure, in differentiating the West from its new adversary, there was a stress on differences in internal public order and "freedom," and, significantly, this message was contained in important internal documents of the time. For instance, NSC 68, often treated as the master plan of the Cold War contained the following language: "There is a basic conflict between the idea of freedom under a government of laws, and the idea of slavery under the grim oligarchy of the Kremlin.."[17]

The point here is not to excoriate Kennan and other realists for their insensitivity about international human rights, but to make a stronger point.

Namely, the U.S. leadership role in the post-1945 period, during the Truman and Eisenhower presidencies, was forward-looking and preoccupied by the challenge of Soviet expansion. It did not want to be diverted by the Holocaust, an emphasis on which would be seen as a moralist regression that was not particularly relevant to meeting present challenges. To the extent that the Holocaust was considered by those involved in the inner circles of foreign policy, it was viewed as either irrelevant to the future because it was an anomaly of pathological politics or inconvenient in relation to "the new thinking" about Germany, not as a defeated enemy, but as a divided country that was the most dangerous potential flashpoint for the onset of World War III. In Washington's view, Germany needed to be rehabilitated as quickly as possible, and not reminded of its criminal past. Indeed, the quiet reintegration of Nazi officials into the new democratic Germany was indicative of how soon and fully the Holocaust was "denied" policy relevance.

For all of these reasons associated with "containment" and a realist foreign policy, it seems quite understandable that an international human rights regime would have trouble gaining serious credibility within U.S. government policy circles. How this credibility was later achieved, especially during the early years of the Carter presidency, is not part of the story being told here, but it is a propos to observe that this unexpected foregrounding of human rights in the mid-1970s had virtually nothing to do with a belated effort to restructure international relations in light of the Holocaust. In essence, the origins and early development of human rights, as generally understood, had little to do with the Holocaust until the change of global political and moral climate took place in the 1990s.

The Positive Holocaust Legacy

The *direct* bearing of the Holocaust on human rights, as generally understood by the international law and NGO community, is marginal. But if "human rights" is enlarged in scope to encompass "genocide" and criminal account-ability of leaders, then the Holocaust played a crucial, direct foundational role in the immediate post-World War II period. It was a matter of planting several seeds that lay almost dormant in the soil of international life for more than 40 years, but burst forth into the sunlight of prominence in the 1990s. There is little doubt that, but for this historical experience, these later developments would not have occurred, or would have occurred in a less impressive manner.

I have in mind here the Nuremberg Judgment and the Genocide Convention. Arguably, both of these historic responses to the Holocaust were less about "human rights" as generally specified and more about "aggression" or what Nuremberg regarded as "Crimes Against Peace." On a far lesser scale of concern was the "criminality" of governments, whether the official behavior of Nazi Germany being challenged was delimited as "Crimes Against

Humanity" or "Genocide." The ambit of human rights has been gradually enlarged, in the course of decades, to encompass these forms of criminality. For instance, Human Rights Watch and Amnesty International both devoted major attention to "ethnic cleansing" in the Balkans and Rwanda, as well as to the legal pursuit of General Pinochet. Beyond this, the human rights community has been mobilized during the 1990s to lend support, as its highest priority, to the establishment of an International Criminal Court (ICC). The negotiation of the Rome Treaty in 1998 and its widespread ratification were viewed as major victories for global civil society that led directly to the establishment of the ICC in 2002.

The Nuremberg Judgment (along with the Nuremberg Principles that distill its essential jurisprudential meaning) was at the time, and remains, a crucial challenge to the Westphalian ideology of unconditional territorial sovereignty with no legal accountability beyond the law of the state. Also challenged at Nuremberg was the closely related idea that leaders enjoy immunity *outside* their territory for acts performed *within* the boundaries of the state. The Nuremberg proceedings also authenticated and illuminated for world public opinion the full range of horrors comprising the Holocaust. Such a powerful narrative of mass genocide tended to neutralize more legalistic objections to criminal accountability based both on contentions of "victors' justice" and on the retroactivity of the standards being imposed.[18] These objections were not without merit, being partially acknowledged by the American prosecutor at Nuremberg, Justice Robert Jackson, in his celebrated "promise" that the principles being applied to assess the German defendants would in the future provide a legal basis for judging the actions of all governments, including those sitting in judgment. The accusers at Nuremberg were vulnerable to allegations of war crimes, especially in relation to the conduct of strategic bombing campaigns against German cities that were indiscriminate and deliberately aimed at causing maximum disruption of civilian society. To some slight extent, this controversy deflected attention from the causative impact of the Holocaust on the development of norms and procedures for international accountability, but the main deflection was due to the intrusion of geopolitical considerations associated with the Cold War and as a result of the resilience of a Westphalian world order.

These intrusions, aside from what has been discussed in prior sections, took two main forms: according priority to mobilizing resources and support for Cold War goals, which meant (1) not dwelling on the German past, and (2) implicitly accepting the Kennanesque conclusion that it was not possible to live within the Nuremberg framework while upholding strategic interests in a world of contending ideologies, alliances, and powerful states. To the extent that the Nuremberg ethos was kept alive at all, it was entirely due to individuals of conscience in civil society who invoked notions of accountability derived from international law to validate their own legally grounded resistance to governmental policy. Principled civilian resistance based on Nuremberg reached its climax during the Vietnam War, and was in a sense dramatized by the publication of Telford Taylor's *Vietnam and Nuremberg*, which argued that the United States was acting in Vietnam in a manner that contradicted the letter and spirit of the Nuremberg Principles.[19] What gave this assessment its dramatic effect was the identity of Taylor, a member of the prosecutorial staff at Nuremberg, a military officer with the rank of general, and a respected and conservative constitutional law professor at Columbia Law School.

The Genocide Convention would not exist but for the Holocaust. This treaty of universal reach was brought into being by the dedication of a single person, Raphael Lemkin, who was intensely motivated by the idea that the existence of a legal barrier to the commission of future genocides would have a preventive impact. But the Genocide Convention was itself a creature of larger forces and could not be expected to live up to very high expectations. Its own text betrayed deep ambivalence with respect to implementation. Article VI limits prosecutions to competent tribunals in the state where the genocide took place or in an international tribunal whose jurisdiction has been accepted by the relevant states, both with respect to allegation and defendant. And the United States, the leading state and the champion of the Nuremberg approach, did not get around to ratifying the Genocide Convention until 1988. Beyond this, there was a reluctance to allege genocide unless it was consistent with geopolitical priorities and strategic interests. The refusal to challenge the legitimacy of the Khmer Rouge regime as the representative of the Cambodian state reflected an unwillingness to disturb the American strategic partnership with China. Similarly, the failure to act effectively in response to "ethnic cleansing" in Bosnia and the refusal to act at all in response to full-fledged genocide in Rwanda, further confirm this refusal of leading states to compromise their strategic postures or commit their manpower and resources for the sake of opposing genocide or other acute violations of human rights. This refusal is even evident at the symbolic level, as illustrated by the successful Turkish effort as recently as 2008 to dissuade the U.S. Congress from censuring Turkey for its failure to acknowledge as "genocide," the Turkish killings of the Armenian people in 1915.

Nevertheless, these two streams of normative activity taking place immediately after World War II persist as important influences. It may be that a perspective of centuries rather than decades will be needed before the extent of the Holocaust (and parallel experiences) upon the evolution of this enlarged corpus of human rights can be fully realized. In the meantime, it needs to be acknowledged that this normative imagination (of accountability) has been kept alive mainly by the initiative, energies, and dedication of individuals and groups in civil society. Part of this effort is attributable to the academic and cultural efforts to sustain the relevance of the Holocaust through "Holocaust Studies" and Holocaust museums. Another part of the picture, but a more confusing part, is the extent to which the state of Israel acts, and even exists, in conscious relation to, and is perceived to represent and protect, the victims

93

and survivors of the Holocaust, and their descendants. On the one side, Israel's success as a state among states, as well as its close relationship to the United States, gives the Holocaust a geopolitical underpinning that ensures its influence and salience. On the other side is the controversial character of Israel's main policies that make its own behavior, especially in relation to the fundamental rights of the Palestinian people, the subject of widespread international criticism that complicates the legacy of the Holocaust.

The Holocaust and the Redress of Grievances

A contention being made in this chapter is that the memory of the Holocaust has been kept alive primarily by the forces of civil society and, to a confusing additional extent, by the existence of the state of Israel. A second contention is that the Holocaust influenced the origins of the movement to establish an international human rights regime, but not nearly as much as might be expected. To the extent that this regime has evolved, and gained in strength and stature, it has been primarily due to the interplay of civil society initiatives based on secular values (without much historical consciousness) and the periodic pragmatic moves of key governments, especially of the United States. For instance, the embrace of human rights by the Carter presidency resulted from many influences, but certainly one was the search for the moral rehabilitation of America in the aftermath of the dispiriting outcome of the Vietnam War. The opportunistic nature of this embrace was disclosed by the downgrading of human rights by the Carter administration in light of the strategic setbacks associated especially with the opposition to the Shah of Iran and flaring of the Cold War as a result of the Soviet intervention in Afghanistan. Carter's advocacy of human rights was blamed for emboldening the opposition to the Shah, and was alleged to contribute to Moscow's miscalculation as to the United States response to its Afghanistan policy on the theory that a human rights presidency was not likely to be confrontational when it came to international relations.

Intriguingly, the various moves toward reparations and redress that have been so impressive in the 1990s are of a different character. True, their emergence was delayed by the onset of the Cold War, and its tendency to suppress justice claims that might dilute alliance cohesion. Unlike Nuremberg, the animus of these claims rested directly on the undeniable justice of seeking recompense in various forms for wrongs done in the Holocaust setting. This setting was paradigmatic, with an array of comparable claims for redress and accountability around the world gaining political credibility and leverage by analogy.

A concluding point is that the Holocaust played a surprisingly small role in accounting for either the origins or the further development of international human rights. Initially, this small role can be best understood as a consequence of a state-centric world not genuinely ready for the imposition of human rights standards upon states on the basis of external sources of authority. Later on, when the human rights movement gained unexpected strength, the relationship to the Holocaust was also left in the background partly to avoid the impression that the promotion of human rights was a Western project and partly to avoid linking support for human rights with the various controversies raging in relation to the state of Israel. The main political levers relied upon in relation to the promotion of human rights were transnational social forces that worked via human rights NGOs, Cold War arenas such as those associated with the Helsinki Accords that turned out to be so influential in East Europe, the various constituencies around the world that were mobilized around the Anti-apartheid Campaign, and such other initiatives as were fashioned by the international women's movement, by coalitions of indigenous peoples, and by a variety of pro-democracy movements in Third World countries, especially in Asia.

The redress initiatives seem to have followed a different course, although emanating from the same set of historical circumstances. The traumas of the Nazi experience, together with the dilemmas of the Cold War, conspired to keep these issues at a low profile for decades. Germany made a variety of arrangements on its own for the monetary compensation of Holocaust survivors and their families, as well as offering a variety of symbolic statements and acts of contrition, apology, and remembrance. For many years there was little indication that the redress agenda would achieve its goals in relation to banks, museums, governments, corporations that in some way reacted to or sought to give recompense for Holocaust-era policies. To the extent these issues were kept alive, however, it was on the basis of the unhealed wounds of the Holocaust; thus when the political climate of the 1990s became more therapeutic, the moral space available to address them expanded. In this atmosphere these claims began to engender positive responses involving acknowledgments of responsibility and negotiations leading to the resolution of outstanding claims. In such settings, there is no doubt that the original context of harm and suffering is causally linked to the whole process of redress of past or historic grievances. The Holocaust has operated as the master example of such a dynamic, and parallel efforts have drawn on whatever historical circumstance of severe wrongdoing provides the foundation for the legitimacy and credibility of an insistence on some form restorative justice, no matter how long the passage of time since the offending acts took place. It is likely that if intellectual and political efforts are made to theorize this trend toward redress, the overt links to the Holocaust will be muted for some of the same reasons noted in relation to the development of the human rights tradition.

Professor Barkan, toward the end of his thoughtful and challenging book, poses the following question: "Are we to celebrate the proliferation of restitution as a modest beginning of a new international morality, or is it merely the latest twist in contemporary escapism from moral responsibility?"[20] My own answer to this question is that the current redress trend needs to be understood as a political as well as a moral phenomenon. Its prospects, beyond certain situational openings at the present time, will depend on the success or failure of a wider movement of global civil society to bring about a people-oriented world order, embodying the norms, procedures, and institutional arrangements appropriate for the realization of "humane governance."[21] I believe it is premature to suppose that a threshold has been crossed so that it can be confidently concluded that "a new international morality" beyond realism is emergent. Such a hopeful possibility cannot also be altogether excluded at this point, although it has certainly been sidelined, at least temporarily, by renewed security concerns since the 9/11 attacks and the American response by way of a "global war on terror." Contradictory trends in world politics are producing what I have in the past called "a geopolitics of ambivalence," which disguises realism without abandoning it. Such a disguise is more evident in relation to the complicated discourse of the past decade that has grown up around the debate about "humanitarian intervention," especially in relation to the NATO War of 1999 over Kosovo. Was it, as some have claimed, the first humanitarian war in history, or was it a use of force that invoked moral factors but was responding to a wide range of considerations? A change in leadership in the United States in 2001, together with the 9/11 attacks, moved this influential country away from its reliance upon humanitarian justifications for global policy, and has returned strategic calculations of national interests to their earlier position of dominance, although somewhat disguised beneath a veneer of ideological claims about promoting democracy and ending tyranny.

I tend to think, therefore, of the future of redress and restitution, and the whole pursuit of inter-temporal justice, primarily in relation to the ongoing struggle between democratizing initiatives associated with "globalization-from-below" and market-guided neoliberal and related geopolitical postulates of governance associated with "globalization-from-above."[22] The democratizing perspectives are animated by justice in relation to the past and future (especially pronounced in environmental circles due to concerns about "sustainable development"), and will inevitably lend support to the wider satisfaction of redress claims, while the corporate and militarist globalizers will generally be reluctant to validate a process of governance that accords priority to moral factors, given the emphasis placed on the efficient uses of capital. Of course, the ultimate form of redress for Holocaust victims would be the secure establishment of a world without genocide, ideally through preventive and anticipatory responses, and to the extent necessary, by way of collective global action. Unfortunately, that prospect remains a rather distant dream, given the persistence of realism, and its cohabitation with a new globalizing phase of geopolitics, yet it is a resilient dream that is likely to animate future action when conditions again seem receptive as they did in the 1990s.

7

The Pinochet Moment

Whither Universal Jurisdiction?

A Jurisprudential Bombshell

The drama associated with the attempt to hold General Augusto Pinochet, the notorious former Chilean head of state (1973–1990), legally accountable for crimes of state was widely shared around the world. Typical of the comments on this legal pursuit of Pinochet were the following: "breathtaking,"[1] "a decision without precedent . . . [a] beginning for what can and should be justice without borders,"[2] and a course of litigation that has "already revolutionized international law."[3]

Whatever else, then, the Pinochet legal proceedings that stretched out over a period of several years, fueled the moral, political, and legal imagination relating to accountability of political leaders, but divergently. For many it was a step forward in the struggle against impunity with respect to severe crimes of state. For others it was the related breakthrough associated with piercing the veil of sovereignty that had insulated dictators and tyrants from criminal responsibility for their criminal deeds. For still others it was the fruition of a long enduring effort to gain some redress of grievances in relation to the specific ordeal of Pinochet's oppressive rule in Chile, a simple matter of historical reckoning by a particular people, especially former victims and their families. For still others, it was the moment when the technical lawyers' concern with "universal jurisdiction" made headlines, moved international criminal law to a new level of seriousness, and demonstrated the vitality of national courts as potential enforcement agents for several of the most crucial norms in the area of international law, thereby making the prospect of a genuine international criminal law a meaningful global project. Of course, the Pinochet litigation in Britain was an assemblage of all these things, and, for many close observers, their fascination with the case arose because it has so many dimensions, and contains so many intriguing loose ends.

To some extent, the media response to the Pinochet drama was an instance of hype and spin, as well as a display of the absence of much historical consciousness. There was very little made of the fact that a series of domestic courts had over the years imposed standards of criminal responsibility or cooperated with extradition requests for Nazi perpetrators of atrocities wherever they were to be found. The Eichmann and Barbie cases had certainly laid the groundwork for proceedings against Pinochet, although there were significant differences. To begin with, there was an intense moral and political consensus about the Nazi regime that was much less clearly established in relation to the Pinochet dictatorship. This consensus had been authenticated by the outcome of World War II, being vividly confirmed at the war crimes trials of surviving German leaders held at Nuremberg. In contrast, Pinochet was an anti-communist ruler who came to and remained in power with Washington's blessings, and continued until his death to have support from a substantial minority in Chile who believed that he had rescued the country from its slide toward communism, chaos, and economic collapse by overthrowing the Allende government of the left. Beyond this, Pinochet was the leader, the symbol of ultimate authority, and not a loyal lieutenant as in most of the other prominent cases, and this represented the first time that such a notable head of state was being directly challenged in a domestic court.[4] Even Nuremberg never had the opportunity to prosecute Hitler, and although the Tokyo Tribunal came closer by prosecuting several top wartime leaders, it exempted the Japanese Emperor from indictment out of respect for his place in the hallowed traditions of his country, as well as the sacrosanct relationship of the emperor-system to the Japanese people. Thus it can be said that proceedings against Pinochet, even with the qualifications of historical recollection, does represent a watershed. Here, for the first time, a leader who was on the winning side in the Cold War, who had voluntarily and nonviolently given up power to enable a return to constitutionalism in Chile, was being criminally charged for crimes of state committed during his period of leadership. The Pinochet case did seem to emerge in a global setting in which adherence to minimum human rights standards by governments were becoming obligatory for even the head of state. In this regard, the case against Pinochet seemed at the time to be symbolic of a transition to a period of more cosmopolitan values as the underpinning for the rule of law.[5] The 1999 indictment and later prosecution in the Hague Tribunal of Slobodan Milosevic for serious international crimes while he was a sitting head of state is further evidence of what seemed, in the late 1990s, to be a trend toward the accountability of the highest political leaders. Unlike the Pinochet case, the Milosevic proceeding was organized under the auspices of an international tribunal, the International Criminal Tribunal for the former Yugoslavia, and, as with Pinochet, health considerations cast doubt on whether the lengthy legal proceedings would lead to conviction and punishment or to the natural demise of the defendant. In fact, Milosevic died before the trial could be completed, and the proceedings were frequently suspended due to his failing health.[6] This matter of the medical condition of the defendant was also a continuing feature of the Pinochet case almost from the first moment of his London detention. Pinochet's ill health was controversially relied upon by the British Foreign Office in the end to justify a denial of Spain's extradition request.

Pinochet was sent back to Chile, where he survived for several years before dying in his native country. To some extent the Chilean courts were somewhat less prepared to grant Pinochet medical impunity, but in the end came to a similar conclusion. In June 2002 the Supreme Court of Chile ruled that Pinochet was suffering from a severe form of dementia rendering him unable to stand trial on charges of human rights abuses during his time in power. To lend credibility to this assessment, and to meet the criticisms of Pinochet's opponents—who argued that if he was too ill to stand trial he was unfit to remain in the Senate—the 86-year-old former dictator resigned his lifetime seat. These developments brought the legal soap opera to an apparent end, which resulted in neither satisfaction nor complete disappointment for either side in the controversy over fitness.

There is little doubt that the Pinochet legal proceedings will be long studied as a momentous "case." Indeed, it may serve as a defining, if ambiguous precedent, for an expanding activist role of domestic courts with respect to challenging those forms of international criminality done under color of authority by the state, and its maximal leader. Perceived more critically, the Pinochet litigation, with its numerous sites of legal articulation (multiple judicial decisions in at least six countries: Spain, France, Belgium, Switzerland, Britain, and Chile, as well as formal legal proceedings and inquiries in several others), also illuminates the weaknesses and limitations of a strictly juridical approach to the underlying quest for an *effective* and *fair* regime of universal jurisdiction. Such a regime in relation to such serious crimes as genocide, crimes against humanity, torture, gross violations of human rights and of international humanitarian law is beset, to begin with, by the divergences associated with a decentralized world order of distinct sovereign states exhibiting dramatically uneven records of adherence to the rule of law, as well as highly subjective political appreciations of alleged criminality. Despite these concerns, given the current outlook of several major countries, including the United States, the path of universal jurisdiction may be more promising than the main alternative, the institution-building path of an International Criminal Court. More optimistically, building on the Pinochet experience could emphasize the *complementary* roles of domestic courts in a global setting, in which the very young International Criminal Court (ICC) has become an institutional reality of uncertain impact at this time.

In the background of this view is the current realization that the International Criminal Court, despite establishing its formal existence as of July 2002, is most unlikely in the foreseeable future to provide an effective and sufficient enforcement framework for many of the most serious crimes of state. It will take years, possibly decades or more, for many important states to make a firm commitment via ratification. Some key states are likely to remain outside, and opposed, indefinitely. As the ICC attempts to operate, it is likely to be severely constrained in its applicability by the primary authorizing role entrusted to the United Nations (UN) Security Council, and due to the constraints on prosecutorial initiative.[7] Adequate funding is also far from assured.

Under these circumstances, whatever happens, national courts will continue to have a dominant role for the foreseeable future in the development of international criminal law. Yet this vital role could be easily beset by a sense of chaos, arbitrariness, and partisanship unless the present disarray left behind by the Pinochet precedent is not mitigated in the near future. Justice Richard Goldstone suggests most hopefully that the Pinochet detention and litigation provides both "a new urgency" for the ICC and may well have served as "the catalyst" for "more frequent use of the civil and criminal courts against alleged war criminals."[8]

Above all, the Pinochet experience underscores the importance of establishing a more coherent regime for administering claims associated with universal jurisdiction over behavior that qualifies as international or global crimes. In other words, those who seek to close loopholes of impunity would be well advised to do more than celebrate the impressive pursuit of Pinochet, and welcome jurisprudential scrutiny given by various courts to such statist staple notions as "immunity," "double criminality," "extradition," and "amnesty." The weaknesses of the current decentralized international legal order were exhibited as well as its capacity for evolution in response to growing support around the world for the "globalization" of accountability for crimes of state, or put differently, a backlash against earlier tendencies toward de facto impunity for high government officials. The strength of the human rights discourse as the foundation of normative unity also supports judicial initiatives that impose enhanced standards of individual accountability.[9] In effect, those responsible for extreme violations of human rights should be held accountable to the extent possible, or else the regime of human rights will not seem to represent much of a challenge to state power where and when it is most needed, that is, in relation to a government and its leadership which deliberately embarks on a path of brutal oppressive rule. Ideally, of course, the prospect of accountability would be sufficiently robust to appear a consistent prospect that might even exert some deterrent impact upon would-be oppressors.

This chapter examines the successive stages of the Pinochet litigation from the perspective of generating an effective and fair regime of universal jurisdiction, suggesting the relevance of what was achieved, a realization of the insufficiency of the scope and methodology of judicial inquiry as it was delimited, and a concern about the inconsistent pattern of disposition at the level of judicial practice. As such, the inquiry here will not dwell on the detailed legal argumentation pertaining to such doctrinal matters as extradition, amnesty, and immunity, but will rather explore in a general way how the Pinochet case helps us identify the contours of an appropriate role for national courts. This exploration is inseparable from some view of the preferred relationship among the criminal legal systems of territorial states, and the link between states and the wider international community, given the current condition of global politics, morality, and law. In the background, as well, is the degree to which the international challenge to Chilean embrace of impunity with respect to the Pinochet era was itself seemingly influential— along with such other developments as the emergence of a new generation of military leaders in Chile and the assumption of the Chilean presidency by Ricardo Lagos, who was known to be in strong sympathy with the victims of the Pinochet dictatorship—in helping to lead Chilean courts to back away from their earlier embrace of impunity in relation to Pinochet, although this effort was partially nullified by the Supreme Court dismissal of claims against Pinochet due to its finding of his unfitness. Also of great importance for this Chilean process was the political impact of Pinochet's detention and legal proceedings in foreign courts and attendant publicity. The denial of immunity to Pinochet was apparently a crucial influence on the willingness of Chilean courts to consider complaints that sought to deny Pinochet the immunity that had been conferred in Chile as accompanying his status as "Senator-for-Life."[10]

The Chilean Backdrop

As is generally known, General Pinochet while leader of the Chilean armed forces organized a violent coup that successfully wrested control of the government in Santiago from the democratically elected president, Salvador Allende on September 11, 1973. Pinochet led a military junta that initially ran the country, and some months later proclaimed himself as president of Chile. He continued in that role until 1990 when he relinquished power under growing domestic pressure, and with the assurances of a self-amnesty decree, on the basis of a negotiated series of arrangements with opposition leaders that included leaving him in charge of the military and granting him a permanent position in the Chilean Senate. It had become clear through the results of a crucial plebiscite in 1988 that Pinochet had lost the confidence of the majority of the Chilean populace. It also became evident that important sectors of elite opinion, including much of the business community that had initially welcomed his takeover, now wanted a return to civilian government and the rule of law. According to Human Rights Watch:

> [t]he military regime he headed dismantled Chile's long-established
> democratic institutions, privatized its economy, and tried to eradicate
> left-wing parties and organizations in a reign of terror that claimed
> more than 3,000 lives, involved the torture of tens of thousands more,
> and forced over a quarter million Chileans into exile.[11]

Despite Pinochet's departure from the presidency in 1990, Pinochet remained head of the armed forces for eight more years, and then, by virtue of a constitutional provision, became a senator for life, thereby enjoying full parliamentary immunity. Pinochet's level of support in Chilean society as measured by referenda and elections remained in the vicinity of 40 percent, the armed forces continued to be a potent political force, and Pinochet himself exerted enormous influence on the military and, behind the scenes, on the exercise of authority by the elected civilian government.[12] The military remained unrepentant regarding the policies pursued in the 1970s, which they credited with saving the country from left extremism. In such an atmosphere it is hardly surprising that a general acceptance of impunity would emerge in Chile with respect to past offenses that might be attributed to the Pinochet period of rule. That is, the early years of transition to democracy were fragile and uncertain, and definitely did not include a mandate to apply constitutional standards retrospectively to the Pinochet period. At the same time, there were continuous urgings from human rights groups, activists, and representatives of the victims to inquire into the past, to tell the story, to find out what had actually happened, and to the extent feasible, to impose criminal accountability.

Responding to this welter of contradictory pressures, while walking a tightrope between reconciliation and disclosure, the Aylwin government in Chile did establish a National Commission of Truth and Reconciliation in 1991, known as the Rettig Commission. There was also a second official inquiry known as the National Corporation of Reparation and Reconciliation. Together these two bodies established an extensive record narrating the experiences of those political adversaries who were killed during the Pinochet regime. These extensive reports detailed the loss of life on the part of 3,197 individuals who were in this form officially recognized for the first time as victims of human rights abuse. These inquiries operated within strict limits and did not have the authority to consider torture or abuses other than killings, or to name names of the perpetrators of abuse. The military leadership and its numerous political allies menacingly rejected even these findings along with the recommendations of the Rettig Commission to take various steps to strengthen human rights. At the same time, such findings confirmed the suspicions of many Chilean citizens and strengthened civic demands that justice be done in relation to past wrongs.

It was not until the late 1990s that the issued of the "disappeared" entered into the mainstream political debate in Chile, becoming a strong moral challenge to the democratically elected government, although human rights groups associated with the families of victims had kept the issue alive all along. By 1998, in a more secure democratizing atmosphere, even some military leaders were beginning to cooperate with political parties and human rights groups, and agreed to provide information about the "disappeared." It had become clear to all parts of Chilean society that reconciliation with the past would not be possible without addressing this set of concerns that remained open wounds for many families in Chile. The Defense Minister Pérez Yoma in late 1999 took the rather amazing step of arranging meetings under his auspices between members of the armed forces and relatives of the "disappeared" and other victims. This initiative was itself controversial as some of the human rights lawyers and organizations in Chile thought that such events might interfere with the increasingly assertive approach being taken by Chilean judges in the new atmosphere of enhanced constitutionalism that included more openness to human rights and issues of governmental accountability.

The Pinochet government had done its best to prevent its criminality from ever being legally challenged. By virtue of a government act proclaiming the end of a state of siege in April 1978, Decree 2, 191, amnesty was granted for all serious crimes committed between September 11, 1973 and March 10, 1978. This "amnesty law" was described by the government as a reconciliation initiative at the time, and its coverage was extended to opponents of the Pinochet regime, resulting in the release of several hundred political prisoners with leftist orientations from Chilean jails. There has been continuous controversy about this amnesty initiative, with both the Aylwin and Frei at various points proposing in their electoral campaigns annulment of the decree, and then backing away from such a commitment under pressure from the military, and refusing to support legislative efforts aimed at annulment.

In the 1980s and into the 1990s courts in Chile, dominated by Pinochet appointees, generally applied the amnesty law to block investigations into the alleged criminality of the dictatorship. But increasingly in relation to unresolved "disappearances" some Chilean judges started to view the absence of the body of the victim as creating a continuing crime, and hence its occurrence as not covered by the amnesty decree even if the original disappearance occurred in the 1973–1978 period.

The atmosphere in Chile changed dramatically in the late 1990s, especially after the start of the Spanish criminal investigations. In this period numerous Chilean legal initiatives were instituted in relation to the alleged crimes of Pinochet and other important military figures active in his regime. The main investigation was being conducted by Judge Juan Guzmán Tapia as to the merits of a series of criminal complaints by individuals and organizations, including more than 40 against Pinochet himself. This investigation was encouraged by a unanimous ruling of the Supreme Court of Chile in July 1999 that Guzmán was correct to exempt from the amnesty law all cases in which the fact of death could not be authenticated, with the result that victims of abduction were treated as still missing. In this new atmosphere even such notorious incidents from the past as the "Caravan of Death" came under review, and the Fifth Chamber of the Santiago Appeals Court applied what came to be known as the Guzmán doctrine, removing disappearances from the amnesty law, but refusing to extend scrutiny to allegations of torture and murder.

It is against this background that it is necessary to understand Chile's response to the Spanish proceedings against Pinochet, as well as his subsequent detention in Britain pending the outcome of an inquiry as to whether the extradition request from Spain should be honored. The Frei government in Chile refused to cooperate with Judge Balthasar Garzón in Spain, regarding the Spanish proceedings as "an illegitimate invasion of the jurisdiction of the Chilean courts."[13] Chile also formally objected to the British detention of Pinochet as a violation of his immune status as a "special envoy" of the Chilean state. It is difficult to assess the real motives for this Chilean stand, especially whether it primarily reflected concerns that any proceedings against Pinochet abroad would result in intense agitation in Chile. It may also have expressed the sentiment that in the new atmosphere in Chile it was possible to deal with charges against Pinochet within the Chilean legal system, that Chile was legally entitled to take control over any criminal proceedings as it was on its territory that the supposed crimes took place, and that it would consolidate the transition to democracy through a clear repudiation of criminality associated with Pinochet and his years of rule. As such, questions of sovereignty and nationalist prerogatives were engaged, as well as respect for a former Chilean head of state who continued to hold an official title and office, but also issues about the comparative merit of competing claims to assert criminal jurisdiction.

This interplay between Chile and Britain and Spain does raise issues of importance. To what extent should the representations of the territorial government, particularly if it is currently operating as a constitutional democracy, be entitled to respect and deference by foreign governments and their judicial bodies? Specifically, should foreign courts affirm the primacy of territorial claims of jurisdiction where the defendant is a national and where the crimes at issue were committed? And should foreign governments take some sort of notice of purported dangers to the stability of a democratic regime if there is a failure to respect an agreed earlier policy of impunity in relation to past crimes? Should the primacy of Chilean jurisdictional claims be respected if prospects for prosecution and conviction seem strong and the atmosphere is conducive to judicial independence? Or disregarded if such prospects seem dubious?

The evolving Chilean withdrawal of impunity from Pinochet and his regime underscores both the importance of a more authoritative international law approach to these issues and its difficulties. Arguably, in the fragile early period of the transition in Chile it was prudent to avoid challenging amnesty and the ethos of impunity, acknowledging the wisdom of President Aylwin's pledge to pursue justice in relation to the past "to the extent possible" (*en la medida de lo posible*).[14] A more directive approach based on canons of universal jurisdiction would have placed the Chilean political leadership and judiciary in an untenable position of either provoking renewed military interference or repudiating the framework of inquiry and accountability embodied in international law.

This complex Chilean experience during these years of restored democracy is suggestive of both the need for flexibility, and the importance of initiatives taken in foreign national courts with respect to past official criminality. There seems little doubt that the Spanish proceedings, reinforced by those in several other countries, to impose criminal accountability, strengthened the Chilean resolve to seek a higher standard of justice within its own legal system. The passing into history of the Cold War, a gradually more secure democratic order in Chile, a displacement of the earlier Pinochet generation of leaders in the armed forces, the ascendancy of post-Pinochet judges, the persisting activism of human rights groups, and the pressures of international public opinion have together facilitated a greater use of Chilean courts to address unresolved grievances of past victims. At the same time, counter-pressures have also been mobilized, particularly in the armed forces, generating doubts about the degree of autonomy that can be expected in relation to the Chilean judicial process.[15] These changes of circumstances in Chile lent weight to the Chilean request for Pinochet's return, and weakened somewhat the foundation underlying foreign criminal prosecution, but not entirely due to the uncertainties of the Chilean situation. There remained ample room for assessment and debate. Should a jurisdictional challenge be resolved in favor of a foreign court that has ample grounds in law for determining criminal allegations against such a defendant as Pinochet or does his special relationship with Chile give that country priority in determining his degree of accountability? And should such a determination be made on strictly legal grounds by judicial institutions or should it be decided, or at least shaped, by the views of the political branch of government. For instance, in American practice, the State Department's Legal Advisor has the authority to communicate to the court its views on granting or withholding immunity or diplomatic recognition. Similarly, challenges based on international law directed at American foreign policy have been habitually disallowed by U.S. courts, which have invoked either the doctrine of "political questions" or denied that the initiating plaintiffs possessed the legal standing to pursue such an allegation. A more robust role for national courts would suggest greater judicial autonomy in resolving jurisdictional challenges, but not necessarily unlimited autonomy.[16] A nuanced approach would clarify the considerations that would justify departing from normal expectations of deference by political branches of government to the autonomy of domestic courts.

The Spanish Request and Inquiry

These issues of jurisdictional propriety were all present in relation to the approach taken by various non-Chilean legal authorities in deciding how to respond to the interplay between the attempted initiation of criminal proceeding against Pinochet and the objections raised by the government of Chile. The Spanish proceedings, although complex, seemed to treat the controversy surrounding jurisdiction in a legalistic manner, that is, giving no overt attention to the political context.

The Spanish legal process had been initiated in 1996 by the Progressive Union of Prosecutors of Spain in the form of criminal complaints against the military leadership of Argentina and Chile for their role in "disappearances" of Spanish citizens in both countries. Subsequently, the charges were expanded to include torture, terrorism, and genocide. The prosecutors, in accordance with Spanish law, were joined by private complainants acting on the basis of *actio popularis*, which allows individuals and citizen organizations to bring criminal charges without any demonstration of a connection to the events. In the Chilean initiative the actions in Spain were brought by the Salvador Allende Foundation and by the Chilean Group of Relatives of Detained and Disappeared Persons (Agrupación de Familares de Detenidos y Desaparecidos de Chile). The allegations were initially made before two quasi-judicial bodies, so-called Investigating Courts No. 5 and No. 6, subordinate units of the Spanish National Court, which is known as Audiencia Nacional. Both of these courts issued orders confirming their jurisdiction to investigate genocide and terrorism, which were in turn unanimously upheld on appeal by the Criminal Division of the National Court in a plenary session in which eleven magistrates participated. All along, the Spanish Public Prosecutor—acting not on behalf of the government, but given the role of enacting legal conscience as pertaining to both sides—raised a series of objections relating to jurisdiction, in effect, arguing the case for and against those accused on the basis of both procedural and substantive considerations.[17]

These cases were initiated before there was any prospect of obtaining the physical presence of Pinochet, but included the investigation of "Operation Condor," which had been organized by the Chilean National Intelligence Directorate (DINA) acting under a mandate from Pinochet to work toward "the elimination of communism" and for the sake of "Western-Christian society." Judge Garzón presiding over Investigating Court No. 5, acting in accordance with a decision by the Spanish Supreme Court, issued orders confirming jurisdiction based on the principle of universality associated with the crimes charged. These orders also stressed that the Spanish identity of victims of these policies in both Chile and Argentina, while not jurisdictionally necessary, added what was described as "a legitimate interest" to the Spanish proceedings.[18] After learning of Pinochet's presence in Britain, extradition was formally requested by Garzón on the basis of both the Spanish Criminal Procedure Act and the 1957 European Convention on Extradition. The Spanish government was instructed to proceed diplomatically to request extradition of Pinochet to face charges relating to genocide, terrorism, and torture specifically associated with the activities of Operation Condor. On November 6, 1998 the Spanish Council of Ministers sent the extradition request to London, and a month later Judge Garzón formally initiated the prosecution of Pinochet in relation to the crimes alleged.

Several features here are worth highlighting. First, the grounding of criminal jurisdiction on Spanish legislation that affirms the universality of the alleged crimes, regardless of the time and place of their occurrence. Second, the reinforcement of jurisdictional claims based on universality with the idea of a distinct "legitimate interest" based on the national identity of some of the victims. Third, a procedural framework in which the absent accused's legal interests are protected by the assigned role of the prosecutor to serve the cause of justice with impartiality. Fourth, the availability of procedural access to any concerned party without any particular showing of a relationship to a victim; in effect, civil society and its representatives are given legal standing. Fifth, and most radically, the extension of the crime of genocide to encompass a deliberate plan to eliminate a *political* group, rather than being confined to ethnic, racial, and religious attributes.[19]

Other Responses by Foreign Domestic Courts

It is notable that several other criminal complaints were lodged in domestic courts in Europe once Pinochet had been detained in Britain.[20] It is also relevant to recall that, in 1994, during a private visit to the Netherlands, the public prosecutor dismissed a criminal complaint against Pinochet that had been filed under the UN Torture Convention. The grounds for dismissal given were the absence of an extradition request, lack of jurisdiction, head of state immunity, lack of Dutch public interest, and difficulties of proof.[21] It seems natural to wonder whether the response in 1998, a mere four years later, given changes in the global climate of opinion on such matters, would have been the same. In any event, although there were legal proceedings of some sort in several more European countries in 1998, responding to the British detention and the Spanish request, only those in France and Belgium appeared to have reached some degree of resolution. It appears that, in view of the priority in time of the Spanish request, other potential extradition claimants gave way and did not formally request that extradition be granted by the British courts. If correct, this raises the question as to whether, in the event of multiple requests for extradition, a response should be based purely on priority in time. It is arguable that other factors deserve to be given greater weight under certain circumstances, such as the relative degree of interest in prosecution, availability of evidence, and the persuasiveness of the various jurisdictional claims. For instance, if a claim based on universal jurisdiction is reinforced by the nationality of the victim(s) of the alleged crimes, then a presumption of validity might be attached to a jurisdiction claim, with timeliness of the extradition request being taken into secondary account. Arranging a hierarchy of jurisdictional claims might deserve inclusion in any articulation of a principled approach to universal jurisdiction.

In France, several French citizens who claimed to be victims of Pinochet crimes filed complaints requesting the Prosecutor to initiate criminal proceedings against Pinochet for crimes against humanity, torture and disappearances.[22] In French practice the Prosecutor decides whether the facts deserve investigation, and if so, issues an *instruction*, which in effect declares that the complaint should be evaluated by an examining magistrate, *juge d'instruction*. At the end of this procedure, Judge Roger Le Loire, *juge d'instruction du Tribunal de instance*, of Paris issued international arrest warrants in two of the five cases presented for consideration. The reasoning relied upon is of interest.

Both arrest warrants issued related either to French leftist students living in Chile or individuals associated with the government of President Salvador Allende in the 1973–1977 period. They were French citizens at the time of their arrest and "disappearance." The jurisdictional foundation of the case rested on the nationality of the victims, known technically as "the passive personality" principle. Universal jurisdiction is not available for crimes against humanity in France unless the accused is present in the country. Even then there would be a problem unless the acts complained about qualified as crimes against humanity, as otherwise prosecution would be barred by "time prescription," known in the United States as the statute of limitations. It was thus necessary to examine the substantive character of the crimes. The French court refused to extend the concept of genocide in the manner done by the Spanish court, restricting genocide to deliberate undertakings to exterminate "a national, ethnic, racial or religious group." It also refused to consider such charges in relation to Pinochet as a French law governing crimes against humanity was not passed into law until 1994, making the attempt to apply it to the crimes alleged against Pinochet retroactive, which would violate the maxim *nullum crimen sine lege*.

Such a ruling made the time prescription relevant. If the crimes were classified as murder and torture, then jurisdiction lapsed due to time. The French judicial authority refused to regard the Chilean amnesty decree as operative in French courts, and thus French citizens if their contentions were otherwise acceptable could have proceeded. However, in relation to the cases of disappearance, the time prescription does not begin until the person who disappeared is found, whether dead or alive. This approach is supported both by Article 17 of the United Nations General Assembly Declaration on Protection of All Persons from Enforced Disappearances and by the Inter-American Convention on Forced Disappearances. As a result, Judge LeLoire, ruled that for the crime of "sequestration and disappearance, the time prescription does not apply."[23]

The Belgian court proceeded somewhat differently. First of all, the criminal complaint was filed by six Chilean exiles living in Belgium, charging crimes committed under international law as specified in the Belgian statute implementing the Geneva Conventions of 1949 and Additional Protocols of 1977 comprising international humanitarian law. The magistrate addressed issues of public immunity, universal jurisdiction for international crimes, and the matter of time prescription.

On the matter of immunity, the magistrate concluded that Pinochet was immune for all official acts arising from the exercise of his role as head of state. Relying on Nuremberg and the authority of legal scholars, the magistrate decided that Pinochet was not immune in relation to torture, murder, and hostage-taking, which could not possibly be considered as falling within the scope of official acts. Unlike the French approach, the Belgian law was deemed to confer universal jurisdiction on the Belgian courts, allowing prosecutions to take place even when the accused is not present in the country and the victims are not Belgian. Such prosecutions were only allowable if the evidence supported allegations of severe violations of international humanitarian law. The magistrate also overcame the objection based on retroactivity by concluding that the crimes charged to Pinochet were common crimes in Belgium at the time of their commission in Chile, even though their occurrence was prior to the 1993 enactment of the Belgian implementing statute. The magistrate did finally conclude, however, that the absence in Chile of an armed conflict as defined in Geneva Additional Protocol II of 1977 meant that there was no basis for an exercise of legal authority resting on charges of violating international humanitarian law.

The only remaining issue was whether an international arrest warrant could be issued on the basis of the contention that these complainants had been victims of crimes against humanity. Here, the difficulty was that the Belgian criminal law statutes made no explicit reference to crimes against humanity.[24] The Belgian magistrate, nevertheless, found a legal basis to proceed:

we find that, before being codified in a treaty or statute, the prohibition on crimes against humanity was part of customary international law and of international *jus cogens*, and this norm imposes itself imperatively and *erga omnes* on our domestic legal order.

The magistrate added, "[c]ustomary international law is equivalent to conventional international law and is directly applicable in the Belgian legal order."[25] There were several other statements in this opinion that are relevant, in the spirit of the Spanish judicial response and far less positivistic than either the eventual outcome in the House of Lords or in the French legal system. For instance, the Belgian magistrate accepted the mission of "combating impunity" and the relevance in such circumstances of the principle of general international law, *aut dedere aut judicare*. One more assertion is worth quoting to give the flavor of the Belgian response:

The struggle against impunity of persons responsible for crimes under international law is, therefore, a responsibility of all states. National authorities have, at least, the right to take such measures as are necessary for the prosecution and punishment of crimes against humanity.[26]

This leads to the conclusion that universal jurisdiction is firmly established in relation to crimes against humanity in customary international law, and exists "even more strongly as a matter of *jus cogens*." Luc Reydams notes the contrast between the Belgian and French approaches, associating, with implicit irony, the former approach with the celebrated advocacy by the great French jurist, Georges Scelle, of *dédoublement fonctionnel*—insisting that those who act for the state have a dual function of representing their particular state and acting as an agent on behalf of the international legal order.[27]

The British Response

Most of the attention given to the pursuit of Pinochet has focused on the British response to the Spanish extradition request. I believe this is somewhat misleading in relation to the underlying issues of universal jurisdiction. The legal developments in Chile, Spain, and Argentina with respect to the criminality of the Pinochet regime seem as important, or more so, in relation to the fundamental jurisdictional and substantive questions at issue. The British role was in a sense peripheral and quite accidental, revolving around its willingness to respond to an extradition request, and hence focused on the collateral issue of whether the charges against Pinochet in Spanish courts were "extradition crimes" from the perspective of British law. Part of the explanation for the disproportionate interest in the British treatment of these issues is undoubtedly the journalistic dimension relating to the sudden legal vulnerability of this former military dictator, an interest deepened by Margaret Thatcher's expressed solicitude for Pinochet who she defended as a personal friend, a guest of the country, and an ally of Britain at the time of the Falklands crisis. More relevant here is the fact that the British legal system, due to his physical detention, was in a position to determine the fate of Pinochet outside of his own country, and that it did so in a series of carefully argued and reasoned legal decisions.

Following the useful lead of Professor Christine Chinkin it seems helpful to distinguish within the British sphere three phases of litigation: *Pinochet 1*, *Pinochet II*, and *Pinochet III*.[28] Most attention will be devoted to *Pinochet III*, the final determination of a judicial character taking place in the House of Lords, and followed by the determination of the Home Secretary (also called Secretary of State) to send Pinochet back to Chile on grounds of health, concluding that he was unfit to stand trial by British standards.

Pinochet I

In response to the Spanish international arrest warrant, dated October 16, 1998, relating to a series of crimes alleged to have been committed by Pinochet, a London magistrate issued a provisional warrant the next day for Pinochet's detention at a clinic where he was undergoing medical treatment. The warrant was issued under the Extradition Act of 1989. There was a second international arrest warrant issued by Spain a few weeks later that dealt with the additional enumerated crimes of torture and conspiracy to commit torture, detention of hostages, and conspiracy to commit murder.

Pinochet responded by seeking a writ of *habeas corpus* and leave for judicial review of his detention. The Divisional Court of the Queen's Bench Division unanimously quashed both warrants, partly by regarding Pinochet as immune during his period as head of state and partly by refusing to regard extraterritorial claims to prosecute for a murder committed in Chile as entitled to be treated as an "extradition crime." The Crown Prosecution Service was given leave to appeal, on behalf of Spain, to the House of Lords because there were issues of general importance presented relating to immunity and extradition. In the meantime, Spain expanded once more its extradition request to include genocide, torture, murder, and hostage-taking in Chile and elsewhere. Reflecting concern that the legal issues had not been fully addressed in the Divisional Court, the House of Lords instructed the Attorney General to appoint an *amicus curiae* to examine the international law issues at stake. As a result, Amnesty International, Human Rights Watch, and several other individuals and organizations, including the Association of the Relatives of the Disappeared Detained, were treated as "intervenors" and distinguished in British usage from "neutral jurists" who could only file amicus briefs. Intervenors are entitled to provide oral testimony, as well as to offer independent written submissions. The House of Lords panel also appointed "a neutral jurist" to provide legal advice on the case in the form of written submissions.

By a vote of 3–2 on November 25, less than two weeks after the appeal was heard, a specially constituted Appellate Committee of the House of Lords upheld extradition on the ground that Pinochet was not immune in relation to crimes committed under international law.[29] The main argument had revolved around the issue as to whether the alleged crimes could be assimilated into the official functions of a head of state, and thereby preclude prosecution due to the applicability of immunity. The narrow majority decided, in the words of Lord Nicholls, that:

> international law has made plain that certain types of conduct, including torture and hostage-taking, are not acceptable conduct on the part of anyone. This applies as much to heads of state, and even more so, as it does to everyone else; the contrary conclusion would make a mockery of international law.

Lord Steyn added that, since the criminal charges against Pinochet were "international crimes deserving of punishment," it was "difficult to maintain that the commission of such high crimes may amount to acts performed in the functions of a Head of State."

The arguments favorable to Pinochet were articulated by the two dissenting judges. Lord Slynn was unconvinced on the core issue of universal jurisdiction. In his words:

[i]t does not seem to me that it has been shown that there is any State practice or general consensus let alone a widely supported convention that all crimes against international law should be justiciable in National Courts on the basis of the universality of jurisdiction.

His Lordship went on to say, "[n]or is there any jus cogens in respect of such breaches of international law which require that a claim of State or Head of State immunity, itself a well established principle of international law, should be overridden." Although basing their decision on the availability of immunity to Pinochet as head of state, these two dissenting judges also stressed several other factors. They made reference to the eleven pending prosecutions in Chile, as well as the relevance of the amnesty decree, the impact of the 1990 Commission on Truth and Reconciliation, and the ruling of the Chilean Supreme Court that the amnesty decree did not apply to crimes that occurred or persisted after 1978.

The Home Secretary, Jack Straw, days later, on December 9, authorized a magistrate to proceed with extradition for the crimes alleged in the Spanish request, but deleted genocide on the grounds that it was not an extradition crime under British law. It seems that Straw did not consider whether the Spanish charge of genocide was conceptually acceptable, but rather that, regardless of the factual grounds, extradition for this crime was unavailable. It should be noted that it was the Home Secretary who possessed the authority to bring diplomatic and other extra-legal considerations to bear, even to the extent of disregarding the judicial outcome, if it was found to harm national interests. In this setting, the Chilean objection to extradition could be considered, both with respect to whether there was any serious prospect of bringing Pinochet to justice in Chile, the repercussion for British/Chilean relations of rejecting the Chilean government's intervention in the case, and assessments of how a prosecution of Pinochet anywhere might affect the orderly transition to democracy in Chile.

Pinochet II

Pinochet's counsel filed a petition with the House of Lords contending that *Pinochet I* be set aside on the grounds of the undisclosed connections between one of the judges, Lord Hoffmann, and Amnesty International.[30] Lord Browne-Wilkinson presided over a new panel of Law Lords that unanimously set aside the earlier determination, calling for a new hearing before a new group of judges. The reasoning was based on the idea that since Amnesty International, as an intervenor in favor of extradition, was in effect a party to the appeal, this meant that Lord Hoffmann must be disqualified from participation. He was in effect acting simultaneously as party and judge in the same case, and this was deemed unacceptable. At the same time, the government of Chile formally entered the judicial arena, not to support Pinochet's claim of immunity, but to insist that it possessed a sovereign right and interest in having the question of Pinochet's accountability resolved in Chile, where its courts were considering a series of criminal charges brought against the former leader.[31] This point had been disputed by the human rights community, which expressed the view at the time that, on the basis of past performance and future prospects, it was virtually inconceivable that courts in Chile would have the independence and political will to address adequately the charges against Pinochet.[32] Also, the charges against Pinochet for which extradition was being requested were again amended, being narrowed and expressed with greater specificity in relation to time and place.[33]

Pinochet III

The original appeal to the House of Lords was reargued, but more elaborately. This time a panel of seven Law Lords was convened, excluding Lord Hoffmann, but including the other four Law Lords who had participated in *Pinochet II*. The enlargement of the panel to seven was unusual in the practice of the House of Lords, and apparently reflected the sense that the issues posed were of great importance, and needed to be resolved as authoritatively as possible. In this setting hearings commenced on January 18, 1999, and lasted two weeks. The same intervenors as in the earlier hearings were allowed to participate, but were now joined by the government of Chile, which put forward an argument in support of Pinochet's claim of state immunity, as well as its claim of sovereign prerogative to prosecute alleged crimes committed on its territory. The judgment of the House of Lords on March 24 denied the claim of immunity by a 6–1 majority, and held Pinochet extraditable, but only for the commission of torture subsequent to September 29, 1988, the date on which Britain enacted Section 134 of the Criminal Justice Act, making torture a crime in the United Kingdom regardless of where it was committed or the nationality of the perpetrator. In this sense, the crux of the criminality associated with the Pinochet regime, even as to torture, was not accepted as a valid basis for extradition. The majority rejected the view that there was any basis for charges of criminality under international law in British domestic courts other than for crimes that had been formally and explicitly incorporated into British positive law. It was a narrow, legalistically framed judicial response to the Spanish request. The decision does at least stand substantively for the proposition that international crimes, to the extent that they are incorporated into domestic law, are not shielded from judicial prosecution by state immunity or by notions of the territoriality of criminal law.

The lead Law Lord in *Pinochet III*, Lord Browne-Wilkinson, offers an interesting comment as to both the Spanish venue of potential prosecution and the proper domain of legal inquiry in the setting of assessing an extradition request:

It may well be thought that the trial of Senator Pinochet in Spain for offences all of which related to the state of Chile and most of which occurred in Chile is not calculated to achieve the best justice. But I cannot emphasise too strongly that that is no concern of your Lordships. Although others perceive our task as being to chose between the two sides on the grounds of personal preference or political inclination, that is an entire misconception. Our job is to decide two questions of law: are there any extradition crimes and, if so, is Senator Pinochet immune from trial for committing those crimes?[34]

In effect, then, the British inquiry is whether under *national* law in all three countries it is permissible to assert universal jurisdiction for crimes essentially committed within Chile, and even then, whether the crime alleged is such that its commission is not barred from prosecution because of an immunity enjoyed by this defendant who was head of state at the time. Another stage-setting conclusion was the decision to grant the Republic of Chile "leave to intervene" on the ground that the claim of immunity by Pinochet is for the benefit of the state rather than the person. The charges against Pinochet for which the Spanish warrant requested extradition had been changed several times, but what was forwarded finally to the House of Lords was the following series of crimes: conspiracy to commit torture between 1972 and 1990; conspiracy to take hostages between 1973 and 1990; murder in connection with torture committed in various countries including Italy, France, Spain, and Portugal between 1972 and 1990; torture at various times during 1973; conspiracy to murder in Spain between 1975 and 1976, and in Italy in 1975; attempted murder in Italy in 1976; torture between 1973 and 1977; and torture on 24 June 1989. Note that the Home Secretary omitted on his own authority presentation of the genocide charges—although they were contained in the Spanish request, and had been unanimously affirmed over the prosecutor's objections by the highest court in Spain—presumably because of the British view that the facts alleged in relation to Operation Condor did not appear to constitute "genocide" as the crime had been generally understood. On November 5, 1998, the eleven-member Penal Chamber of the Audiencia Nacional upheld the novel idea put forward by Judge Garzón of "political genocide." In the language of its decision the following reasoning was relied upon: "It was an action of extermination, not done by chance, in an indiscriminate manner, but that responded to the will of destroying a determinate sector of the population, a very heterogeneous, but distinctive, group."[35]

It is important to appreciate the narrowness of the eventual British authorization for extradition as compared to the breadth of the Spanish request, which had received such strong judicial backing despite the legal arguments against asserting jurisdiction being fully presented on behalf of Pinochet by the chief prosecutor of the Spanish Public Prosecutor's office. Aside from torture the charges against Pinochet were not extraterritorial crimes according to British law, and hence could not qualify as "extradition crimes." The only other offense that seemed on its face to qualify, the allegation of hostage-taking due to the extraterritorial reach of the UK law Taking of Hostages Act of 1982, did not do so because the facts presented in support of the charge related to the disappeared, and that was a conception of a hostage not embraced by British law, which regarded a hostage as a person detained with the intention to compel someone who is not a hostage to do some act or refrain from a particular course of action.[36]

The majority of the panel of Law Lords followed the view on extradition most carefully articulated by Lord Browne-Wilkinson, who also invoked and relied upon the legal opinions written by his colleagues on the panel. He made it plain that it was not only that the crime of torture must be currently an extradition crime under British law, but also the facts need to satisfy the double criminality rule so as to demonstrate that it was such a crime *at the time of its commission*. Since the UK did not incorporate the 1984 UN Convention on Torture into British internal law until September 29, 1988, only acts of torture or conspiracy to commit torture that were subsequent to that date were subject to extradition. At the same time, Lord Browne-Wilkinson affirmed in strong language the evolution of international criminal law as establishing "the jus cogens nature of the international crime of torture," which "justifies states in taking universal jurisdiction over torture wherever committed." Representatives of the government of Chile joined in accepting this jurisdictional analysis of legal authority as it pertained to torture.

The Torture Convention was viewed as providing a system of enforcement that would discourage an alleged torturer from moving around the world in an effort to avoid detention and prosecution. This essential idea of the Convention is expressed by the Latin maxim *aut dedere aut punire* (either extradite or punish). It was also relevant that the three countries involved in the British litigation had all ratified the convention by 1988, and that if the state with the most obvious claim based on territoriality does not assert it, then the state where the individual is found must either prosecute itself or grant extradition. Such a view would suggest that Britain itself might have had a duty to arrest and prosecute Pinochet for the post-1988 torture had there been no extradition request, although such a possibility does not seem to have been discussed or considered.

The issue of immunity was also important. The definition of torture in the Convention makes it necessary that the perpetrator be a public official. As Lord Browne-Wilkinson notes, "if Senator Pinochet is not entitled to immunity in relation to the acts of torture alleged to have occurred after 29 September 1988, it will be the first time . . . when a local domestic court has refused to afford immunity to a head of state or former head of state on the grounds that there can be no immunity against prosecution for certain international crimes."[37]

Thus, in relation to reliance upon torture and conspiracy to torture by the Pinochet regime, the House of Lords decision denies the Spanish request for all but the most marginal instances, isolated incidents occurring at the end of his presidency, and quite likely the most difficult to connect with prevailing government policy in the 1988–1990 period. In this regard, if Spain had been given the opportunity to proceed with a criminal trial of Pinochet it would have been, at best, a highly artificial event that might have turned out to be a fiasco from the perspective of substantive justice, especially if a Spanish court came to believe that the post-1988 allegations of torture were either not sustained by sufficient evidence or too tenuously tied to the authority of Pinochet. Beyond this, if the Spanish court had felt that Britain had unduly narrowed their request, it is possible that evidence of the whole pattern of torture from 1973 onwards would have been considered so as to substantiate the post-1988 incidents of torture, and thereby put Pinochet indirectly on trial for a portion of the real criminality of his regime. In turn, such an expanded inquiry might have exerted a downward pressure on future extradition requests of this nature, undermining confidence that the requesting government would not exercise authority to impose its criminal law beyond what was approved when extradition was granted.

The issue of public immunity was treated within the narrow scope afforded by the decision as to extradition crimes. Lord Browne-Wilkinson set forth in his opinion the views on immunity accepted by the majority judges, although elaborated on in various ways in their separate opinions. The major premise is that public immunity applies to both civil and criminal acts performed by officials of a state, extending both to actions performed (*ratione materiae*) and to the person who acts officially (*ratione personae*). Pinochet is entitled to full immunity during his tenure as president of Chile, subject only to the exception associated with international crimes that qualify as crimes against humanity and are violations of norms with a jus cogens status. Lord Browne-Wilkinson accords decisive weight to the impact of the Torture Convention, advancing the view that without its existence the status of torture as an international crime would not have been of sufficient weight to compel the curtailing of immunity. In his words, "[n]ot until there was some form of universal jurisdiction for the punishment of the crime of torture could it really be talked about as a fully constituted international crime."[38] The Torture Convention required all parties to establish torture as an international crime and to make it enforceable via domestic courts. Lord Browne-Wilkinson goes on to demonstrate that there is no way to give such a directive coherence without denying the claim of immunity to a head of state. It needs to be recalled that torture as defined is a crime that can only be committed by a public official, and thus the directive in the Convention would be meaningless if immunity could be invoked, and it would be ridiculous to conclude that such immunity would be denied to lower officials of the state but accorded to the leader who authorized and oversaw the pattern of criminality. The opinion notes, in contrast, that there is no reason why immunity should not be accorded in relation to the charges of murder and conspiracy to murder, which fail to qualify as extradition crimes, but separately are not established as "international crimes" whose enforcement is mandated by treaty.

Lord Goff provides a comprehensive argument in support of the views taken in the earlier House of Lords dissent by Lord Slynn and Lord Lloyd to the effect that there is nothing in the Torture Convention that justifies the conclusion that public immunity is to be withdrawn from an accused head of state.[39] Lord Goff distinguishes those cases before *international* tribunals that impose criminal accountability on public officials for their governmental activity. His argument, in its essence, is that extending this accountability to *domestic* courts cannot be presumed, was not properly argued by the lawyers on either side, and is not implied by the logic of the Torture Convention. Although none of the Law Lords supported Lord Goff, his reasoning is careful and should form part of the Pinochet experience that guides future under-standing of controversies concerning the unavailability of an immunity argument. A lengthy opinion by Lord Hope addresses the complexity of the immunity question, concluding narrowly that the Torture Convention does have the effect of withdrawing the immunity of a head of state charged with the international crime of torture provided its occurrence had a sufficient seriousness of impact to have had a disruptive effect generally on international society, which in this instance appears to have been the case.[40]

Only Lord Millett among the Law Lords situated the whole judicial inquiry within the context of the post-Nuremberg evolution on an international level of criminal accountability. As a result, for Lord Millett the whole train of developments within the United Nations and especially the International Law Commission, are relevant to the dispute over the availability of immunity to Pinochet. Also relevant is the experience of domestic courts, and in particular, "[t]he landmark decision" in the Eichmann case.[41] Lord Millett takes particular note of the linkage between "the scale and international character of the atrocities" and the "fully justified . . . application of the doctrine of universal jurisdiction."[42] Drawing from this past experience Lord Millett concludes that "crimes prohibited by international law attract universal jurisdiction under customary international law if two criteria are satisfied."[43] First, the crime must be contrary to a peremptory norm, thereby infringing jus cogens; second, the criminal allegations "must be so serious and on such a scale that they can justly be regarded as an attack on the international legal order."[44]

A major point advanced by Lord Millett is as follows: he believes that universal jurisdiction is validly available either on the basis of statutory incorporation or via common law, and that customary international law is part of the English common law. This enables Lord Millett to draw a far broader conclusion as to jurisdictional authority than that reached by his brethren:

In my opinion, the systematic use of torture on a large scale and as an instrument of state policy had joined piracy, war crimes and crimes against the peace as an international crime of universal jurisdiction well before 1984. I consider that it had done so by 1973. For my own part, therefore, I would hold that the courts of this country already possessed extra-territorial jurisdiction in respect to torture and conspiracy to commit torture on the scale of the charges in the present case and did not require the authority of statute to exercise it.[45]

Such a view would, of course, have enabled a far less restrictive response to the Spanish request at least as far as torture was concerned, and would have placed the approach taken toward universal jurisdiction in these two countries closer to parity.

Lord Millett also takes a corresponding view of the availability of immunity on behalf of Chile. He rejects the idea that Chile has the exclusive right to prosecute Pinochet, but agrees that it enjoys a primary right under the Torture Convention and in customary international law. All states, whether territorial or not, have a right and obligation to proceed if the acts qualify as a jus cogens crime of sufficient magnitude, which torture in this instance does. In other words, Chile conceded that the statutory directive to prosecute under the Torture Convention would be a valid basis for proceeding against Pinochet absent the immunity plea. This meant that if foreign courts would grant immunity it would acknowledge and confirm the Chilean right and duty not to apply the Convention. Lord Millett joins with the others in rejected such reasoning.

The opinion of Lord Millett ends with an emphasis on the role of customary international law as an evolving process that is fundamental to its development in this setting of individual liability for international crimes. He believes that the disallowance of immunity to Pinochet adds to international custom by confirming that "the exalted rank of the accused can afford no defence."[46]

From the perspective of the future of universal jurisdiction, it would be useful to highlight the arguments presented on both sides of this exemplary judicial encounter on matters of fundamental principle relating to universal jurisdiction. Of particular importance is the relevance of customary international law to the exercise of universal jurisdiction absent reinforcing statutory enactment. To the extent that customary international law is accepted as sufficient grounds for a domestic court to address the jurisdictional issue, it contributes to both a standardization of approach and to a generally expanded role, although of course important differences as to the perceived content and authority of customary international law would be almost certain to persist. For instance, domestic courts might generally accept the jus cogens status of genocide in customary international law, and yet disagree as to the scope of the crime, as in relation to such an accusation being directed at Pinochet and his regime.

Concluding Note

Despite the narrowness of authorization for extradition, the contributions of the House of Lords' 6–1 decision should still be viewed as groundbreaking. It was the first time that a former head of state was being potentially held legally accountable before a domestic court for alleged criminal activity of a political character during his period of rule.[47] The public understanding of the case was inevitably organized around either/or outcomes relating to extradition, making the British final result a smashing victory for accountability and a decisive defeat for impunity. The fact that Pinochet was made subject to extradition and potential criminal liability was virtually all that mattered in the critical arena of public opinion. Such an outcome seems also to have greatly strengthened the resolve of both the Chilean legal system to overcome their past embrace of impunity and encouraged the international community to move elsewhere against tyrants accused of massive crimes against humanity. At the same time, as indicated, counter-pressures to prosecution remained strong in Chile, and the final outcome of declaring Pinochet medically unfit for trial should not have come as a surprise. The legal proceedings of the Hague International Criminal Tribunal for the Former Yugoslavia involving Milosevic undoubtedly appeared more appropriate in light of the Pinochet case, and could not be so easily criticized as nothing more than an expression of anti-Serbian geopolitics or as a thinly disguised American tactic to vindicate the NATO War over Kosovo in 1999.[48]

Jurisprudentially, the Pinochet experience has opened up the issue of universal jurisdiction to an unprecedented degree. It is not only the passions aroused by the person of Pinochet, and the differing views as to whether he should be held individually accountable in a judicial setting other than Chile (or possibly an international tribunal). It is also that the domestic courts of several countries were engaged in assessing whether to seek extradition, and if so, on what basis, with what scope. In this regard, it is important to insist that the final House of Lords disposition was particularly caught up by the characteristically British positivistic emphasis on statutory authority. It does not seem to provide a generalized model for how domestic courts should respond to claims of universal jurisdiction. Perhaps the unevenness of the Pinochet legal outcome in various judicial bodies does strengthen the argument for agreeing upon a global framework for the application of universal jurisdiction. Such an agreement might have minimized the divergences of approach that emerged in the different countries faced with assessing criminal charges directed at Pinochet. What the House of Lords decision also suggests is that such a framework, even if widely endorsed and ratified by official state action, would not necessarily govern the operations of domestic courts unless specifically incorporated by enabling legislation.

The health and age of Pinochet left in doubt all along the final outcome of current Chilean efforts to roll back impunity in relation to their former dictator. At the very least, the decision by the Chilean Supreme Court to strip away his personal immunity represented a historic move and precedent of lasting significance. What is unclear is the scope of accountability that would be available in Chilean courts for potential liability of Pinochet for crimes during his period of leadership, including the applicability of immunity for some part of the charges on the grounds that the wrongs were not established as international crimes at the time of their commission. In other words, there remain important loose ends of a conceptual nature in what has ended up being permanently unresolved (failing health bringing the Chilean proceedings to a premature halt) with respect to the depiction of "the Pinochet precedent."

Beyond this ambit of uncertainty lie other concerns. When the Pinochet experience is broadened to encompass the world as a whole, issues of judicial unevenness and political outlook assume great prominence. It should be remembered that all the action in the Pinochet litigation occurred within European Union countries, that is, within legal systems with strong credentials of constitutionalism, judicial independence, shared democratic values, and a common geopolitical outlook. But what if criminal charges are brought in a state where courts lack autonomy and where the government is authoritarian and intensely anti-Western? Such factors raise a fundamental issue as to whether the world as a whole is ready for universal jurisdiction in criminal proceedings based on Pinochet-like charges. Without considering the viability of implementing universal jurisdiction on a global scale, enthusiasm for the Pinochet experience seems unwarranted, or, at best, lacking the political preconditions needed to establish general guidelines.

If anything, this prematurity has been accentuated by the effects of September 11, as well as by the blatant opposition of the U.S. government during the Bush presidency to all facets of legal internationalism. For now, the Pinochet litigation stands as a legal milestone, but for the time being, despite hopes having been raised a few years back, the struggle for individual accountability on the part of public officials remains stalled. Maybe, the establishment of the International Criminal Court will insert new life into the struggle, and even embolden domestic courts here and there to surprise the world as much as did Spanish and British legal proceedings did back in 1998 when General Pinochet was first detained.

8

Genocide at the World Court
The Case Against Serbia

Widespread disappointment greeted the near unanimous decision of the World Court in The Hague, formally known as the International Court of Justice (ICJ), to the effect that Former Republic of Yugoslavia (FRY; i.e., Serbia) was not guilty of genocide in Bosnia during the 1990s.[1] The outcome, although troubling in some aspects and complex overall, should not be viewed as a defeat for the Bosnian side just because of this failure to hold Serbia *legally* responsible for genocide. The World Court did decide that the 1995 massacres at Srebrenica resulting in the deliberate killing of about 7,000 Bosnian Muslim males was "genocide." It also held that the Serbian government in Belgrade failed to fulfill its duties under Article I of the Convention on the Prevention and Punishment of Genocide (1951) by not doing what it could to prevent these events.[2] And further that the Serbian refusal to arrest General Ratko Mladic, the commander of the Srebrenica operations who was known to be present in their territory, and turn him over to the criminal tribunal in The Netherlands for prosecution was a further breach of its legal duties.

Unfortunately, the world media did not report the outcome in this balanced manner and created confusion that was discrediting to the World Court. The major headline produced by the World Court decision was that the FRY (Serbia), despite common understanding, was after all not guilty of or responsible for genocide despite its seeming close connections with the overall pattern of mass killing and systematic abuse of the Bosnian Muslim population throughout Bosnia during the early 1990s. It seemed perverse for a respected judicial body to conclude that this barbarous Serb behavior did not add up to a finding of genocide aside from the isolated incident at Srebrenica, and even that was treated as the legally distinct work of Srpska armed forces. Well-documented Serb behavior in Bosnia established the occurrence of many incidents of mass civilian killings, cruel detention centers, and widespread rape and sexual violence against Muslim women.

The World Court's failure to hold Belgrade responsible for the conduct of the Bosnian Serbs also challenged these strongly held views that had been largely accepted by European public opinion. The relationship between the Belgrade government headed by the arch Serbian nationalist, Slobodan

Milosevic, and the events in Bosnia seemed completely intertwined, with Belgrade calling the shots. For the World Court to decide that the evidence did not support a finding that the FRY was legally responsible for what its subordinate Serbian allies in Bosnia were doing seemed either completely artificial legalism or exhibited a judicial sub-text to minimize Serbian responsibility so as not to produce an ultra-nationalist backlash. The World Court was persuaded that Belgrade substantially financed, supplied, and admini- stered Serb activities in Bosnia, but remained unconvinced that that such connections were sufficient proof that FRY was *legally* responsible. Some commentators also felt that an unfortunate implication of the legal reasoning of the World Court was to benefit Milosevic, who died before his criminal trial before the International Criminal Tribunal for the former Yugoslavia (ICTY) had reached any conclusions. If the FRY was not criminally accountable for what was done in Bosnia then Milsosevic also would seem entitled to an acquittal despite his blatantly obvious role as the mastermind of what went on in Srpska.[3]

Of course, these were two different tribunals operating in quite different judicial atmospheres, and without any need to arrive at consistent results. The ICJ was a non-criminal proceedings in which the only participants were sovereign states, while the ICTY was a criminal prosecution in which the defendants were persons. This means that in the ICJ the entire viability of the institution depends on sustaining respect for the sovereign rights and status of states, whereas for the ICTY the participation of the accused individuals is involuntary, a matter of governmental cooperation with a tribunal imposing international criminal law.

However disappointing these results, we should not be too quick to condemn the World Court. After all, this judicial arm of the United Nations is composed of highly qualified and distinguished jurists from all parts of the world, drawn from a variety of legal traditions. This judicial body has reached courageous and unpopular legal conclusions (that is, decisions in disputes between states and advisory opinion on legal questions submitted by organs of the United Nations) in recent years that are counter-hegemonic in spirit and substance.[4] In the 1980s the ICJ ruled against the United States in a case involving American military support for the Contras, an insurgency trying to overthrow a leftist government in Nicaragua.[5] It also issued an Advisory Opinion in the 1996 on the legality of nuclear weapons that came close to declaring that these weapons were unlawful and that the nuclear weapons states were failing in their obligations to pursue nuclear disarmament in good faith.[6] And most impressively of all, back in 2004 the World Court issued an Advisory Opinion that held by a 14–1 vote that Israel's controversial security wall built on occupied Palestine was not only unlawful, but that it should be dismantled and reparations paid to the Palestinians for the damage done.[7]

In other words, this is a judicial body that has consistently in recent years demonstrated its political independence from geopolitics and hegemonic international law. Beyond this, its various decisions and opinions exhibit both a high quality of legal reasoning and a diversity of viewpoint that reflects the realities of international life. This willingness of the ICJ to render geopolitically unpopular decisions because of its adherence to a professional ethos based on the discipline of law should increase confidence throughout global civil society that this institution can over time contribute usefully to world order, a more peaceful world, and global justice. Of course, the issues of "confidence" touch on bitterly contested matters of the relations between law and power in world politics, with those who favor greater responsiveness to power disappointed by these displays of geopolitical independence and those who are supportive of an enhanced counter-hegemonic role for the UN system, and the World Court in particular, are delighted by displays of judicial behavior that flouts geopolitical pressures.[8]

For these reasons, critics of the World Court in the Bosnia case should avoid the temptation to explain the outcome as one more example of Islamophobia or its obverse, Serbophilia. Or similarly, to contend that the failure to hold Serbia responsible for genocide in Bosnia was a reflection of unacknowledged political pressures that somehow swayed the judges to overlook convincing evidence and the relevant legal norms. Despite personally wishing that the case had been decided more in accord with public perceptions of the underlying realities, I maintain that the World Court was acting in accord with its *principled* understanding of the requirements of legality for a case of this kind in a judicial arena that depends on the voluntary participation of sovereign states. Such an assessment is strengthened by the one-sidedness of the outcome that reflected the supportive votes of judges from Morocco, Mexico, Venezuela, Sierra Leone, Madagascar, and China. True, the only dissenting judge, other than the Bosnian ad hoc judge who was expected to represent Bosnia's views, was Awn Shawkat Al-Khasawneh, a jurist from Jordan who was the Vice-President of the World Court. But overall, such a high degree of consensus among the judges could not be achieved without a strong jurisprudential belief on their part as to the correctness of their approach and findings.

It is helpful to understand the legal reasoning of the World Court before offering any critical commentary. The Bosnia decision makes very clear that when evaluating a complaint about the behavior of a sovereign state, the World Court should demand a very high level of proof from the complaining state. The majority decision also explicitly declared that this demand is even greater when the case involves charges of wrongdoing against the government of a sovereign state as serious as "genocide." In these respects the decision is indirectly acknowledging that the authority of the World Court ultimately depends on the confidence of the states that make up international society. In this sense, it is unlike courts in national legal systems, whose authority derives from a governmental system with assured jurisdiction and an effective enforcement capacity. The World Court, in contrast, is a voluntary institution available to states as a way of solving disputes with other states, but not mandatory. Its judicial authority depends on some indication of consent by the parties. Here, for instance, by ratifying the Genocide Convention, participating states agreed in Article IX to resolve any dispute among the parties by having recourse to the World Court and accepting the possibility of being required to defend a course of official behavior before an international judicial body. If states doubted the legitimacy of the World Court or suspected it of an anti-state bias, such a provision would have made it impossible to agree during the treaty negotiations to insert such a dispute-settlement mechanism in the text of the Genocide Convention.

In addition to this concern about the identity of the World Court as a judicial institution serving sovereign states and the United Nations there were reinforcing considerations associated with the special character of the crime of genocide. Among international lawyers generally there is resistance to the tendency of the media and public opinion to label any pattern of widespread killing of civilians as "genocidal" or "genocide" without regard to the characteristics of the crime as it is defined in the Genocide Convention. The *legal* conception has been interpreted to require an overwhelming demonstration that takes a documentary written form of a *specific intention* "to destroy, in whole or in part, a national, ethnical, racial or religious group" by the commission of acts specified in Article II. In this regard, the decision distinguishes "ethnic cleansing" from "genocide," deciding that using horrible means to coerce the Bosnian Muslims to leave the territory of Bosnia claimed to belong to the Republic of Srpska, and elsewhere, is not genocide, although its enactment unquestionably involves the commission of crimes against humanity and war crimes. A severely abusive set of practices designed to coerce dispossession is thus treated by the World Court majority as having an intention that does not qualify the behavior as genocide within the meaning of the treaty. The World Court decision describes the evidence of Serb wrongdoing in the greatest detail, largely accounting for why its text runs to 171 single-spaced pages. The main effort associated with this extensive exercise in legal reasoning is to show that, apart from Srebrenica, the evidence presented to the World Court does not support a legal conclusion of genocide. The decision also notes that it has only been asked to determine the existence of genocide, and as a civil tribunal lacks the authority in any event to identify individual perpetrators of international crimes, which is the role assigned to criminal tribunals. In this case, the International Criminal Tribunal for former Yugoslavia, established by the United Nations Security Council in 1992, and, more generally, the International Criminal Court (ICC), both of which are also located in The Hague, are the relevant tribunals capable of identifying such crimes as are alleged to have been committed by Serbia. In this instance, the ICC is not available for behavior resulting from the breakup of Yugoslavia as its authority does not extend to crimes committed before its establishment in 2002.

Yet having decided that the events at Srebrenica did constitute genocide, the most puzzling feature of the decision is its reluctance to draw the circle of accountability wide enough to encompass Belgrade.

Why was Serbia not held at least responsible for Srebrenica where genocide did occur even by the strict legal test applied by the World Court? Here too the tribunal leans over backwards to withhold adverse judgment against the government of a sovereign state in a setting where the allegation being made is of such a serious nature.

The majority decision of the World Court argues that since Serb control over the military and paramilitary forces was "not conclusively shown," legal responsibility cannot be attributed to Belgrade. This is so even though the decision acknowledges that some potentially incriminating documents demonstrating the linkage between Belgrade and Srpska, as well as highly relevant evidence of Serb governmental complicity in the Srebrenica genocide were withheld from the World Court and from the complaining Bosnian side. Such incriminating considerations should not be allowed to alter an assessment of the insufficiency of the evidence needed to hold FRY responsible for the Srebrenica massacre.

True to its juridical identity as an institution that reflects the realities of law and facts, the World Court does not let Serbia off the hook altogether. The decision takes seriously the Article I obligation of "Contracting Parties" to "undertake to prevent and punish" the crime of genocide in those instances where they are not responsible for the crime itself. There are two applications of this obligation to prevent and enforce that are substantively important in relation to Bosnia and significant for our wider understanding of the legal duties of states in relation to other instances of alleged genocide, e.g. Darfur. Serbia was held by the World Court to have sufficient knowledge and influence in relation to the Bosnian Serb political leadership and military forces as to have a duty to do what it could to prevent the genocide from happening at Srebrenica, and this it failed to do, thereby violating Article I of the Genocide Convention. Similarly, its refusal to arrest General Mladic, despite his known presence in Serbia, in order to transfer him to the ICTY for trial, represented a failure by the FRY to uphold its legal duty to take steps to facilitate the punishment of those properly accused of genocide.

The dissenting judge, Al-Khasawneh, does not disagree very sharply in method and assessment with the other judges. He is somewhat more willing to draw inferences of legal responsibility from patterns of Serb behavior on the basis of strong *circumstantial* evidence, and, more significantly, believed that the Serb failure to make known documentary evidence available to the tribunal should have eased the burden of proof imposed on Bosnia in relation to providing proof of genocidal intent on the part of FRY. In this respect, Judge Al-Khasawneh's view would have corresponded more closely with world public opinion than did the decision reached by the great majority of the judges, but the margin of support among the judges for the narrower findings should at least be understood from the perspective of legal craftsmanship in an *international* judicial tribunal before it is repudiated because the decision avoids a clear condemnation of the Serbian role. Beyond this need to take account of what kind of court the World Court is, there is presented by this decision relating to the charges against Serbia an occasion to ponder a vital continuing question about the future of the Genocide Convention that has legal, political, and moral aspects: what should all states be doing *as a matter of law* to prevent and punish clear ongoing and historical instances of genocide. This question touches on the extent of human solidarity in circumstances of incipient massive vulnerability to genocidal behavior. It also raises prudential issues about whether international society is at the stage where it can bring capabilities to bear except on rare occasions, as some have claimed in support of the NATO War of 1999.[9] Difficult legal issues are also raised with respect to balancing respect for sovereignty against the duty to prevent genocide. There are a variety of current conflict situations that raise these concerns in various configurations, including Darfur, Gaza, and Kenya.

I believe that the World Court's cautious and conservative reading of responsibility for genocide should not be understood as extending to the moral and political duties to act preventively and reactively in the face of firm, internationally validated instances of imminent or ongoing genocidal behavior. The World Court has good reasons for adopting an approach protective of its institutional role within the United Nations system, but the UN Security Council has a wider institutional mandate, as do, under certain conditions, regional organizations. At the same time a highly pro-active approach needs to avoid being coopted into the service of hegemonic international law. The Kosovo instance is so perplexing because it can be understood as such an instance of co-option.[10]

Part IV

Human Rights After 9/11

9

A Descending Spiral

Scope of Inquiry

This chapter is written in the context of discussion within the United States, but seeks to be sensitive to what might be described as "a global perspective." In this regard, the central point is the degree to which much of the rest of the world, especially at the level of civil society, has grown over time far more disturbed by the American response to the September 11 attacks than by the attacks themselves, and the continuing threat posed by such forms of non-state political violence. In this regard, the impact of September 11 on adherence to human rights standards and on American foreign policy is different than in any other country, including the main American ally, Britain. In one sense, this uneven response is an understandable reflection of the degree to which the United States, its people and interests around the world, are the main target of Al Qaeda-type political violence as exemplified by the 9/11 traumatic experience and by the emphasis given to the United States as "the head of the snake" in the diatribes of Osama Bin Laden. But in another more important sense, this unevenness expresses the critical view of the American governmental response as exaggerated and manipulated, primarily motivated by a geopolitical project to achieve global domination, and related domestic initiatives that inflate the terrorist threat to justify suppressive legal moves within the United States. The overall tactic is to gain a free hand for the government, especially the executive branch, by inducing and sustaining fear of further terrorist attacks among the citizenry.

In view of such considerations, it seems worth questioning whether the label "Age of Terror," so widely used in American discussions of world order since September 11, including as the subtitle of Michael Ignatieff's influential *A Lesser Evil*, is a helpful reminder that there has occurred a seeming shift in perceptual focus from globalization to terrorism.[1] Or is this supposed shift motivated by hegemonic ambitions? I believe it is. To describe the global setting in this period as "an age of terror" tends to bias discussion by adopting the rhetorical stance of the U.S. government, which tends to validate a mobilization of energies and resources to conduct the supposed "global war on terror," conveniently ill-defined as to scope, enemy, and duration. My skepticism about such an attempted centering of terrorism on the global policy agenda serves as the background for assessing the diminished adherence to the core norms of international human rights, especially overseas, as integral to the American response to 9/11. The most truculent of neoconservative militants have provided a rationale for this wartime approach that includes the encouragement of a jingoistic mentality.[2] A concluding section depicts three alternative patterns of counter-terrorist policy, each with practical advantages as compared to the American approach: the Turkish push for human rights, the Spanish response to the Madrid train attacks of March 11 (2004), and an enhanced law enforcement model.

An "Age of Terror"? Before moving on it seems helpful to clarify what is the likely effect of an acceptance of the label an "Age of Terror" as the defining dimension of our historical moment. If it is intended to refer only to anti-state political violence, then I find the use of the word "terror" not only misleading but regressive, as it seems to invalidate all struggle for self-determination no matter what the circumstances. It is further misleading if anti-state political violence that is directed at military or government targets is described, as routinely occurs in the mainstream media, as terrorism, while state violence that does massive damage to civilian society is explained as "collateral damage." Terrorism, a slippery term at best, seems polemical unless it consistently refers to state and anti-state political violence directed against civilians and non-governmental targets, that is, in a broad sense political violence against "innocence." Of course, problems remain, and it is not just an American problem. The character of innocence is contested, manipulated, and far from transparent. Are armed settlers living in West Bank settlements innocent in relation to Palestinian resistance? In Iraq, Turkey, Israel, India, and elsewhere, those who attack soldiers are routinely characterized by the media and government officials as "terrorists." This use of inflammatory language helps to construct a political and moral climate that denies to those involved in movements of resistance and self-determination, and their political organizations, normal rights as civilians, combatants, and as political actors.

The issues here are far more important and complex than matters of semantics, and pre-date the preoccupation with "terrorism" that has transpired since 9/11. By describing all Palestinian or Kurdish political violence as "terrorism" the official authorities in both Israel and Turkey sanitize their own violence as well as invalidate *any* form of armed struggle in settings of resistance to an oppressive occupation or in relation to efforts by dissatisfied "captive nations" to exercise their right of self-determination.[3] Of course, the opposite point of sanitizing all non-state violence undertaken in a resistance mode by claiming an unrestricted "right of self-determination" or a legal exemption for "a war of national liberation" is not supported by either legal or ethical reasoning.[4] Assuming the retention of "terrorism" as a descriptive term, *some* anti-state political violence is properly described as terrorism, as for instance, suicide bombing deliberately aimed at civilian targets. And certainly not all state political violence directed at non-state opposition is terrorism, if resulting from isolated instances of excessive police violence or if military and para-military violence is directed in a proportional and discriminate manner at anti-state combatants actively engaged in armed struggle that amounts to an insurgency. These definitional concerns have never been trivial, and the varying approaches to "terrorism," even at the level of state policy, has been so great as to prevent an agreed definition that could underpin a global anti-terrorist treaty. But certainly it is true that such concerns have grown in magnitude since 9/11, not least because of an extremely unpopular and unsuccessful American diplomacy around the world that stridently insists that those who do not side with the United States in its global "anti-terrorist policies" will be treated as siding with "the terrorists."[5] To the extent it is implemented, such an approach—prominently endorsed immediately after 9/11 by President Bush—challenges the sovereign right, protected by international law, to be neutral in relation to a foreign war.

This emphasis on terminology has assumed a more significant form since 9/11. American leaders immediately declared war on "terrorism" in general, which was meant to encompass both anti-state violence and state support for only such violence.[6] This unspecified American mandate was immediately seized upon to validate escalating violence by the Russian and Israeli governments against long-standing internal adversaries under the banner of anti-terrorism. This mimicry raises a fundamental point. The attacks of 9/11 involved a novel, and potentially fundamental, challenge to world order, raising issues of the severity and scale of harm, as well as the apocalyptic methods and goals of Al Qaeda. As such, the 9/11 challenge deserves to be treated as a distinctive threat to future security. To merge this threat with the many pre-existing issues of unresolved resistance and self-determination struggles going on around the world is to denigrate indiscriminately the character of these anti-state movements, and, at the same time, to authorize oppressive or beleaguered governments to rely on whatever suppressive violence seems useful in defending the status quo. This issue of merger has also been posed by the American encounters with armed resistance in Afghanistan and Iraq. It is possible to draw some distinctions, including the need and reasonableness of treating definite Al Qaeda fighters and jihadist operatives as "terrorists." At the same time, it is misleading to brand organized movements of resistance, especially in Iraq, as inherently "terrorist," even when the main goal of this political violence has been to end a foreign occupation of the country—although this goal has over time become intertwined with an internal Iraqi struggles for influence and power. It should also be acknowledged that this occupation is a violation of Iraqi sovereign rights, and was preceded by an invasion undertaken in a manner contrary to international law and the United Nations Charter.[7] To the extent that any actor in Iraq relies on tactics that cause harm to civilians and their property, it is appropriate to regard such political violence as terrorism, but to single out the resistance fighters and their tactics is to mislead and distort perceptions of the conflict.

With these considerations in mind, is it still clarifying to speak of this epoch as an "Age of Terror"? This question hovers ambiguously over any deliberation as to the effect of 9/11.[8] It is true that the declared *American* preoccupation since 9/11 has been officially focused on restoring global security by destroying Al Qaeda. At the same time, many critics here and abroad, challenge this official version of American policy, and are far less concerned with the Al Qaeda threat to world order than with the American project, which is most often discussed under the rubric of "empire," making "Age of Empire" a more fitting sequel to the 1990s, which was widely regarded as the "Age of Globalization."[9] From this perspective, to accept blandly the designation of an Age of Terror is to allow official Washington (and its societal collaborators) to frame and distort the historical moment, especially if terrorism is limited in its usage, as has been the case in governmental usage, to anti-state violence by non-state political actors.[10]

I believe that we cannot properly assess the human rights impacts of 9/11 without taking a position on these broad contextual matters. For purposes of the discussion in this chapter only, I accept conditionally, and with the serious qualifications noted, the American insistence that the defining idea of our present era is terror, and that we are thus justified in reaching a conclusion that we are living in an Age of Terror, rather than, say, the Age of Empire or the Age of Globality.[11] As argued, my discomfort would be greatly reduced if the Age of Terror was generally understood as an acknowledgment of the salience of indiscriminate political violence, including the continuing retention and development of weapons of mass destruction by leading states, particularly nuclear weapons. Yet it is here that labeling is subject to political control, reflecting the capacity of the U.S. government, as well as its supporters in a series of think-tanks, or well-placed throughout the media, to restrict unacceptably the general comprehension of "terrorism" and "terrorists" to the enemies of the United States. For this reason, in part, I do not believe that the label will travel well beyond the territorial confines of the United States, even if it is understood in the more critical fashion being proposed here. It will also not travel well because, for most other parts of the world, "terror" in either the narrow or broad sense is not the primary worry of most of the peoples in the world and their leaders, faced as they are with multiple forms of human insecurity.

This consideration of labels also bears on the perspective taken on human rights. By highlighting "terrorism" there is an almost unavoidable tendency to perceive issues through the lens of the 9/11 attacks, and to downplay such other issues as are associated with the inequities arising from the operation of the world economy, from local corruption, and from an array of practices that produce environmental decay on a daily basis. In these respects, from the perspective of human rights priorities, the highlighting of the security agenda inevitably leads to a downplaying of economic and social rights, the right of self-determination, health issues, and rights associated with environmental protection. It is to be expected that academic discussions of security would take different forms in other parts of the world, and that the American context of discussion is in this respect rather the exception than the rule.

Overall Adverse Effects of 9/11

Even assuming a prudent and ethically sensitive American response to 9/11, which by now is entirely implausible, some serious adverse effects would have inevitably occurred in any country experiencing such severe and unexpected attacks. First, the severity, shock, and fears associated with the attacks would have induced *any* American leadership immediately to put the security of the society at the center of its political agenda and, by so doing, diminish the attention and priority accorded to the protection of international human rights as a matter of national policy. This generalized impact was reinforced by the assertion by government officials that "sleeper cells" of Islamic terrorists likely exist within American borders and that high-profile soft targets abound in the country. For these reasons, it was reasonable to expect greater security precautions impinging on human rights in America, especially as associated with air and sea travel and access to high-value soft targets. In this regard, it was reasonable to expect enhanced efforts to keep individuals believed to be dangerous on the basis of evidence from entering the country or operating freely within it. This inevitable impact of 9/11 was soon made unacceptable from a human rights perspective, however, by the *gratuitously* abusive treatment of individuals, especially of Islamic males, detained on the basis of scant suspicion or deported for trivial technical infractions of immigration regulations entirely irrelevant with respect to homeland security. This flagrant series of failures to show minimum respect for the rights of individuals was deeply disturbing, especially as this governmental behavior seemed to flow from the highest levels of authority at the White House and Department of Justice, and could not be convincingly rationalized as necessary for "security," even taking into account the anxieties associated with the post-attack atmosphere in America, which included the anticipation of further attacks of comparable or greater magnitude.

Also, given the leading position of the United States both as political actor and as promoter of human rights, its new preoccupation with security—under any political leadership—would have probably diminished the emphasis previously accorded to human rights in American foreign policy, most notably during the 1990s.[12] The focus by the Bush presidency on its security agenda, including the significance given to the acquisition of allies in its "war on terror" inevitably meant turning a blind eye toward oppressive practices of countries that were also claiming to act under the banner of anti-terror. This was the case with respect to countries with serious ongoing self-determination struggles, but also such recently acquired strategic partners as Uzbekistan and Pakistan, both having very poor human rights records. In effect, American foreign policy in the period since 9/11 has reverted to a Cold War strategic outlook in which *geopolitical* considerations take consistent and decisive precedence over *normative* (that is, the norms of law and ethics) considerations.

Again, as during the Cold War, "freedom" is used as a code word by American leaders to mean "on our side." The supposed promotion of freedom and democracy became a large part of the rationale for interventionary wars as in Afghanistan and Iraq. Such a calculus also substitutes self-serving geopolitical criteria for normative criteria, that is, assessing policy outcomes by reference to the strategic goals of Washington rather than by standards embodied in the norms of international human rights. Again, the Cold War rhetoric of "the free world" and "free elections" reminds us that authoritarian leaders such as the Shah of Iran and Pinochet were strongly favored by the United States over democratically inclined leaders such as Mosaddegh and Allende.[13]

We are faced with difficult issues of assessment. Are the people of Afghanistan and Iraq beneficiaries of war and occupation from the perspective of human rights? It would be premature to offer a definitive answer at this stage, although the future looks more and more dismal for both countries with each passing month. The costs imposed on both Afghanistan and Iraq by prolonged foreign occupation can be best measured by the civilian casualties estimated in the hundreds of thousands, as well as the additional millions who have fled the country or been internally displaced. It can be observed that a major incidental cost of the Iraq War, in particular, has been to weaken the role of United Nations authority and international law, and to discourage humanitarian diplomacy.[14] These issues are confusingly entangled with a discussion of the inability to explain the Iraq War convincingly as a response to global terrorism, or as an engagement with the emancipation of oppressed peoples. This war, at least initially, could be most persuasively explained as an aspect of the wider American drive for Middle Eastern and global domination. The difficulties of the occupation have led the United States government to strike a posture of deference to Iraqi sovereignty and of attempting to solicit the widest possible United Nations and international participation. Whether this altered American posture might eventually allow for self-determination on the part of the Iraqi people remains doubtful, as does the political outcome in Iraq as measured by the yardsticks of human rights and democracy. It is possible, of course, that despite imperial objectives that originally motivated the war, the impact of these wars and subsequent occupations will eventually produce a net gain if appraisal is narrowly based on human rights and democracy, and the disruptive traumas of transition by foreign military occupation are ignored.

Such a narrow appraisal of the Iraqi future is not adequate, and due account must be given to the negative effects of loosening the bonds of international legal, moral, and political constraints on recourse to aggressive war. This loosening cannot be disregarded even if the following insistence by President Bush on behalf of the war is accepted, namely, that the people of Iraq, the region, and the world are better off having Saddam Hussein deposed and dead, instead of in power. To endorse such a post hoc justification of an aggressive war would be an exceedingly dangerous precedent, given the unwillingness to provide a *prior* green light for humanitarian intervention using available international procedures under UN auspices, given the regional and popular opposition to the war, given the absence of a palpable humanitarian emergency in Iraq, and given the lack of an established internal opposition to the regime of Saddam Hussein.[15] Such factors should be contrasted with the situation that existed in relation to the NATO Kosovo War of 1999, which itself posed a series of difficult issues because recourse to a non-defensive war undertaken at that time without a proper legal mandate by the UN Security Council, was then invoked as a precedent by those advocating the attack on Iraq.[16]

Some Specific Adverse Effects

The specific adverse effects on human rights are associated with developments that are not derivative from more general policies adopted, especially the priority accorded to security and geopolitical goals, but rather are reflections of deficiencies in the human rights culture of the United States and to varying degrees in other countries. This is a large subject by itself, and can be encompassed by the rapid and uncritical omnibus legislation known as "The Patriot Act," which empowered the government to carry out, in the name of anti-terrorism, a series of previously prohibited activities intruding on the privacy and liberties of citizens, and even more so, non-citizens. As earlier suggested, there were grounds for tightening security at the expense of rights in light of the severe threats to homeland security posed after 9/11, but such initiatives could have been mainly taken on the basis of pre-existing legislation and carefully crafted supplemental laws.

There has been a notable neoconservative push to provide the government with extensive administrative powers of surveillance and detention of citizens. Further, a stream of supplementary proposals been presented from time to time to add still further instruments of control to the arsenal already available to the state. Revealingly, there has been an abusive pattern of practices disclosed, especially in relation to Arab-American and Muslim males. Many instances of detention and harassment have taken place on the basis of unsubstantiated and vague allegations and suspicions. These abuses have been frequent and cannot be explained away as exceptions or examples of bad judgment by field personnel. Especially in the period shortly after 9/11, reflecting the agitated atmosphere, these detentions were often accompanied by a seemingly vindictive denial of rights to contact with lawyers and family that caused great anxiety and deep resentment. Such behavior has revealed attitudes of anger, revenge, and racism on the part of law enforcement officials, and has undermined the claims by politicians that there was only of prudent law enforcement respectful of individual rights.

This picture of a gratuitous and vindictive approach to security at home was strongly reinforced by the style of detention and interrogation adopted by the Pentagon toward individuals detained in combat zones in Afghanistan and Iraq. From the very outset of this process arising out of the Afghanistan War, the establishment of Camp X-Ray in the Cuban enclave of Guantánamo disclosed an American refusal to deal with its prisoners in a manner prescribed by international humanitarian law. The legalistic justification given by government lawyers was that these detainees were "enemy combatants," and not as such entitled to be treated "prisoners of war." Such individuals allegedly were outside the protection of the Geneva Convention. This contention was problematic. But even accepting this unilateral and illegal reclassification of these detainees as enemy combatants, the manner of their treatment aroused worldwide concerns about the inhumane and unlawful practices of the prison authorities. This disturbing and discrediting approach was coupled with the attempted presidential establishment of military commissions for prosecuting detainees accused of crimes. These commissions were above the Rule of Law as generally understood in the United States, operating in secret, without the right of habeas corpus, without appellate procedures for review, with loose rules of evidence, and armed with the authority to impose capital punishment. There was no review of prisoner abuse, coerced confessions were admissible, and the accused had no rights of cross-examination, or even to examine the evidence used by the prosecution. The whole structure of such an ad hoc criminal process expressed, above all, a disregard of the rights of the person, and especially a completely intimidating approach to individuals who were completely vulnerable in view of their conditions of detention and confinement that included harsh methods of interrogation generally regarded as constituting "torture."

What was first disclosed in Guantánamo, and justified by the urgency of obtaining information (so-called "actionable intelligence") relating to Al Qaeda, has been confirmed many times over by the pictorial evidence of abuse at Abu Ghraib prison in Iraq, and other U.S.-administered prisons in Afghanistan and Iraq. A particularly disturbing aspect of these disclosures, which came to light indirectly and accidentally in the form of leaks to the media, is the degree to which they represented dysfunctional exercises in sadism and humiliation, which were, indirectly at least, being encouraged at the highest levels of government. The great majority of the inmates of Abu Ghraib were not even connected with the Iraqi resistance, much less Al Qaeda or kindred organizations, and possessed no useful information. The depth and breadth of abuse reveals an alarming indifference to human rights, or more basically, to the dignity of the human person. True, these practices have been officially repudiated by American leaders, but only after their reality was made public in a manner that could not be doubted. Some of those involved who were at low levels in the hierarchies of authority have been prosecuted and given minor punishments considering the gravity of their deeds. There seems to be no willingness within the United States at either the grassroots level or among elites to impose standards of criminal accountability on the higher officials responsible. Donald Rumsfield seemed secure in his job so long as his tactics for the invasion and occupation seemed headed for success and enjoyed public support. At the same time, General Sanchez, the commander in Iraq, apparently was deprived of a fourth star, because he spoke critically and in the open about these detention policies being promoted by the civilian leadership at the Pentagon. The overall picture sends a message that the denial of the most fundamental human rights will be tolerated if takes place in a counter-terrorist setting.

These disclosures contradict in disturbing ways the American insistence that it is liberating Iraq and Iraqis from governmental oppression, as well as the related claim that it is the bearer and self-designated custodian of values diametrically opposed to those of the previous regime of Saddam Hussein. These publicized abuses contributed to an unexpected moral erosion among Iraqis of the American plan to hold Saddam Hussein responsible for his massive perpetuation of Crimes Against Humanity. Part of this moral erosion was the manifest double standards associated with prosecuting Saddam Hussein and his leadership cadre while exempting George W. Bush and his entourage from scrutiny for their own flagrant violations of international humanitarian law and, more generally, the laws of war. If Abu Ghraib represents what freedom and democracy mean for the new Iraq, the whole credibility of American qualifications for global leadership is drawn into most serious question.

Even leaving aside issues of moral and political credibility, the discourse of democracy, so prominently highlighted in the foreign policy pronouncements of the Bush administration with respect to the Middle East, has always seemed puzzling, especially when strongly espoused by neoconservative strategists who are known to be such militant supporters of Israel.[17] Such pro-democracy polemics ignore the established reality that "the Arab street" is fervently anti-Israeli and anti-American, and that democracy for the Middle East in the central respect of responsiveness of government to popular will, would directly challenge the most prized features of the grand design of American policy for the region and the world. This neoconservative advocacy only makes political sense for American foreign policy if "democracy" for the Middle East resembles what the Soviet Union had in mind for its satellites in Eastern Europe when it spoke of "people's democracy" and "socialism."

Three Alternative Response Patterns

The Turkish Exception

It is interesting to reflect that there is nothing pre-determined or inevitable about encroaching upon human rights in the aftermath of 9/11. Turkey is an interesting case. The country was faced with a temporarily dormant insurgency involving the future of the Kurdish minority. As well, several terrorist incidents associated with international jihadism have occurred in Turkey since 9/11. Turkey is a country with a strong so-called "deep state" controlled by a non-accountable or minimally accountable military, and Turkey is a member of NATO, a neighbor of Iraq, a site for important American air bases, and a regional strategic ally of the United States. Such a combination of circumstances gave rise to expectations that Turkey would seize the occasion of 9/11 to justify a tightening of the grip exercised by the Turkish state on society, and ignore domestic and international pressures to improve the protection of human rights.

And yet this expectation has proved to be wrong. Turkey has moved in the period to grant language and cultural rights to the Kurdish minority, it has encouraged the expansion of the right to freedom of expression along with other civil and political rights, it has worked with Europe to improve prison conditions, it has abolished capital punishment, it has enacted a series of laws that strengthen the position of the individual in relation to the state, and, most impressive of all, it has made significant reforms intended to weaken the role of the deep state, especially by measures mandating the civilianization of the Turkish National Security Council. This latter important symbolic and substantive step was taken with the approval of the military leadership. It may be explained, in part, by the strong Turkish support around the time for moves to convince the European Union that Turkey is qualified to become a member.

Given the lengthy Turkish experience of subordination in its strategic relationship with the United States, it is also relevant to note that Turkey did not succumb to American pressure in 2001 to declare "war" on terrorism, and despite intense lobbying by and inducements from the U.S. government, Turkey refused to allow its territory to be used to invade Iraq in 2003. In this respect, the Turkey in the end deferred both to its public opinion, which was overwhelmingly opposed to the Iraq War, and to the Parliament, which rejected the recommendation of the Turkish Prime Minister. This exercise of constitutional democracy, although called "disappointing" by a high official (Paul Wolfowitz) in the Pentagon, was an impressive exhibition of political independence on the part of Turkey, but also a revelation that democracy-in-practice is not welcomed in Washington whenever it collides with the pursuit of U.S. strategic objectives.

A leading Turkish official associated with the development of these policies maintains that: "Turkey is the only country in the world that can claim to have improved its human rights record in the period since September 11."[18] Of course, there are reasons for this Turkish accomplishment, especially the then powerful push/pull influence of the European Union, which the recently empowered Justice and Development Party (AKP) leadership was eager to satisfy in the hopes that it would lead by stages to Turkish membership. Further, the deep state controlled by the Turkish military supported the effort to join the EU, as does the United States. Beyond this, the AKP leadership was sensitive about its own legitimacy. The AKP wanted to demonstrate the compatibility between its presumed soft Islamic identity and its commitment to pluralistic democracy and the rights of individuals to pursue their own beliefs.

What is important under these circumstances is the conclusion that Turkey, despite its encounters with terrorist attacks in its leading city of Istanbul, appears no less secure because of having taken these impressive steps to strengthen human rights. During this period the Turkish state has been vigilant in seeking to use law enforcement methods to prevent and apprehend those engaged in terrorism, and to improve its capacity to prevent terrorism and to apprehend perpetrators. There has been a noticeable tightening of security arrangements in hotels and public buildings, involving monitoring of entry and nearby parking, but without inducing the sort of collective fear spread in America. Recourse by the U.S. government to such measures as the use of color-coded alerts by the Office of Homeland Security conveyed to the public from time to time a sense of heightened vulnerability. Would the United States have been less secure if it had taken an approach resembling that of Turkey? I think not. That is, there is no evidence to support the claim that the abridgement of human rights and the abusive treatment of detainees and suspects enhance security, and even if some evidence did exist, it would not on its own justify official behavior that violates basic rights. The social and political costs of sacrificing the protection of human rights must also be assessed. Such supposedly "lesser evil" tactics put any government on a slippery slope that generally ends badly and lacks a convincing security rationale. The revelations of abuse and torture of detainees in Abu Ghraib, Guantánamo, at CIA "black sites," and through "extraordinary rendition" (transfer of suspects to foreign prisons where torture is relied upon as an interrogation technique) have badly damaged America's reputation to an extent that appears to exceed the usefulness of information so obtained.

The Spanish Response to March 11

On March 11, 2004, several commuter trains heading for Madrid were blown up by terrorist bombs. The Spanish government, headed by one of the few major European governments to support the Iraq War, initially blamed the explosions on the radical Basque separatist organization ETA. This explanation was quickly shown to have been a false allegation, probably deliberately so. Angered by the spin and by Prime Minister Azner's pro-Bush foreign policy, which in relation to the Iraq War ignored the wishes of the overwhelming majority of the Spanish people, the citizenry surprised public opinion polls a few days later by voting socialists back to power in general elections. The new leadership, headed by Prime Minister Zapatero, immediately indicated that it would withdraw the Spanish contingent of troops from Iraq, and at the same time would increase police efforts to protect Spanish society by taking steps to apprehend those responsible for the attacks and preventing future attacks.

In subsequent weeks, many arrests were made, and the impression created that the new Spanish leadership had fashioned a creative policy that was anti-war *and* anti-terrorist at the same time.

By coincidence I arrived in Barcelona on the day of the attacks to take part in an academic conference. On the following day I marched in a large solemn demonstration of one million or so persons, and was moved and impressed by numerous banners that read "No to war, No to terrorism," "Azner, your war, our lives," and "No to Terrorism by the State." The central mood, also expressed at the conference, by the Spanish media, and a few days later by voters in the national election, confirmed these sentiments. It supported a conclusion that it was entirely feasible, and quite beneficial, to insist that anti-terrorism did not require a transnational war of undetermined scope.

Again, the question presents itself: would the United States have less security internally and internationally if it had relied on the Spanish response after 9/11? Of course, the facts were different. The attack on the United States was more severe symbolically and substantively, and was accompanied by Al Qaeda declarations of war against the United States and against Americans. The nerve center of the perpetrators was immediately identified as situated in southern Afghanistan, supporting the seemingly plausible contention that it would improve global and American security to embark upon a regime-changing war against the Taliban regime in Afghanistan, with the accompanying goal of wiping out the Al Qaeda redoubt and capturing or killing its leadership and cadres. In retrospect, it now seems that the rush to war against Afghanistan was uncritical and possibly counter-productive, especially given the mode of implementation and post-war reconstruction. It might well have been worth exploring the Taliban offer, immediately after 9/11, to cooperate in a law enforcement undertaking to apprehend Osama Bin Laden and cohorts, and end the Al Qaeda presence in the country.

But certainly, after Afghanistan, the Spanish model seems far more likely to reconcile security interests with human rights than the American model. As argued above, the transnational scope of the American model can only be understood in relation to goals of foreign policy associated with a grand strategic design, which makes it additional to, and in central respects antithetical to, a genuine counter-terrorism campaign. The wider goals of neoconservative grand strategy require reliance on the tactics of fear and oppression, while distracting American citizens with manipulated fears of terrorism, and thereby avoiding most criticism of an approach that otherwise would be widely seen as linked to a politically controversial, and possibly unacceptable, agenda of global domination.

A U.S. Response Based on Enhanced Law Enforcement

Implicit in the prior discussion is a radical questioning of the immediate adoption of a response model based on *war* rather than *law enforcement* by the

U.S. government and the mainstream media. It is understandable that this reaction occurred, given the combined sense of urgency and trauma that was associated with the circumstances prevailing on the day after, September 12, as well as the war consciousness long associated with the Westphalian approach to world order and deeply inscribed in American political culture, perhaps epitomized by the jingoist slogan "Don't tread on me!" I confess to my own early failures of discernment, moving too quickly to accept the rationale for war against Afghanistan, and overlooking the unrealized potential of diplomacy and an enhanced law enforcement model.[19] This potential for intergovernmental cooperation was itself greatly increased by the initial sentiments of solidarity with the United States in the immediate aftermath of the attacks, a solidarity partly based on empathy for the tragedy and its victims, but also reflecting a shared statist opposition to anti-state political violence, especially as was the case with 9/11, which seemed unconnected with any relevant concrete grievance.[20] There existed in that period an unprecedented opportunity for international cooperation in a genuine effort to protect the basic structure of world order against what might be described as the menace of "mega-terrorism." Of course, the law enforcement model as a counter-factual is purely speculative with respect to its effectiveness and effects. Unrepentant advocates of the war approach, such as John Yoo, continue to insist that the law enforcement model had been tried in the 1990s, and that 9/11 by its occurrence proved that it was a failure. The answer to such contentions is that the law/diplomacy approach had never been tried in a committed way, and that the post-9/11 international climate made possible intergovernmental counter-terrorist collaboration on a scale that would have been unthinkable previously.

However one bemoans these lost opportunities, what is not speculative are the costs and harms associated with reliance on the war model, especially as extended to Iraq. Part of these costs involves the sacrifice of human rights, and the difficulty of stopping such a slide once it is underway. It is well accepted that a war mentality tends to displace and overwhelm a human rights mentality, both in tightening restraints on freedom in the name of security at home and with regard to the ranking of priorities in foreign policy, and this is precisely what has occurred.[21] Such a displacement was particularly unfortunate considering the extraordinary pro-human rights momentum that had developed in the decade following the end of the Cold War.

It is also not speculative to conclude that the war model as applied to this new form of global conflict has produced many difficulties, some of which seem to have actually augmented the mega-terrorist danger. And it is not speculative to take note of the non-territorial locus of international jihadism, making war against a sovereign state an indiscriminate and grossly ineffective instrument of response. Even from the perspective of the wider strategic design of regional and world influence and control it is not at all clear that the militarist strategies favored by the neoconservative worldview are more effective than the economistic and soft power strategies of the liberal internationalists of the Clinton presidency that were designed to reach the same goals.[22] What seems evident is that the nature of mega-terrorist threats mounted from concealed and dispersed sites anywhere gives a new primacy to information and accurate intelligence even as compared to its vital role in traditional state-to-state conflict, especially with respect to the possible acquisition of weaponry of mass destruction and missile technology by non-state political extremists. Such intelligence is exceedingly difficult to achieve and often exceedingly unreliable. Revealingly, it seems that American leaders were reluctant to act on intelligence assessments and a variety of warnings of mega-terrorist threats with respect to the 9/11 realities, while being eager to rest their case for recourse to war against Iraq on highly questionable intelligence.[23] How can we explain such an inconsistency? Can we?

In criticism of the law enforcement/diplomacy model it is widely believed by the public and many mainstream commentators that it was tried and failed in the 1990s, and that, in any event, it is not responsive to the magnitude and originality of the threat posed by mega-terrorism. It is even being claimed that the United States is now engaged, whether it realizes it or not, in World War IV, which supposedly can only be waged by the sort of full-scale mobilization associated with prior major wars, most notably World Wars I and II.[24] I find such a defense of the war model of response dangerously unconvincing and a recipe for a self-defeating approach to security. It transposes the old thinking about international conflict in a statist world onto a more complex template of global society that must adapt to the participation of powerful non-state actors. It combines such outmoded thinking with an unacceptable form of new thinking that aspires to establish by coercive means the first global empire. At the same time, the unreflective dismissal of a law enforcement/diplomacy approach is insensitive to the possibilities of enhanced law enforcement based on full-scale global cooperation and on finding diplomatic space for negotiation.[25]

The adoption of the law enforcement/diplomacy model would be greatly facilitated if it would also move toward the recognition of the importance of addressing the roots of political and religious extremism, including especially the *legitimate* grievances of the Islamic world against an American-led world order. Such grievances include the failure to promote a just solution regarding Palestinian self-determination and the embrace of predatory globalization that disadvantages the poorer segments of humanity. Such adjustments should not be presented or understood as an acquiescence to the demands of political extremists, but would involve taking steps that should have been undertaken long ago. Moves in these directions might also create opportunities for tacit diplomacy involving reciprocal de-escalating moves in a shared effort to restore political normalcy to the global setting. *Illegitimate* grievances, including those relating to the existence and security of Israel and other sovereign states, should be rejected as before. What constitutes a legitimate grievance is itself a matter for negotiation and compromise, especially on such matters as foreign bases, oil revenues, and extra-regional links to existing governments.

In favoring enhanced law enforcement plus diplomacy, there is also implicit a wide series of opportunities to contribute simultaneously to the establishment of the sort of global architecture required for global governance in a post-Westphalian world, in which sovereign states are losing control over many tendencies threatening their wellbeing, including crime, environment, migration.[26]

Conclusion

I believe that, with some minor exceptions, the cause of human rights has been set back by the American response to 9/11. This setback was not a necessary effect of the attacks. It was a choice shaped as much by geopolitical ambitions as by the security challenges posed by mega-terrorism. As long as these geopolitical ambitions are combined with a war model of response, the prospects for human rights will remain poor.

If consideration is given to the wider impacts of the attacks and the U.S. response it might have some unanticipated positive effects of a dialectic character. It could move Europe to contrast its political identity with that of the United States by moving even further toward an ethos based on international law and human rights.[27] It could stimulate the growth of a global anti-war movement that showed signs of robustness by way of the huge demonstration prior to the Iraq War on February 15, 2003, held in hundreds of cities in more than 60 countries. It could also produce an internationalist backlash in the United States that would create a political climate allowing a new leadership to move toward an abandonment of the war model and a concerted effort to address legitimate grievances unilaterally and diplomatically, as well as through tacit negotiations. An altered American political leadership and popular mandate could make such initiatives plausible, but despite the failures of a militarist approach these recommended moves remain, as of now, remote political possibilities. The more likely political scenario is a continuing downward spiral of political violence and state repression that continues to erode the protection of human rights at home and as a dimension of U.S. foreign policy.

10

Encroaching on the Rule of Law
Counter-Terrorist Justifications

There are several distinguishing features of the American response to the 9/11 attacks that should be considered in evaluating subsequent U.S. governmental encroachments on the rule of law. These contextual elements suggest that the natural urge to compare this American pattern with the counter-terrorist practices of other countries must proceed with caution, but the effort should certainly not be abandoned. The specificities of the American situation are notable and relevant. These distinctive elements help us understand somewhat better the approach chosen by the Bush administration after 9/11, which, if detached from this context, remains virtually incomprehensible from a counter-terrorist perspective.

Most prominent among these elements was a pre-existing neoconservative blueprint for an increasingly interventionary and pro-active American foreign policy, especially in the Middle East. Also important were strong neoconservative views as to the proper role for the United States to play on the global stage given world conditions. An emphasis was placed on the status of the United States as the one and only *global* state, with strategic interests and military deployments spread around the entire globe. This ideological framing of foreign policy helps explain why goals other than counter-terrorism became so influential in shaping the American response to 9/11, often diverting attention and resources from the manifest security concerns raised by persisting terrorist threats of unprecedented magnitude emanating from overseas. Adding to the confusion is the continuing attempt of the Bush presidency to validate its controversial policy moves by relying upon a counter-terrorist rationale, even when other explanations are far more convincing. Increasingly, the official justifications of the Iraq policy by the Bush White House seem less persuasive than the explanations of harsh critics who emphasize the undisclosed motivations (oil, Israeli security, regional hegemony) of the attack on Iraq. Such a depiction of the policies being pursued by the U.S. government in the Middle East is one way of demonstrating how misleading it is to take counter-terrorist justifications at face value.[1]

Such considerations show us why comparisons with the counter-terrorist approaches adopted by other countries are bound to be misleading. Other governments, although each acting within a given set of circumstances, have been guided by straightforward counter-terrorist objectives preoccupied with the use of police methods to reducing the terrorist threat to the extent possible. My main contention is that the United States government, at least after the Afghanistan War, was pursuing several additional and incompatible strategic goals under the rubric of "counter-terrorism." And furthermore, that its leadership, whether consciously or not, jeopardized counter-terrorist goals in its pursuit of a far wider world order design: achieving and sustaining regional supremacy for the United States in the Middle East; ensuring maximum influence with respect to regional energy supplies and pricing; promoting long-range Israeli security; avoiding any further proliferation of nuclear weapons in the region; and containing the challenge of political Islam, especially as associated with Iran.

At the same time, because American society was mobilized and propagandized around an essentially counter-terrorist agenda, the steps taken to impair the human rights of its citizens, and especially of non-citizens, do resemble the circumstances of other countries in some respects. This seems especially true for Israel, whose government did apparently feel that the very survival of the country was being threatened a few years ago by the violent tactics adopted by its Palestinian adversary, above all by suicide bombings. Beyond this, the nature of Al Qaeda and the threats it poses are elusive in nature and changing through time; and, despite being seemingly serious, have been manipulated so often by American leaders to facilitate the undisclosed pursuit of more controversial strategic goals as to be difficult to assess. It remains difficult to tell whether there exists an authentic basis for concern about the vulnerability of American society to future terrorist attacks of a magnitude similar to or greater than that of 9/11, or whether such alleged threats are being hyped for political effect by government officials and their friends in the media.

If due account is taken of this background, comparisons with the responses of other governments to major terrorist incidents may be illuminating. This seems particularly so in relation to the questionable functionality of the immediate American decision to treat its post-9/11 counter-terrorist campaign as a species of warfare, as in "the war on terror," rather than as a challenge calling for enhanced law enforcement, heightened intelligence activity, and recourse as necessary to paramilitary operations undertaken cooperatively with or on the basis of the consent of the territorial government. It seems likely that many of the worst excesses of governmental abuse in the United States might have been avoided if the attacks had been described as massive crimes to be addressed by appropriate counter-terrorist law and order mechanisms. The international legal framework applicable to war is premised on armed conflict between sovereign states, and is not suitable to govern interactions in conflicts involving non-state actors that lack territory or diplomatic status.

While favoring an approach rooted in criminal law, and reliance on law and order techniques, is preferable to war, past practice suggests that even this more constrained approach would likely also have produced several forms of abusive behavior, which would undoubtedly have raised a series of human rights and related concerns. The many documented abuses of governmental authority by Britain, France, Germany, and elsewhere in the treatment of terrorist suspects by national police and intelligence forces suggest that whenever security pressures become intense they almost always erode human rights, even if "war" is not declared. The United States, perhaps because of its geographic position, history, and self-righteous political culture, seems somewhat more inclined than other states to resort to unrestrained behavior once it crosses the threshold, regarding itself "at war." This appears to be especially so if the war was initiated by an adversary that is not a foreign state, and this non-state enemy has been officially depicted as "evil."[2]

Also, it is true that the spectacular character of the 9/11 attacks, as well as their transnational locus and the inflammatory war discourse of Osama Bin Laden, made the American response by way of war seem more appropriate than in the circumstances of other countries, with the possible exception of Israel, which faced a Palestinian war of liberation that pursued its goals by traumatizing tactics, including a wave of suicide bombings aimed at the civilian heartland of Israeli society. For these reasons, too, it is necessary to condition comparisons with respect to counter-terrorist policies by reference to the national context of the United States, reinforced by the unique circumstances surrounding the 9/11 events.

Yet despite this need to treat American counter-terrorism as *sui generis*, certain comparisons can be instructive, and useful in the future. The counter-terrorist experience of other European countries suggests the wisdom of non-war approaches. This non-war option, remarkably enough, was not put on the table by the United States, and was avoided even by the opposition political party. The strategic stakes of the Iraq War were regarded by virtually the entire American political mainstream as justifying support for it, although some doubted the wisdom of its initiation. As the Iraq War drags on year after year it becomes plain that it diverts resources and energies from the more efficient pursuit of counter-terrorist objectives, and domestic opposition grows. As of early 2008, the rising costs of the American occupation of Iraq may be approaching a tipping point that will swing the policy in the direction of phased withdrawal. Yet this is by no means assured, especially as the recent decline in violent incidents and American casualties is being interpreted as a demonstration that finally American occupation policy is "working."

There are further troublesome uncertainties associated with the war approach that continues to govern American counter-terrorist thinking and policy. The Lebanon War in the summer of 2006 demonstrated the volatility of political life in the region, as well as reminding the world of the persisting

Israeli-American strategic commitment to reconfigure the politics of the region.[3] The currently escalating confrontation with Iran could easily produce a new cycle of political violence, with extremely dangerous regional, even global, implications.

This chapter is divided into two main parts. In the first section, several areas of American distinctiveness are identified as relevant for an understanding of both its particular approach to counter-terrorism and as the foundation for comparison with the policies adopted by other like-minded countries faced with terrorist threats. In the second section, some of the inroads on human rights are discussed, being regarded as fallout from the intensity of the counter-terrorist campaign, as well as the seeming authoritarian predispositions of influential bureaucrats serving the Bush presidency.

General Considerations

The Pre-9/11 Atmosphere

It is misleading to associate the totality of pressures on American freedoms as following from 9/11. In direct response to the Oklahoma City bombing of 1995, the Clinton administration responded by enacting in 1996 the Anti-Terror and Effective Death Penalty Act. In many ways this pre-9/11 law anticipated the looseness of definitions associated with Bush-era criminalization, especially of what constitutes "terrorism," as well as the comprehensiveness of governmental authority so widely criticized and ardently defended. This controversy has continued, surrounding the enactment and implementation of the Patriot Act of 2001, which was renewed by Congress in 2006 despite a much sharper debate than in 2001, when Congress acted as a virtual rubber stamp. The new legislation retains most of the features of the earlier version of the Patriot Act, but there are a few minor modifications that were designed to address concerns about civil liberties.[4]

There was in 1995 little criticism of a governmental response that seemed to ignore the menace posed by purely domestic sources of the extremist violence, the work of right-wing militias that had been directed at important civilian and governmental targets, and could be again in the future. In retrospect, it seems odd that although a federal office building was the target of the Oklahoma City bombing, there was immediately fashioned a counter-terrorist response directed at purely *international* sources of terrorism. What still seems surprising is the apparent indifference in Washington to the continuing threats of political violence stemming from American right-wing militias, as well as the preoccupation even in the 1990s with terrorist threats emanating from Arab countries in the Islamic world. In this respect, the American legal system was predisposed to erode rule-of-law constraints on enforcement activities *prior to* 9/11, and prior to the arrival of a Republican president at the White House. After 9/11, especially if the deprivations of individual rights involved Islamic suspects who were foreign nationals, there were few voices of protest raised. In contrast, in the British response to the July 7, 2005 London bombings, which were the work of young Islamic extremists who were born and raised in Britain, the British government concentrated its energies on the domestic locus of the main terrorist threat now confronting the country.

Perhaps, more to the point is the long period of the Cold War where, directly and indirectly, especially under CIA auspices and in the course of a series of Third World interventions, many abuses were committed in a manner that prefigures the patterns of abuse that have taken place since 9/11.[5] The Cold War atmosphere of conflict waged on the global stage provided a strategic rationale for the adoption of tactics inconsistent with international humanitarian law, a dynamic that reached its climax in the course of more than a decade of warfare in Indochina.[6] Employing a tactical logic that closely parallels the current counter-terrorist discourse, think-tanks in the United States during the 1960s and 1970s were working on aspects security policy emphasizing the specific challenges of what was then being described as "counter-insurgency warfare." As in Iraq these days, it was often then impossible for American firepower to distinguish enemy soldiers from the civilian population in Vietnam. There were at the time elaborate justifications put forward for coercively separating the population from insurgents by relocating them into strategic hamlets, and the like. This perspective on the nature of the conflict led to the adoption of legally and morally dubious practices such as the Phoenix Program of large-scale civilian assassination designed to intimidate and coerce the civilian population. Systematic interrogation of captured enemy combatants was followed by many criminal practices, including the notorious act of throwing selected Vietcong detainees to their death from helicopters to terrify other prisoners to such an extent that they would divulge information about the enemy. As in the war on terror, the Vietnam War showed the limitations of military superiority when the stakes of conflict involve the *political* future of an occupied country that mounts a strong nationalist resistance. The frustrations of such a stymied war effort exerted strong pressure on the United States to abandon the laws of war so as to either gain information about their Vietnamese adversary or to ignore the distinction between civilian and combatant because the information needed to confine firepower to genuine military targets was either unavailable or treated as irrelevant. There too the enemy was accused of deliberately intermingling weapons and combatants with the civilian population. It is instructive, and somewhat discouraging, to look back to the Vietnamese War to gain insight into the encroachments on international humanitarian law that have been associated with the ongoing war on terror.

The Primacy of Geopolitics

In decisive respects the geopolitical tail has been wagging the counter-terrorist dog during the Bush presidency. The domestic intensification of a politics of fear and anger seems mainly associated with mobilizing American society to support a much more militant and controversial global security strategy that had been articulated and advocated by prominent neoconservatives well before George W. Bush was elected president in 2000.[7] A notable feature of the Project for a New American Century (PNAC) blueprint was the recognition that the pre-9/11 political climate in the United States was not conducive to such an aggressive geopolitics unless "a new Pearl Harbor" awakened the American people to the dangers (and opportunities) of the post-Cold War world.[8] Significantly, the neoconservative worldview prior to 9/11 was not at all preoccupied with the threats posed by international terrorism, but its attention was primarily focused on so-called "rogue states," especially, Iraq and Iran, and to a lesser extent China and North Korea, which were seen as posing obstacles to the favored course of American global grand strategy.

The contention here is that the 9/11 attacks provided the political cover and support needed to launch a militant foreign policy, which was based on grandiose global security goals. A previously reluctant American society was effectively mobilized for a generalized "global war on terror," that, despite its label, was used by the Bush presidency as a mandate to pursue the neoconservative grand strategy that accorded priority to the political restructuring of the Middle East, starting with Iraq, but always with an eye on Iran as its culminating goal.

Counter-terrorism was part of the policy mix, to be sure, especially in the immediate response to 9/11 in the form of the Afghanistan War. The exaggerated and misdirected response to global terrorism was effective in giving the Bush presidency a blank check for several years in foreign and domestic policy. The prevailing rationale being that it was permissible for the U.S. government to do whatever it takes to make America and Americans as secure as possible. In the years after 9/11 color-coded alerts and government warnings about imminent attacks were seemingly manipulated by Washington officials to sustain anxiety levels, creating a mood in America of aroused collective fear from time to time. These tactics helped build bipartisan Congressional and media support for intrusions on the privacy and liberties of Americans in general, and Muslim male residents in particular. At the same time, the liberal opposition to such governmental tactics was marginalized through a skilful playing of the "security" card by the Bush leadership. As public opinion began to turn against the Iraq policy in 2005, this security card became less effective, particularly as coupled with Bush's declining popularity as a leader. This change in the political mood certainly reflected the public's growing sense of failure and futility in Iraq, but it also resulted from such seemingly unrelated issues as the inept and regressive governmental response to Hurricane Katrina and the rising cost of gas at the pumps due to escalating oil prices.

Lawyers in Government

It needs to be appreciated that the structure of legal argument and normative architecture is such that it is always possible for a seasoned lawyer to present a logically coherent legal argument to support a preferred political course of action. Government lawyers generally view their professional role, especially in the context of foreign policy or national security, to be one of facilitating official policies rather than positing restraints, although this is a contested point prior to the Bush II presidency.[9] This use of lawyers and legal analysis to lend an aura of legality is nothing new, but it has been carried beyond the outer limits of plausibility during the Bush presidency. This vocational orientation toward facilitating political initiatives has been reinforced by recruiting to government service neoconservative legal specialists known to share the policy agenda of the political leadership. Most neoconservatives in the United States have a highly skeptical attitude about whether international law should ever be allowed to override foreign policy goals. This skepticism is not very far removed from standard realist thinking that affirms the primacy of national security in foreign policy settings. In addition to this skepticism about law, neoconservatives favor a strong executive, and believe that a wartime president possesses virtually unlimited constitutional authority with respect to national security policy.[10]

This attitude is further reinforced by America's imperial geopolitics, which simultaneously enforces legal standards rigorously against adversaries while exempting itself. Such patterns of legal exceptionalism are particularly flagrant in the setting of international criminal accountability (for instance, prosecuting Saddam Hussein as a war criminal, while insisting on impunity for American officials) and the implementation of the treaty regime governing nonproliferation of nuclear weaponry.[11] In the first instance, Americans are exempt but enemies are held accountable, in the second instance, the United States sets the rules, and enforces them selectively

The Magnitude of 9/11

The European terrorist incidents, however traumatic and cruel in their impacts, were minor in comparison with the 9/11 attacks, which were spectacular events of an unprecedented symbolic and substantive magnitude. The World Trade Center (WTC) and the Pentagon were the prime symbols of American power, economic and military, and by striking them so effectively in a manner suitable for TV, American vulnerability was shockingly and undeniably established. Beyond this, the real-time image of the plane crashing into the WTC tower created an unforgettable image of the attack that was repeated over and over for tens of millions of TV watchers. This extraordinary visualization of the attacks was given a further gruesome resonance in the form of immediate eye-witness accounts offered by survivors and victims of bodies falling from the towers and the many human tragedies associated with the event. And finally, the early identification of Al Qaeda, and its telegenic and charismatic leader, Osama Bin Laden, as responsible for the attacks undoubtedly helped to ensure that the memories of the 9/11 experience would be lodged deep in the political imagination of the American people and their leaders.

Cumulatively, this was a terrorist event unlike any other, and seemed at the time to make an American recourse to "war" an appropriate, even an inevitable response, foreclosing the "law enforcement" option, or some intermediate response, that had been relied upon by other countries when faced with major and sustained terrorist challenges to their home security.[12] World public opinion, including as expressed at the United Nations, seemed to underscore this dual reality: that 9/11 was a terrorist incident of such unprecedented ferocity that a response based on recourse to war, at least against Afghanistan, seemed unavoidable, reasonable, and even appropriate. Such a response was also congruent with the extremist language of Osama Bin Laden who had previously declared a war without limits against all Americans, indeed against Jews and Christians everywhere, who were described by the Al Qaeda leader as "crusaders." President Bush made effective use of this understanding of 9/11 to rally the country around a response based on declaring and waging war on a global scale against terrorism in general in which foreign countries were denied the option of neutrality. There was also a widespread American fear that 9/11 would be soon replicated, perhaps causing even greater harm and havoc, a prospect given credible backing by the menacing rhetoric and statements of Bin Laden, as well as by the daring plan of multiple hijackings and suicide tactics used to such great effect on 9/11. This prospect of further attacks was constantly invoked by Bush in the months and years ahead to claim the need for a variety of extraordinary powers for the government, and especially for the executive branch. After 9/11 Bush repeatedly asserted that the dangers of nuclear weapons technology falling into the hands of anti-American terrorist groups posed the greatest of all threats to national and global security. Furthermore, it was not reasonable to wait until such a threat materialized in the form of an attack, or even involved the acquisition of the knowledge and capabilities that could be used to mount an attack at some future time. With this new mandate, this kind of threat needed to be dealt with *preemptively*, not reactively. Bush continuously argued that this situation created truly apocalyptic dangers for the future that must be reduced to the extent possible.

Such dangers laid the foundations for dramatic doctrinal moves by the U.S. government, including a claimed right to engage in preventive wars at times and in places of its own choosing. This doctrine was given a misleadingly somewhat less provocative label by being associated with the right to wage "preemptive" wars, that is, initiating a war when faced with an *imminent* and severe threat of major attack.[13] Again, seeking to identify distinctive American preoccupations, this fusing of counter-terrorism with the dangers associated with the proliferation of weapons of mass destruction (WMD), especially nuclear weapons, provided the essential rationale for the Iraq War, which even at the time proved convincing only to portions of the American public and to a few foreign governments. No other country, again with the possible exception of Israel, insisted that the WMD threat was so closely interwoven with the terrorist challenge.[14] Bin Laden's statements and Al Qaeda moves to acquire WMD did lend some credence to this concern, but its application to the situation of Iraq in 2003 seemed far-fetched even if the Baghdad regime had been found to possess some kind of WMD arsenal. The point here is that the American concern with WMD and proliferation is, at most, tangentially related to counter-terrorism. If these fears were what they claimed, then the biggest danger would have been Pakistan, due to its possession of nuclear weapons and the strong extremist presence within the security apparatus of the Pakistani state. Instead, U.S. policy on nuclear weapons was mainly a reflection of pre-9/11 grand strategy, which was based on the pursuit of counter-proliferation objectives as the basis of regional security in the Middle East.

In this period, as well, there were elaborate legalistic efforts made to cut corners in view of the special security demands attributed to this new kind of warfare, where the enemy lacked a true home base and remained hidden underground until an attack was launched. Government lawyers in the Bush administration argued that normally applicable international rules governing the treatment of foreign fighters should be cast aside, that these suspects (most of whom were, it turns out, completely innocent of terrorist connections) were "evil" and "bad guys," and that the need to obtain information from detainees justified the use of much more coercive forms interrogation.[15] A principal rhetorical device in lowering the threshold of public and professional resistance to torture was an extremely manipulative reliance on the so-called "ticking bomb" scenario to explain recourse to inhumane forms of interrogation whenever a suspect may possibly have time-urgent counter-terror information. Almost anyone detained could, by this logic, possibly be hiding some key information, and thus becomes a potential subject for the harshest forms of interrogation.[16] Experience at Guantanamo and Abu Ghraib confirm the view that abstract justifications for abusive treatment to deal with exceptional instances of potential immediate jeopardy (threats of weapons of mass destruction about to be used against heavily populated targets), are converted into implicit permission to engage in severely abusive behavior on a routine and comprehensive basis.

There were from the outset concerns, given a muted voice by moderates and principled persons inside and outside government, about Bush's posture of globalizing counter-terrorism as a global war on terror. Limitations could have been introduced by confining the struggle to the organizations backing the 9/11 terrorists or by reference to the geographic locus of the political violence, but in the anxious and patriotic atmosphere that prevailed after 9/11 there existed an uncritical acceptance of all official pronouncements. This was initially true across virtually the whole of the American political spectrum. Such a broad undertaking as embarking upon a war against terror on a global scale was without precedent in the history of counter-terrorism. Bush never limited counter-terrorist war to Al Qaeda, and thus all forms of non-state political violence could be considered as falling beneath the counter-terror umbrella being raised above the entire planet by the American political leadership. As might have been expected this broad American approach encouraged various embattled leaders of governments around the world to claim that their struggles against self-determination movements were part of this wider global war on terror.

By moving American counter-terrorist policy from a backburner of neglect so rapidly, massively, and unconditionally into the war domain, it became far easier for the government to insist upon and acquire extraordinary authority to act as it saw fit inside and outside the country without encountering any serious objections stemming from legal and moral considerations. At first, in public space, it was only civil society organizations such as the American Civil Liberties Union and the National Lawyers Guild that expressed strong opposition to security measures involving dramatic intrusions on privacy or unrestricted authority to detain and deny due process rights to terrorist suspects. Later on, when the abusive conditions of detention at Guantanamo became better known, and especially after the Abu Ghraib pictures found their way into magazines and onto TV, the government found itself under serious pressure from many legal professionals in government and private practice to justify its actions and modify its policies. The U.S. government response was to deny wrongdoing, and to deny all allegations of officially sanctioned torture, while ordering a series of formal inquiries into the allegations that restricted nominal accountability to very junior levels. The resulting reports placed most of the blame for the worst outrages perpetrated on detainees on unauthorized and improper behavior of deviant low-level military personnel (so-called "bad apples"), some of whom have been subsequently prosecuted for dereliction of duty. In effect, the top civilian and military policymakers responded to the pressure by scapegoating those at lower levels of the military/civilian hierarchy, while relying on impunity for themselves.

The main point here is that the peculiarly traumatizing character of the 9/11 attacks, unlike terrorist experience elsewhere and previously, made the adoption by the United States of this dysfunctional war modality an almost foregone, politically unchallenged conclusion. The dysfunctionality of this response only started to become apparent to most Americans, including opposition political figures, several years later, in the deep *aftermath* of the Iraq invasion, when the costs of changing the course of American foreign policy had become very high, although the costs of persisting seemed even higher. By then, also, the defining steps taken to erode the rule of law had been put into practice. The dysfunction in relation to addressing the terrorist threat associated with 9/11 is significantly different from the dysfunction arising from a reliance on inter-state war as an instrument of grand strategy, closely connected with the project of American global dominance.

External Location of Threats and Grievances

Unlike most political struggles involving non-state actors, the locus of the threat that materialized on 9/11 cannot be easily situated in geographic space, nor can the grievances of the attackers be clearly identified. Also, for reasons suggested earlier, the priority given to removing the threat is uncertain due to overlapping, yet distinct and somewhat contradictory, geopolitical objectives. At the same time, this vagueness encourages a variety of apprehensions of attack from within and without that made the American public willing to accept most measures taken in the name of lessening the risk of successful future attacks. Seven years later, the Bush administration contends that the absence of subsequent attacks is due to this tightening of control over people and activities in the United States, making curtailments of liberties seem worthwhile.

The focus on minimizing the terrorist threat was combined with the perception of the terrorists as evil extremists. This perception discourages any moves to defuse the conflict by addressing, or even perceiving, the *root causes* of terrorist violence. There appears to be an attitude among the American leadership that all efforts to explain or understand the motives of the attackers or to account for the high levels of support enjoyed around the world for extremist anti-American politics, are misguided, signaling weakness or a lack of resolve. Such efforts are alleged to divert attention from the only path to restored security, namely, the extermination of the threat. The former Conservative Prime Minister, John Major, speaking in London to a small gathering of invited guests in 2005, strongly disagreed. Major said about how important it became for him, while in government, to understand that counter-terrorism measures to thwart the IRA would only be successful over time if supplemented by efforts to deal responsibly with the root causes of terrorism that had afflicted Northern Ireland for decades. Major said he found it crucial to acknowledge and remove these roots, while doing his best to implement policies based on prevention and enforcement. Major contrasted this approach with his impression of how the United States leadership was dealing with the Al Qaeda threat after 9/11.[17] In other words, Major was arguing that counter-terrorism cannot succeed in the end if conceived exclusively as the killing and capture of terrorists. According to Major there must be a complementary *political* strategy that recognizes and responds to grievances.

The U.S. government has refused to consider the root causes of the 9/11 attacks for several reasons. To do so would challenge various aspects of the American engagement with and presence in the Middle East, including unconditional support for Israel in the conflict with the Palestinians over the future of historic Palestine. It would also raise serious doubts about the wisdom of the American deployment of military forces in areas close to sacred Islamic sites, as well as question continued support for corrupt and oppressive governments throughout the Arab world. This unwillingness to look at root causes also means that any serious dissent questioning the American response to 9/11 will be automatically looked upon as evidence of disloyalty and a lack of patriotism, which has intimidated voices in opposition. This intimidation has been reinforced by mainstream media in the United States, especially by talk show hosts, who monitor the narrow parameters of permissible counter-terrorist debate.

There is always some resistance to examining the grievances that might have provoked terrorism as it may be seen as an expression of weakness or as giving incentives to terrorists to inflict more harm. In the American case after 9/11 this resistance was particularly strong because the Bush presidency immediately adopted such a self-righteous position by its insistence on the unprovoked and barbarous character of the attacks. It described the conflict in the meta-political language of good and evil. As has been argued, it is reasonable to suspect that the Bush leadership wanted the terrorist threat to persist so as to provide necessary cover for going forward with the neocon-servative project for global domination, which was much more controversial than counter-terrorism. These pressures, while not entirely expressive of rather unique American circumstances, have not existed to nearly the same extent in other countries facing serious terrorist threats that were in some respects as formidable as what the United States faced after 9/11.

Counter-Proliferation

The United States has incorporated into its broad counter-terrorist approach a heavy emphasis on counter-proliferation in relation to countries seen as hostile to its view of future world order. As the Iraq War illustrates, and the threat of the use of force to destroy Iran nuclear program confirms, the implementation of counter-proliferation policy has become a pretext for non-defensive wars that cannot be justified under the UN Charter or international law. It is claimed that preventing such proliferation is integral to prevailing in the war on terror, but the two sets of goals seem to be mainly divergent. As with counter-terrorism, so with counter-proliferation, the primary American goal seems to be associated with reshaping the strategic environment of the world to accord with goals of American dominance. This wider set of global objectives complicates still further comparisons of American counter-terrorist operations with those undertaken by other countries, and may help to explain the escalating implications of declaring "war" rather than relying on enhanced law enforcement.

Of course, conceptually there is a potential link between the terrorist threat and the proliferation of nuclear weaponry. If a country with nuclear weapons is prepared to risk its own annihilation or to transfer such weaponry to non-state actors prepared to attack with nuclear weapons, then the danger exists. At the same time, the effort to preclude acquisition may increase the incentives to obtain such weapons, as once possessed, there is a diminished

155

motivation to rely on force to contain a threat. If the perspective on proliferation is pushed back to the mid-1990s, it would seem rather clear that Pakistan was the most dangerous of the threshold countries, and yet when Pakistan tested, and then acquired, such weapons in 1998, there were no alarmist reactions. Even today Pakistan is likely to be the most dangerous nuclear weapons state from the perspective of counter-terrorism. Its government is vulnerable to overthrow by Islamists, and within its governing process there are elements aligned with anti-American extremism. Despite these considerations Pakistan continues to collaborate with the United States, subscribing formally to the same counter-terrorist agenda.

Creeping Authoritarianism

As suggested earlier, all countries tend to weaken their respect for the rule of law and liberties in wartime. What makes the global war on terror so disturbing from this perspective is the combination of its intangibility and the seeming unavailability of an ending through either victory or diplomacy. Unless the objectives are scaled back and concretely specified this "war" is likely to persist indefinitely.[19] The various elements present create a further vulnerability to renewed attacks at some future point, while the likelihood exists of moves toward a further tightening of governmental control within the United States in response to a real or imagined increased sense of danger. In the event of another spectacular terrorist incident the citizenry might even demand, and certainly would accept, a curtailment of its liberty. In other words, the security syndrome shaped after 9/11 prepares the way for radical future steps toward the weakening of constitutional governance. In this sense, consideration needs to be directed not only at the erosion of the rule of law that has followed from 9/11, but also the degree to which the politics of fear creates the potential for much deeper inroads arising from either a polarization of opinion in American society or the belief by the leadership that the relative openness of a democratic society aggravates the security threat.

A foretaste of this dark set of possibilities has emerged in the course of the intense 2006 debate on immigration policy, with its call for more tightly guarded borders, including the construction of 700 miles of security fences along the Mexican border and reports of government contracts to build large domestic detention centers that would be available in times of crisis. Again, the issue of counter-terrorism is linked somewhat loosely to a variety of social issues associated with illegal entry to obtain employment. Whatever else, so long as the war on terror continues, there will be continuous pressures on democratic liberties and human rights, always with the danger that if matters take a turn for the worse with respect to the struggle, there will be a further tightening of the screws on the home front, either by invoking emergency or war.

Other countries have experienced serious inroads in relation to standards to liberal legality due to prolonged counter-terror campaigns. Among these are Britain (with respect to the IRA), France (in relation to the FLN), and Israel (especially, in relation to the occupation of Palestinian territories since 1967, but even more so during the wave of suicide bombings across "the green line" since the late 1990s). In each of these instances, the struggle eroded constitutional protections for suspected militants, but also for the civilian population as a whole, both those seeking change and those being protected. With the possible exception of a severe threat to public order in France at the end of the Algerian War in 1962, the counter-terrorist policies adopted never threatened the political stability of the country as deeply as have recent American developments. Because these American developments are likely to continue for years, if not decades, almost independent of the orientation of the elected leadership, the danger to political democracy seems particularly severe. This severity also arises from the extent to which security pre-occupations during the Cold War already endowed the U.S. government with vast powers, including a huge intelligence apparatus and a bureaucratic penchant for secrecy.

This discouraging assessment is reinforced by some shortcomings of American political culture, including the impulse to hide the extent to which the success of the terrorist attacks on 9/11 resulted from governmental incompetence or worse. This resistance to transparency is compounded by the extent to which the global domination project is deceptively folded within the counter-terrorist campaign. These deceptions of the citizenry naturally incline government officials to rely on secrecy, disinformation, and suppressive techniques to avoid exposing the full reality at issue. These factors, or some variation of them, may have also been present in other settings involving counter-terrorist agendas, but the special nature of the American relationship to world order makes the stakes higher. The scale and impact of the 9/11 attacks, as well as the perceptions of continuing vulnerability to catastrophic future possible attacks also makes comparisons with the counter-terrorist programs of other countries somewhat misleading.

Eroding the Rule of Law in the Post-9/11 Political Climate

Against the background of the preceding discussion, it is possible to identify the most serious encroachments on the domain of human rights that have been attributed to the distinctive security concerns arising from the 9/11 attacks and the counter-terrorist war pursued in response. The lines of justifying argument relied upon by the U.S. Government fall into three broad categories: (1) 9/11 changed everything, rendering obsolete some prior legal constraints and making the costs of future breaches of security unacceptable; (2) the urgency of obtaining information relevant to counter-terror goals provides valid grounds for engaging in more coercive forms of detention and interroga-tion; (3) the neoconservative dogma that presidential powers are virtually unchallengeable in wartime: even categorical prohibitions on "torture" and "inhumane treatment" should be circumvented, as necessary, by interpretative legerdemain.

Inter Arma Silent Leges (In Times of War the Law is Silent)

It is certainly the case that throughout American history, including during the American Civil War, crucial standards of legal protection of individual rights have been weakened, if not altogether abandoned.[20] Ideas of military necessity and an atmosphere of present danger to national security have been given precedence over restraints on the normal use of governmental power. In World War II the internment of Japanese residents, including citizens, involved imposing a harsh collective punishment that was later the subject of regret, apology, and even symbolic reparations for the wrong inflicted. A U.S. Supreme Court majority upheld the internment in decisions that remain controversial, but is still on the books.[21] As O'Donnell puts it, "[o]nce again, the deafening cry of 'military necessity' drowned out a plea to honor America's commitment to civil liberties and the rule of law."[22]

Unless there is executive sensitivity to civil liberties, human rights, and the rule of law, it is unlikely that *judicial* protection during wartime will be very effective except in extreme instances of abuse where the security justifications seem frivolous. For one thing, there is a judicial reluctance to invalidate government policy in the face of uncertain knowledge as to the level of risk involved, especially when the executive branch purports to have superior secret knowledge that is not shared and an atmosphere of national emergency exists.

The denial of habeas corpus to a U.S. citizen, Yaser Esam Hamdi, held without charges and incommunicado in a naval prison as an enemy combatant where the court said "the federal courts have many strengths, but the conduct of combat operations has been left to others. The executive is best prepared to exercise the military judgment attending the capture of alleged combatants."[23] For another, the president is charged constitutionally with authority and responsibility as commander in chief with respect to the conduct of war. And, finally, this tradition of deference took shape *prior* to the development in the latter half of the twentieth century of procedures of accountability with respect to evolving standards governing the conduct of states during a war. Steps taken by governments during war to implement internal security policies continue to be given a very broad "margin of appreciation," but as even a conservative United Supreme Court has increasingly shown, there are some limits to this deference that neoconservative government lawyers have overstepped in crafting the various aspects of the counter-terrorism program of the Bush White House.[24]

This susceptibility of the rule of law to erosion in wartime is accentuated by the extent to which political leaders and their main advisors adhere to a *realist* view of foreign policy that tends to marginalize considerations of legality and morality, or even more so, if the dominant climate of opinion is characterized by an *evangelical* approach to foreign policy as has been mainly the case during the Bush administration since 9/11. In this regard, whatever facilitates a war effort deemed "defensive," "just," and "sacred," is regarded as *legitimate,* and it is the job of government lawyers to provide a *legal* rationale. The Bush cadre of government lawyers has carried this process to such extremes as to cause opposition from Pentagon legal specialists who are fearful of the bad consequences for military professionalism and a loss of leverage in relation to violation of the rights of American military personnel who claim abuse overseas in future wars.[25]

The War Against Terror Declared after 9/11 Validates Otherwise Illegal Policies

The whole nature of *this* war is alleged to validate the sidelining of prior legal guidelines, especially international humanitarian law as embodied in the Geneva Conventions.[26] In effect, the traditional law of war, including treating captured combatants as "prisoners of war," was based on the reciprocal standards of behavior agreed upon as governing international wars between sovereign states.[27] But if the "enemy" is an invisible non-state actor that can be anywhere and whose "soldiers" are not wearing military uniforms, then legal duties designed for governments seems less applicable. And beyond this, the nature of such a conflict in which the enemy has shown the capacity to inflict severe harm and displayed an ingenuity with respect to tactics that include suicidal commitments, places a premium on "prevention," and that creates special pressures to obtain what the Pentagon calls "actionable intelligence."

It is this logic that has been used to justify "enemy combatant" classifications and "coercive interrogation" methods that are regarded as "torture" by others. Lawyers who defend American detention practices for the government strenuously deny allegations of torture.[28] As President Bush expressed this need to acquire information: "The security of our nation and the lives of our citizens depend on our ability to learn what these terrorists know."[29] In the same speech Bush acknowledged the reliance by the CIA on "an alternative set of procedures" to conduct interrogations of important suspects, but declined to specify what these were. Reliable information as to the techniques that have been used against detainees strongly support the contention that these procedures violate the Torture Convention, a valid treaty binding on the U.S. government.

The unreasonableness of these practices and policies can be reliably assessed even without complete access to the realities. Most impartial reports suggest a dragnet used to hold persons in detention, with many being held without rights within and without America, most of whom are neither threats nor responsible for past wrongdoing nor in possession of vital information. The claim made that there are exceptional circumstances that justify suspending normal legal constraints is rejected for two main reasons: once exceptions are allowed, abuses pile up; and the existence of exceptional circumstances ("the ticking bomb") are rare and contrived, and should be ignored when constructing general rules for behavior.[30] The insidious side of this ticking bomb scenario is that it elicits a grudging admission that torture can sometimes be justified, and as a result, the prohibition on torture is always a matter of context. It can always be claimed that eliciting information from a detainee might just possibly provide information that could be used to save hundreds of American lives.

The Lesser of Evils

There has been considerable overlapping argumentation given by "liberal hawks" who seek to preserve an atmosphere of decency in the midst of the counter-terror campaigns while accommodating to varying degrees the pressure to rely on unacceptable methods to acquire information or to detain. Rather than follow the neoconservatives down the path of limitless presidential authority to set policy, even in secret, and avoid any accountability, this balancing of competing values (decency, rule of law, human rights v. security, strong state) tries to avoid the worst, and moves toward shifting back the burden of persuasion to those claiming exceptional powers.[31] Some commentators in the context of torture believe it is important to make the prohibition as absolute as possible, but would still allow a defense of necessity as mitigating subsequent responsibility if the accused torturer could *demonstrate* that he acted in an exceptional set of circumstances. Another pragmatic proposal has been widely discussed, which allows a judge to issue a warrant authorizing torture for a limited purpose in response to a governmental argument made in secret.

An Imperial Commander-in-Chief

The neoconservative outlook is one that is supposedly deferential to a strict reading of the Constitution, but is at the same time contemptuous of international law or of laws that have been legislatively enacted or judicially interpreted to reflect liberal values.[32] In advancing this viewpoint that applies across the board, but is being more vigorously challenged recently by Congress and in the courts, has to do with the powers claimed for the executive branch, and specifically the presidency, with respect to prosecuting the war against terrorism. The standard view had been that an American president is always accountable to applicable law, including during wartime. Since 9/11 John Yoo in particular has put forward an extreme reinterpretation of the Constitution that accords a president truly unrestricted and unaccountable powers over any undertaking that arises from carrying on the war.[33]

Of course, the expansion of presidential powers during wartime and an accompanying domestic controversy is far from unprecedented. The issue last seriously gained public attention in the latter stages of the Vietnam War, when books with the titles *Arrogance of Power* and *The Imperial Presidency* were written by prominent American citizens.[34] At the time, the president was accused of misleading Congress and the public, engaging in warfare without a declaration of war by Congress, maintaining unwarranted secrecy, engaging in surveillance without proper authorization, and planning detention centers and the like for domestic opponents of the war.

Nixon actually compiled "an enemy's list" of anti-war activists.[35] What is different in the Bush presidency, aside from a Congress and media that has been so far generally supportive, is the elaborate efforts to validate these excessive claims of presidential power as beyond the reach of the rule of law, and as part of a deliberate effort to push the governing process of the country toward the far right for as long as possible. And as mentioned earlier, the uncertain duration of the war means that measures adopted to meet a present emergency are likely to remain operative indefinitely.

Failures to Uphold International Legal Standards as Embodied in International Humanitarian Law and in International Human Rights

An integral part of the rule of law within the United States in the early twenty-first century is the obligation to uphold *internally* applicable international standards, whether in the form of duly ratified international treaties or of norms of customary international law. These standards apply especially to the treatment of persons captured abroad and held in detention as "enemy combatants" or as unspecified suspects in some manner related to terrorism. The most comprehensive and authoritative discussion of these issues is to be found in the report of UN Commission on Human Rights, "Situation of Detainees at Guantanamo Bay," which is extremely critical of U.S. detention policies and recommends closing the facilities, as well as providing compensation to victims of torture and cruel, inhuman, or degrading treatment as prohibited in Article 14 of the Convention on Torture.[36] Guantanamo Bay is situated on Cuban territory leased on a long-term basis by the United States. It was apparently deliberately chosen as a major site for detention of captured suspects precisely because it was thought to be beyond the reach of American courts and not subject to rule of law constraints.

Wiretapping Without a Warrant

One controversial practice has been the recent disclosures that the president has been wiretapping without warrants communications between Americans and overseas contacts who are suspected of being connected with Al Qaeda in some way. Such wiretapping appears to violate an explicit legislative procedure that covers all reasonable surveillance needs as specified in the Foreign

Intelligence Surveillance Act (FISA). The statute already authorizes warrantless wiretaps if ordered by the executive, but only during the first fifteen days of a war. Otherwise, judicial approval must be obtained, not an onerous burden, as the FISA court has consistently and without delay approved of security claims made by the executive branch when it seeks permission to wiretap without obtaining a warrant. In effect, the claim on behalf of this domestic spying program is based primarily on the implied powers of the president as commander-in-chief, and, secondarily, on a strained reading of the authorization for the Use of Military Force against Al Qaeda.[37] The full legal assessment is made in a letter to Congress signed by a distinguished group of constitutional law specialists in the United States reaching the conclusion that the spying program is violating the clear intent of Congress.

Military Commissions

Shortly after 9/11, President Bush, by executive decree, authorized the establishment of military commissions to prosecute "enemy combatants" for alleged terrorist activities. This legal maneuver was obviously designed to circumvent both the protective provisions of the Geneva Conventions, the backbone of international humanitarian law, and to avoid scrutiny by the American judicial system. There are many objections to this procedure from the perspective of human rights: the judges of the military commissions are hand-picked military officers, the accused person has no rights to act in defense or even to attend hearings, there are no rules of evidence, and no right of judicial review. The commission is empowered to impose a death sentence, and the only review is an appeal to the president, or if he decides, to the secretary of defense. The legal status of these military commissions has yet to be clarified. The case of *Hamdan* v. *Rumsfeld* before the U.S. Supreme Court decided by a 5–3 majority that the president violated the separation of powers by setting up the commissions without Congressional authorization and in a manner inconsistent with Articles 3 and 4 of the Third Geneva Convention on the Treatment of Prisoners of War.[38] Clearly the reliance on commissions, as well as locating the site of detention outside of the territorial limits of the United States, reflects the dual position of the Bush administration: to treat those alleged to be associated with terrorism as engaged in "war," and thus not entitled to judicial protection; and then treating the war as being of such a special character that it is not within the domain of the Geneva Conventions, or more generally, international humanitarian law. The underlying issue is whether the president has inherent powers arising from his role as commander-in-chief in wartime or delegated powers deriving from 2001 statute entitled Authorization of the Use of Military Force.[39] Additional legal questions in the case include whether a detainee can be constitutionally denied rights of habeas corpus to assess judicially the legality of confinement and treatment as Congress has attempted in the Detainee Treatment Act and whether the provisions of the Geneva Conventions can be enforced in an American court.

After a considerable struggle in Congress, in which several leading Republican senators broke ranks with the president, a Military Commissions Act was passed by both houses, and then signed by the president. Whether its controversial provisions, which will be tested in courts, will survive judicial scrutiny is difficult to predict. If they do, it will mean that the U.S. government has authoritatively adopted an approach to detainees who are not citizens that cannot be reconciled with international legal norms and procedures.

Patriot Act of 2001, Reenacted with Revisions 2006

The most extensive domestic impact on human rights arising from the counter-terror priority after 9/11 took the form of the very comprehensive legislation known as USA Patriot Act, initially adopted after virtually no debate in late 2001, reauthorized and altered in March 2006 after considerable controversy in the media and Congress. This legislation consolidated preexisting governmental law enforcement authority scattered in many laws, but also added to this authority in controversial ways that have aroused opposition from the American Civil Liberties Union and other groups concerned with human rights. The Patriot Act is very long, covering in its initial enactment 341 pages.

Among its most controversial features is the adoption of a vague definition of "domestic terrorism" that could be used to criminalize activity normally associated with peaceful opposition to government policy. According to section 802 of the Act domestic terrorism include activities that:

> (A) involve acts dangerous to human life that are a violation of the criminal laws of the U.S. or of any state, that (B) appear to be intended (i) to intimidate or coerce a civilian population, (ii) to influence the policy of a government by intimidation or coercion, or (iii) to affect the conduct of a government by mass destruction, assassination, or kidnapping, and (C) occur primarily within the territorial jurisdiction of the U.S.

There is a parallel crime of international terrorism, which is defined in terms identical to that of domestic terrorism, except that its locus transcends national boundaries. This sweeping conception of terrorism is linked to the establishment of a new uniformed police force under the authority of the Department of Homeland Security that allows the arrest of demonstrators at "special events of national significance," and along with expanded arresting authority of the Secret Service, allows felony charges against demonstrators who breach security perimeters with penalties of up to ten years in prison.

The 2006 Act renews the controversial "sneak and peak" provision that empowers the government to gather information from a variety of sources: intercepts of telephone and Internet communications, access to medical and tax records, scrutiny of book purchases and library borrowings. There are various provisions exempting some of these surveillance and search procedures from the requirement of a prior warrant or of notification to the target of investigation and suspicion. The judge issuing the warrant may allow the delay in notification under a variety of circumstances when there exists a risk of "endangering the life or physical safety of an individual; flight from prosecution; destruction of or tampering with evidence; intimidation of potential witnesses; or otherwise seriously jeopardizing an investigation or unduly delaying a trial." These procedures are handled by the Foreign Intelligence Surveillance Court, which has a record of deference to governmental requests, instead of a normal federal or state court. And the basis for granting requests is based on a claim of "reasonable cause" rather than the more restrictive "probable cause." There are some measures in the 2006 version of the Patriot Act that allow challenges to "gag orders" and place some burdens on government agents making requests for intrusions on privacy. For instance, FBI agents who want to search bookstore or library records must now gain explicit permission from one of three designated high government officials.

In essence, the Patriot Act gives to the government wide powers with a serious potential of abuse that has alarmed civil libertarians, especially as this authority has been applied to immigrant suspects detained secretly without charges for long periods of time. The statutory language, which has not been judicially tested as yet, relies on very broad definitions of prohibited activity that could be interpreted to intimidate, and even punish, normal political action. Such legislation would have been impossible to enact in the absence of the post-9/11 climate of fear and anger, an atmosphere that has been sustained by periodic alarms uttered by high officials. The linking of counter-terrorism with the war on terror has been relied upon by the Bush administration and the courts to defer to governmental claims that rely on a national security rationale.

Conclusions

The threat to civil liberties, human rights, and the rule of law associated with developments since 9/11 is complicated by the outlook of the Bush presidency and the deliberate confusion drawn between counter-terrorism and a broader foreign policy agenda unlikely to generate domestic support unless fused in the public mind with responding to terrorist dangers. It is also clear that an authoritarian tendency has been activated, which was partly a dormant predisposition of neoconservative leadership and partly a response to the traumatic attacks of 9/11. This conjuncture has resulted in a series of controversial intrusions on rights, quite unhelpful with respect to genuine counter-terror goals of achieving security without disrupting the democratic fabric of society. In the instance of torture and reliance on cruel, inhuman, and degrading treatment of various categories of detainees the debate as to utility has not been completely settled, although there is certainly no firm evidence that such abuse produces sufficient reliable and strategically useful information to offset the harm done.

The fact that the renewal of the Patriot Act received far more legislative scrutiny than did its initial adoption exhibited both the waning of automatic Congressional approval of whatever the executive branch claims to be helpful for counter-terrorism, as well as the overall weakening of the Bush presidency. The situation remains fluid. Renewed terrorist incidents of any magnitude in the United States would undoubtedly reinforce the disposition to enhance governmental enforcement authority at the expense of human rights, while evidence of governmental abuse and the further withering away of Al Qaeda might produce a push toward restoring normalcy with respect to the rights of individuals. If associated extremist groups do not perpetrate major terrorist attacks, especially in the United States, it might soon convince the legislative, and possibly the judicial, branch, to restore protection of individual rights and take steps to uphold the integrity of the rule of law. These kind of moves seem more likely in the wake of the recovery of control over Congress by the Democratic Party as a result of the 2006 mid-term elections, generally understood to have resulted from a repudiation of Bush's leadership, and of the Iraq policy.

11

Humanitarian Intervention

The Golden Age of Humanitarian Intervention: The 1990s

Humanitarian intervention has never had an easy time gaining broad and deep acceptance among international lawyers. As a doctrine justifying the use of force it has consistently invited skepticism because in practice it often seemed more like a self-interested instrument of power than an altruistic undertaking for the sake of others. Humanitarian intervention was often viewed as geopolitics disguised by the language of legal and moral pretension. After all, it was only weak and non-Western countries that could become sites of humanitarian intervention. Strong and Western countries are off-limits no matter how severe the humanitarian crisis. Besides, with realists of varying stripes shaping the foreign policy of leading states, who but a naïve fool could doubt that beneath the mellifluous rhetoric of humanitarianism were lurking strategic motivations relating to power relationships, foreign basing rights, and access to resources or investment opportunities?

The United States has over the course of its history done more than its share to cast shadows of doubt across the laudable impulse to rescue populations from oppressive rule and to protect minorities from persecution. One thinks of the decades of "gunboat diplomacy" in Latin America, often accompanied by self-serving explanations about the promotion of "democracy," "the blessings of liberty," and the enforcement of the legal obligations owed by lawless dictatorships to foreign nationals.[1] The diplomacy of the Cold War also contributed to a suspicious view of interventions that were claimed by Washington to be undertaken for the benefit of the target society. How many times were Americans told that they were partially fighting and dying in Vietnam to bring "democracy" to South Vietnam, a claim that was never more than a cruel charade, given the governing style of Washington's autocratic allies in Saigon? As well, the ideological interventions of the 1950s in Iran and Guatemala, implemented through reliance on the covert capabilities of the CIA, brought to power oppressive and exploitative elites submissive to American geopolitical priorities, and recipients of American economic and military assistance. Progressive and popular leaders who had placed nationalist obstacles in the way of American economic and ideological goals while seeking to overcome the destitution of their peoples were tossed aside, if not killed outright. Similar interventions occurred in Latin America in the 1960s and 1970s, leading to repressive military dictatorships. Most revealingly, the U.S. government was prominently linked to the military ascension of General Augusto Pinochet to power in Chile on September 11, 1973, displacing an elected and constitutionally observant government! The list of abusive intrusions is sadly far longer than these illustrative cases mentioned here, but the relevance of this background helps us understand the reluctance of many countries in the South to give a green light, or even a yellow one, to humanitarian intervention as an acceptable international practice, much less an established doctrine of international law.[2]

Despite this background, a series of developments in the 1990s began to give humanitarian intervention a better name. Human rights had been steadily achieving greater political and legal influence in the course of the twenty or so preceding years. The international promotion of human rights was widely understood as having encouraged a series of positive achievements in world politics: the rise of nonviolent mass movements opposing repressive regimes in East Europe; the emergence of similar movements in several Asian countries; and the extraordinary bloodless collapse of the apartheid regime in South Africa. The United States' impact on these developments was salient and crucial, generally traced to Jimmy Carter's high-profile advocacy of human rights as a major element in U.S. foreign policy during the early years of his presidency that commenced in 1976. The UN Conference on Human Rights and Development in 1993 gave added attention to international human rights as a genuinely global phenomenon, and led directly to the establishment of a UN High Commissioner for Human Rights that was expressive of an upgrading of the role of human rights within the UN system. Important too was a new globalized media that provided real-time awareness of some vivid instances of human suffering arising from governmental abuse or incompetence—"the CNN factor"—that produced pressures on major governments and on the international community to act in the face of impending humanitarian catastrophes.

The bridge between human rights and humanitarian intervention was being built in this period by increasingly stressing the importance and feasibility of implementation. Earlier, human rights advocacy consisted mainly of lawmaking initiatives by governments to establish international standards and the efforts of human rights non-governmental organizations (NGOs) to spread awareness and to expose certain kinds of abuse, especially the plight of prisoners of conscience and the practice of torture. But the 1990s gave rise to several distinct, although mutually reinforcing, initiatives to achieve global justice, including especially moves seeking the protection of severely abused and vulnerable populations. Among the most important of these initiatives were the following: moves to redress historic injustices (recovery of gold and other assets by survivors and heirs of Holocaust victims; compensation for victims of slave labor during World War II; attention to the grievances of "comfort women" in Asia, of indigenous peoples throughout the world; agitation relating to the payment of "reparations" for slavery); moves to overcome "impunity" for those alleged to be responsible for crimes against humanity (truth and reconciliation commissions; ad hoc international criminal tribunals for former Yugoslavia and Rwanda; prosecutions based on claims of "universal jurisdiction" within national courts, most notably the Pinochet litigation); sanctions and boycotts imposed on countries alleged to be guilty of gross violations of human rights.[3] In the deepest sense, support for humanitarian intervention *from a human rights* perspective was an expression of a new seriousness with respect to possibilities of enforcement in selected instances of severe abuse. The 1990s witnessed a series of settings in which such responses were attempted, with varying degrees of effectiveness and credibility, revealing the ambivalence that officials in leading governments felt toward the doctrine and practice of humanitarian intervention that helped explained inconsistent responses. The most notable instances in this period were Somalia, Bosnia, Rwanda, Haiti, Kosovo, and East Timor.[4]

Several assessments of what now appears to have been, for all of its setbacks, the golden years of humanitarian intervention, can be tentatively offered: (1) the logic of humanitarian intervention was never, during the 1990s, supported by a global consensus of either leading states, a majority of states, or among civil society actors, but represented an American-led world diplomacy; (2) the effectiveness of humanitarian intervention in each instance seemed crucially dependent on the existence of reinforcing non-humanitarian motivations by the principal intervening actors, and especially the United States; (3) the legality of a *particular* instance of humanitarian intervention depended on the receipt of an explicit mandate in advance from the United Nations (UN) Security Council; (4) after its Somalia experience in 1993, the United States would not support humanitarian intervention unless there were also important strategic interests at stake, as in Kosovo; (5) the overall legitimacy of humanitarian intervention was principally shaped by the degree to which force was seen as effective in curtailing severe human rights abuses, especially in the face of genocide and ethnic cleansing, and as leading to a robust and non-manipulative post-intervention reconstruction process carried out under UN auspices.[5]

The battle lines of this policy debate were most sharply drawn by the Kosovo War of 1999 carried on without a UN mandate, under NATO auspices, but successfully protecting a population that had been abused and seemed seriously threatened with massive ethnic cleansing. The NATO war appeared to provide the 90 percent Albanian majority an opportunity to be secure and independent. Some criticism was directed at the sort of precedent that was being created, arguing that any intervention, however humanitarian the justification, that lacked formal approval by the UN Security Council, was unacceptable. Milder criticisms were directed at the means used to carry out the intervention (high altitude bombing sacrificing accuracy to minimize risks to the pilots, and reliance on some legally dubious targets and weaponry) and in relation to the aftermath (failure of NATO peacekeeping forces to protect Serb minority against "reverse ethnic cleansing"; insufficient reconstruction assistance). This debate, never resolved, was between those social forces who resisted encroachments on territorial sovereignty that were not backed by the permanent members of the UN Security Council and advocates of humanitarian diplomacy who discounted the contemporary relevance of international restraints on the use of force and war-making. This latter position supported a disregard of law or contended that the UN legal regime contained in the Charter governing recourse to force had long been in fundamental disarray, giving it little relevance to uses of force in the world of the 1990s.[6]

Less polarized views suggested that the Charter had evolved since 1945 to give the protection of vulnerable populations a status almost equivalent to that relating to prohibitions on the use of force, and that it was important to acknowledge an undesirable uncertainty arising from the tension between viewing the Kosovo undertaking as *legitimate*, although *illegal*.[7] Even supporters of the Kosovo undertaking were uncomfortable about establishing this sort of precedent for future claims on behalf of humanitarian intervention, as it seemed to be opening the Pandora's box containing a categorical prohibition on non-defensive uses of international force.. But how could one avoid some sense of precedent?[8] Another kind of advocacy claimed that a humanitarian intervention conducted without the formal backing of the UN was, at best, a morally justifiable action if the facts did suggest an imminent humanitarian catastrophe, but one lacking a firm legal foundation. This line of explanation does no more than to shift the tension between legality and legitimacy to that between law and morality, and does not overcome the resulting absence of authoritative guidelines. The net impact of such tensions is to enlarge the subjective domain of discretion with respect to recourse to war available to leading state actors, and thus works against the basic effort of the UN Charter as originally drafted in 1945.[9]

This unsatisfactory doctrinal circumstance led to high-profile controversies about the scope of humanitarian intervention, and important articulations, especially by Kofi Annan in his role as Secretary-General of the UN. For instance, in responding to critics of earlier suggestions that sovereignty must be allowed to block action by the international community designed to rescue a people facing genocide or ethnic cleansing, Annan, while acknowledging the continuing weight of sovereignty arguments, sided with the interventionists: "But to the critics I would pose this question: if humanitarian intervention is, indeed, an unacceptable assault on sovereignty, how should we respond to a Rwanda, to a Srebrenica—to gross and systematic violations of human rights that offend every precept of our common humanity?" The Secretary General continued, "[w]e confront a real dilemma.. . . But surely no legal principle—not even sovereignty—can ever shield crimes against humanity." Annan argues that the Security Council has "a moral duty" to act in such circumstances, including as "the option of last resort" a decision to authorize recourse to force "in the face of mass murder."[10] But what if the Security Council fails to discharge this moral duty? Are there residual rights to act via coalitions of the willing or on the basis of a mandate received from a multilateral framework, such as NATO, that is less inclusive than the UN? And what about unilateral claims to fulfill moral obligations when political considerations preclude action under multilateral auspices?[11] This dilemma has never been resolved: countries in the South remain convinced that sovereign rights should never be forcibly breached to enforce human rights, even in extreme situations, without a formal UN Security Council mandate, while the Euro-American countries insist on a residual freedom of action to engage in ad hoc humanitarian intervention if the gravity of the situation merits such action.

What was widely evident, however, was a discernible trend toward human solidarity that included the mobilization of global civil society actors on behalf of selective instances of humanitarian intervention. Generalizing on the 1990s, Mary Kaldor writes: "[w]hat is striking about the last decade is the emergence of what might be called a humanitarian regime . . . above all a significant growth of global civil society groups who focus on the issue of humanitarian intervention in various ways."[12] The argument here is deceptive, conceiving of humanitarian intervention less as a matter for states and international institutions than as a challenge to civil society actors dedicated to the promotion of human rights and the wellbeing of peoples. Such "intervention" may be militant and opposed by territorial authorities, but it is nonviolent in its essence, although it may under some circumstances collaborate with "intervention from above."[13] What emerged in the 1990s was a robust civil society constituency concerned with human rights, and exercising significant roles of relief and solidarity in situations of impending humanitarian crisis, thereby suggesting a post-Westphalian framing of the humanitarian intervention problematic.[14] This framing was significantly different from the Westphalian framing discussed earlier, whether within or without the UN, that was preoccupied with sovereignty and presupposed the monopoly role of states as actors with respect to issues of war and peace.

It is impossible to consider this period of the 1990s without taking into account the global leadership exerted by the United States. The election of George W. Bush as president in 2000 was accompanied by a strong indication that the U.S. government would no longer be at the forefront of humanitarian diplomacy. Such was the implication of the frequent Bush criticisms directed at the alleged "nation-building" undertakings associated with the Clinton years, which were supposedly responsible for inattentiveness to America's strategic interests. Without the active engagement of the United States, humanitarian intervention seemed like lost cause, but history has a cunning that often defies rational expectations, and it was Bush, more than his predecessor in the White House, who became associated with a neo-Wilsonian foreign policy that promised not only to rescue peoples from dictatorial rule but to end tyranny worldwide.[15]

September 11: The Death and Rebirth of Humanitarian Intervention

The 9/11 attacks exerted a profound influence on the global policy agenda. The preoccupations of the 1990s, ranging from the struggles over foreign economic policy and globalization to the various components of humanitarian diplomacy, seemed to dissolve overnight into thin air. Governmental concerns appeared to shift almost totally to the challenge of mega-terrorism and how to organize an effective military response.[16] The United States government immediately sought successfully to focus the attention of the world on the terrorist menace, and to persuade as many foreign governments as possible to join its struggle. President Bush threatened those states that gave safe haven to terrorists, and notoriously insisted that all countries had a defining choice to make—either you are with us or with the terrorists. As might be expected, public sentiments outside the United States, although initially supportive, were soon alarmed by American bellicosity. Concerns mounted as it started to appear that the anti-terrorist campaign was providing cover for an accelerated global dominance project that had been on the drawing boards of influential Bush advisors well before 9/11.[17]

In this new global setting, the initial phase of the American response was directed at Afghanistan, with war initiated on October 7, 2001, seeking both the destruction of the Al Qaeda presence (including the death or capture of its principal leaders) and the replacement of the Taliban regime. Although the war was justified principally as a form of extended self-defense, given the gravity of the attacks and the continuing Al Qaeda capability, there was also an emphasis on the illegitimacy of the Taliban regime due to its abysmal human rights record that included ethnic massacres, horrifying abuses of women, and overall oppressiveness. Because of its extremity the Taliban regime at the time of 9/11 was diplomatically recognized by only three foreign states, Pakistan, Saudi Arabia, and the United Arab Emirates. Immediately after 9/11, these latter two broke diplomatic relations with Afghanistan, leaving only Pakistan, which was strongly aligned with the United States and kept its link with the Taliban to sustain communication.

In the aftermath of the Afghanistan War, the Bush administration claimed, with some merit, that the effect of its military operations was to emancipate the Afghan people from Taliban thralldom, creating the basis for the democratization of the country under new leadership espousing Western liberal values. Such claims were reinforced by the seemingly genuine displays of relief by the Afghan people who lined the streets of Kabul to welcome the arrival of American military forces. There have been subsequent efforts to allow the Afghan people to select their leaders by a collective process based on national tradition that was expected to lead in a matter of years to democratic elections. Over time problems and disappointments mounted, and included indications that the writ of the Karzai government did not extend much beyond the capital city of Kabul. There were also a variety of reports about the continuing abuse of women, indications that the Afghan people are still caught in enclaves of repression administered by warlords, and disturbing signs of a revival of a Taliban presence in the country. Yet, on balance, it remains reasonable to suggest that from the perspective of *consequences* the Afghanistan War could be viewed *at the time* as a relatively successful instance of humanitarian intervention.[18] From the perspective of 2008, the assessment is much more shadowy, with a highly uncertain future for the country.

The Iraq debate is more complicated with respect to its humanitarian side-effects, especially prior to the war. More explicitly than with respect to Afghanistan, partly because the anti-terrorist rationale for war is so much weaker and the governmental and civil society opposition so much greater, the Bush administration has stressed the humanitarian benefits of an Iraq War. The White House rested its major case before invading Iraq on the alleged threat posed by Iraq's supposed stockpiles of undisclosed weapons of mass destruction, especially biological and chemical weaponry, but an emphasis was also placed on the past brutality of the Baghdad regime. The chemical attacks in the late 1980s on undefended Kurdish villages were frequently mentioned, as were the details of cruel and extreme forms of torture used against political prisoners and relied upon to crush any signs of opposition to Saddam Hussein's dictatorial rule. American success in achieving regime change was claimed to benefit the Iraqi people as a whole. These arguments were not persuasive even prior to the 2003 invasion, but were deeply compromised by the failure to find weapons of mass destruction and by the badly mishandled occupation of the country. Above all, the original American claims of defensive necessity seem strained to the point of lacking all credibility, and were never able to provide an adequate cover for recourse to a war that was denied support in the UN Security Council. From the outset there were conflicting accounts of whether the Iraqi people would resist or welcome an American takeover; and the impact of the war is likely to be far more consequential for the population, with reports that Iraqi civilian casualties could eventually be in the hundreds of thousands. Despite these concerns, it remains notable that the target of this dubious war was the displacement of a brutal dictator almost totally lacking in foreign support. The Saddam Hussein regime in Iraq was considered to be one of the most oppressive, and its demise seemed, at first, to be beneficial for the people of Iraq.

Under these circumstances, it can be argued that, regardless of American motives, and even in the face of significant Iraqi casualties, that the Iraq War had the positive side-effect of removing from power an odious government, and therefore should be assessed as a controversial instance of humanitarian intervention. Prime Minister Tony Blair was most insistent in making the humanitarian intervention aspects of the undertaking integral to his support for the war option to resolve the Iraq crisis: "Ridding the world of Saddam would be an act of humanity. It is leaving him there that is in truth inhumane."[19] The argument supporting the Iraq War was never persuasive. It seemed to encourage an empire-building foreign policy by the United States that was opportunistically using humanitarian arguments to hide crass strategic objectives. Recourse to war against Iraq also impaired the authority of international law and the United Nations to a degree that is still not clear. It is important to understand that even if a given war can be regarded as a valid instance of "humanitarian intervention," this may not be enough to outweigh the objections to such a war based on international law, and on the overall costs, risks, and consequences of war, which by now on every count exceed the expectations of the United States government.[20]

There is another important point here that cuts in the opposite direction. The American approach to anti-terrorism sets in motion two sets of responses that work against humanitarian logic in general, and the politics behind the sort of law enforcement implied by "humanitarian intervention." First of all, a series of governments faced with self-determination movements are emboldened to contend that their struggles should be seen and treated from the perspective of "anti-terrorism," thereby blurring the distinction between the visionary mega-terrorism of Osama Bin Laden and the terrorism of anti-state movements with tangible grievances that disregard civilian innocence. The Bush administration has relied on language that has encouraged this confusion, and with it, the intensification of "state terrorism" in such settings as Chechnya, Palestinian territories, Kashmir, and Xinjiang Province. The second detrimental effect relates to "the Faustian bargains" struck by the United States in its search for allies around the world. Several highly repressive Central Asian states became recipients of major aid and diplomatic support in exchange for accepting military bases on their territory and showing support for the American approach to world order.

The effects of 9/11 on this theme of humanitarian intervention will continue to unfold for years to come. This preliminary identification of positive and negative effects is mainly intended to show that the whole debate on humanitarian intervention has shifted quite dramatically. The form of direct discussion prompted by the Kosovo War is no longer relevant. Humanitarian intervention became an *incidental* feature of the heated debate about wars undertaken in the name of anti-terrorism, and especially the post-Afghanistan role of war as an appropriate tactic. By and large, the anti-war grassroots movement around the world, while fully acknowledging the brutality of Saddam Hussein, rejected the claim that humanitarian benefits for the Iraqi people could validate recourse to war. Such a rejection reflected two distinct considerations: a distrust of the claim in the first place, because it seemed to undercut prohibitions on non-defensive war-making and underestimated the problems of invasion and occupation, and second a strong sense that the prospect of civilian devastation and strife overwhelmed any humanitarian claims made to support recourse to such a war. Perhaps if Iraq in 2003 had been in a condition of internal crisis, the perceptions around the world would have been more sympathetic to the American position, but as the country was quiet, the case for intervention seemed weak.

More generally, the early twenty-first-century debate about uses of force seems to revolve around issues of war and peace, and the pursuit of global security, rather than the sort of global justice concerns that were so often highlighted during the 1990s. As a result, humanitarian intervention as an explicit option of policy, either by the United Nations or by coalitions of the willing, seems in a condition of eclipse. The ambivalent international response to the genocidal crisis in Darfur seems to confirm the persistence of this eclipse.

Global Civil Society and the Future of Humanitarian Intervention

Undoubtedly, in the near future, the advocacy of humanitarian intervention will get caught up in the intensifying debate on the American response to the mega-terrorist threat. To the extent that war options are pursued as an anti-terrorism stratagem, there is likely to be a component of the argument that insists that humanitarian effects will follow from coercive efforts to achieve regime change. Because in most settings the avoidance of war will be treated as the highest priority by civil society proponents of humanitarian diplomacy, there will be a tendency by anti-war advocates to reject humanitarian considerations invoked by pro-war forces as being beside the main point. Humanitarian claims will be viewed as a deceptive way to deflect criticism of 'wars of choice' that are objectionable for legal, moral, and prudential reasons.

Mary Kaldor has challenged in a characteristically stimulating way this dualistic logic, suggesting that it was important to oppose the war option while simultaneously supporting the regime change option for the sake of the Iraqi people. In her words, "Those of us who oppose the war, none the less have a responsibility to put forward proposals about how regime change in Iraq might be done in a peaceful way."[21] Kaldor draws on her experience in the last stages of the Cold War, when solidarity of the West European peace movement with the growing opposition to oppressive regimes in Eastern Europe reinforced the changes in the Moscow leadership and the pressure mounted by NATO governments to achieve peaceful regime change without war. This approach then and now is somewhat controversial among civil society actors, as critics argue that it plays into the hands of the warmongers.

The tactical possibilities of peaceful change must be assessed in the particular circumstances. In the 1980s, there was a robust grassroots movement in East Europe, the Soviet Union began changing its approach as soon as Gorbachev emerged as the leader, and the United States was deterred from provocative action by a pervasive worry about an escalation of any confrontation with the Soviet Union. In the early twenty-first century the structure of conflict is entirely different. There was no significant nonviolent opposition movement in the countries that were the leading candidates for regime-changing interventions by the United States. When Iraq was attacked it was not clear whether retaliatory or defensive options existed that might cause great damage, but with Iran the expectation is that strong retaliatory options are possessed by Tehran and would likely be exercised if attacked. After the Soviet collapse the United States seemed undeterred in pursuing its dangerously aggressive project to achieve global dominance. 9/11, and the Iraq quagmire changed this, discouraging further reliance on war as an instrument for extending American influence in the Middle East.

Although Mary Kaldor's approach did not seem very helpful with respect to resolving the crisis in Iraq prior to the invasion, it remains intriguing as a means of reconciling humanitarian goals with respect for international law and the United Nations. Kaldor urged Britain and other governments "to put forward" a new approach so as "to reunite Europe in a way that just might contain the other rogue state, the United States."[22] I think there may be merit in pursuing such alternatives, especially building transnational civic connections with democratizing opposition forces and supporters of human rights for the Iraqi people, while avoiding war as a counter-terrorist instrument.

There are other important avenues open to civil society. Perhaps the most promising is indirect: the continuing demand that global reforms be carried out in such a way as to address the legitimate grievances of peoples situated throughout the countries and regions of the South. Civil society arenas such as the World Social Forum provide opportunities to raise a wide array of concerns, from AIDs in Africa to the terrible plight of the Palestinians. In this regard, the challenge facing global civil society is to promote effective non-military forms of "humanitarian intervention," and to contest the assumption that states are the only actors with the competence and capabilities to intervene on behalf of human wellbeing.

Collaborations between governments and civil society were also a signal achievement of the 1990s, producing some of the most notable steps forward in the direction of humane global governance. Particularly relevant in relation to the present inquiry was the collaborative movement that led to the establishment in 2002 of the first permanent International Criminal Court (ICC) in history, an achievement especially impressive because opposed strenuously by several leading governments. It is now important for civil society actors to make adherence to the ICC as relevant to political legitimacy as acceptance of such principal human rights treaties as the Genocide Convention and the International Covenant on Civil and Political Rights. It could be imagined in the future that systematically holding political leaders responsible for serious violations of crimes of state would greatly weaken moves to engage in humanitarian intervention.

Perhaps the most relevant institutional development would be to provide the United Nations with an emergency reaction force that would be capable of addressing impending humanitarian catastrophes with higher degrees of credibility than depending on states to accept the peacekeeping burden. Although such a force would not circumvent all of the dilemmas associated with humanitarian intervention, it would give the organized international community a valuable tool to deal with the dual dangers of doing too much (Somalia) or too little (Rwanda, Bosnia), both failures reflecting conflicting geopolitical considerations that shaped the response of the U.S. government to crises in the 1990s. In an important respect, the twenty-first-century context makes this insulation of humanitarian intervention from geopolitics even more important than was the case in the 1990s. Without the insulation, and a greater sense of independence from geopolitical manipulation, humanitarian intervention will be seen as little more than an opportunistic rationalization for controversial war-making associated with the war against global terrorism, and may well be completely discredited, especially since the war has already exacted such a high toll of civilian casualties and has failed to deliver on its promises of a democratizing aftermath.

Another complementary approach to reliance on humanitarian intervention was developed by the International Commission on Intervention and State Sovereignty in its report to overcome the problems raised by the Kosovo debate.[23] Partly to avoid the polarization of views by refering to sovereign rights, the Commission adopted the circuitous language of "a responsibility to protect" a population confronted by severe humanitarian dangers. Similarly, to work against the either/or approach taken in relation to Kosovo, the report recommends reliance on "just war" thinking to shape an identification and exercise of responsibility, and proposes a more principled approach in the event that there is an absence of consensus among the permanent members of the Security Council. By affirming that the primary role in discharging the responsibility to protect rests with the Security Council, but acknowledging secondary roles for the General Assembly and regional organizations, and a residual role for coalitions of the willing, the report persuasively balances sensitivity to the sovereignty issue with attentiveness to the needs of endangered peoples faced with ethnic cleansing or genocide. The Commission report can be interpreted both as a conceptual contribution to resolving the humanitarian intervention dilemmas of the 1990s and as a civil society perspective that is credible to most governments because of its composition and the tenor and substance of its proposals and approach. In this sense independent commissions are one way of reshaping global policy by learning some lessons from experience that can clarify the theory and practice of humanitarian intervention. Hopefully, such efforts will encourage debate and action to move beyond sterile rigidities of the past in which both sides often seemed oblivious to the serious concerns and valid objections of their adversary. For instance, with respect to Kosovo, the pro-interventionists seemed insensitive to the risks of creating a precedent for non-defensive uses of force, while the anti-interventionists appeared insensitive to the risks of inaction in the face of impending humanitarian catastrophe. In my view, neither position can be persuasive until it arrives at a recommended policy *after* taking full account of both sides of the debate.

A Concluding Remark

The future of humanitarian intervention is currently under a series of rather dark clouds, but these may eventually pass, and should not be viewed as decisive to an assessment of what lies ahead. At this time, one category of humanitarian issues that should engage international responsibility are given scant attention because they are seen as largely irrelevant to the sort of geopolitical priorities being pursued by the U.S. government. A second category of humanitarian issues are given an artificially inflated status because their presence attempts to add moral weight to anti-terrorist war-making claims that are still being asserted by Washington.

It would be helpful, first of all, for civil society actors to sustain their concern with impending humanitarian catastrophes, seeking as part of their overall support for humane global governance to highlight the need for capabilities and action. In this regard, the humanitarian element in geopolitical controversies can be more objectively balanced and evaluated, and non-military forms of humanitarian intervention from below can be undertaken as appropriate. Médecins sans Frontières has for years been acting on the basis of a responsibility to act that refuses to accord deference to sovereignty rights and geopolitical factors.

There are also important contributions that could be made conceptually and institutionally. It would be useful to erode objections grounded in claims of sovereign rights by stressing an ethos of international responsibility and human solidarity, and by promoting the establishment of capabilities at regional and global levels that would not evoke credible anxieties about the revival of interventionary diplomacy by the North in the countries of the South.

Despite the problematic status of humanitarian intervention on grounds of feasibility and distrust, the idea of "saving strangers" represents part of the growth of a necessary human solidarity in a globalizing world, as well as being an aspect of taking international human rights obligations seriously.[24] It is to be hoped that the institutions and procedures of global governance will find constructive ways to accord a new attentiveness to urgent humanitarian concerns in the greatly altered circumstances of the early twenty-first century.

Part V

Beyond Politics

12

Crimes, Lies, and Law
Human Rights in Adversity

Introductory Remarks

The urgencies of the post-9/11 realities encourage many forms of rethinking, as well as posing largely difficult challenges of personal engagement with the historical moment. I think of "engagement," above all, as a moral/intellectual commitment to bring to the life of the university a sensitive and objective understanding of practices and events, including whatever is topical and controversial.

In this instance citizen engagement includes assessing the tactics, the doctrine, and the policies of our own government, many of which have caused an unprecedented degree of anti-Americanism around the world. These have also managed to shock the conscience of many of us here at home. For useful conversation to ensue this assessment must be done in a manner that encourages dialogue worthy of a more engaged and thoughtful citizenship and favors an approach to the role of teacher/scholar that treats the existence of acute forms of human suffering as central to the very definition of professional identity. In one respect, this posture deliberately challenges the Weberian image of the detached scholar who views knowledge and learning as removed from its social, political, and historical context. Instead, the approach being recommended opts for an interpretation of all phases of academic life in a manner that allows, but does not insist that a good citizen becomes, within her/his sphere of knowing, a public intellectual. Such a posture actively relies on public reason and nonviolent deeds for the promotion of humane politics and stands ready to speak out against the commission of crimes and abuses attributable to governments of sovereign states. Of course, what this implies is an intensely personal process of self-identification that is continuously and reflexively revised. There are surely no generally applicable formulae that prescribe vocational identity as being this rather than that, and surely less public options may be equally valuable if expressive of empathetic values, and somehow exhibiting in everyday encounters a commitment to living well together.

An integral part of such an outlook is to recognize the need for various types of knowing and engagement, imparting these to students as the core expression of academic freedom and responsibility in a democratic society.

This infuses pedagogy and scholarship with the lively awareness that knowledge and study can facilitate constructive participation in the lifeworld. Put more concretely, this means regarding human rights as a pervasive and indispensable dimension of study, whether by those with social science, humanities, natural science, or engineering backgrounds. In posing such questions we are really asking about what we can and should be learning through deliberate cross-fertilization, whether in classrooms or libraries. This outlook is skeptical about those who contend that the deepest academic commitment is to knowledge for the sake of knowledge. I would not rule out such an orientation, but it seems a kind of intellectual luxury that a society in crisis cannot now afford, and likely never could. I am giving the highest priority to those kinds of knowledge that will enhance the individual and collective dimensions of citizenship and enable the pursuit of a humane civic and political life.

As suggested, the immediate context for such a project is a troubled sense of the recent drift of America, especially the behavior of government, as reinforced by a compliant media and a distressing mood of societal complacency. When the general secretary of Amnesty International refers to the notorious prison facility at Guantanamo Bay as "the Gulag of our time" we should all be asking ourselves whether the U.S. government is acting unacceptably in the name of all of us who are citizens. [1] If as citizens we answer this kind of question in the affirmative, then we are challenged to do something to do something to correct the situation. As Jefferson reminded us long ago, "the price of liberty is eternal vigilance."

Of course, it is not just a matter of taking note of harsh detention policies that violate moral and legal norms, but it is a series of related practices associated with such terminologies as "ghost detainees," "extreme rendition," "secret sites," "enhanced interrogation techniques," and "preemptive war." This is language and behavior which, if employed by the adversaries of the United States, would be treated by the American media and public opinion as unmistakable proof of their depravity. The use of such chilling euphemisms reminds us of some of the worst crimes against humanity associated with the "disappearances" that were so much part of the ugly political landscape that existed in Latin America's Southern Cone countries during the latter stages of the Cold War. In these crimes citizens of Latin American countries would typically be seized by state security forces and paramilitary death squads from their homes in the middle of the night or abducted on the sidewalks of a city in broad daylight, never to be seen again. Beyond this, we observe that the United States government, and its supporters, is finding rationalizations for conduct that was previously regarded as unconditionally prohibited and universally condemned. Specious justifications for "torture" have been officially endorsed, or equally disturbing, redescriptions of what would be torture if done to our prisoners has been transformed by Washington bureaucrats and politicians into "legal" modes of interrogation because they are done by us to suspected terrorists.[2] It should always be grounds for suspicion to humane persons whenever a government finds it necessary to exert pressure on other governments to produce formal agreements that would provide soldiers and leaders with immunity from indictment and prosecution by the International Criminal Court (ICC). This is exactly what the United States government has done to ensure that Americans can never be held accountable other than by American tribunals for their international crimes. It should be humiliating for Americans to hear government lawyers argue that the Geneva Convention governing the treatment of prisoners of war is no longer applicable under conditions of the war on terror, or that the UN Charter's prohibition of recourse to non-defensive wars, although applying to other states, no longer constrains international uses of force by the United States.[3] We must ask ourselves at this point whether we can give respect to a government that consistently thumbs its nose at international law and human rights just because it happens to be our government.[4]

This concern with context extends to the constitutional procedures of government, the independence of opposition forces, and the role of the media and the private sector. Courts in this country have been doing horrendous things in the spirit of endorsing presidential claims of unlimited war powers.[5] For instance, in "extraordinary rendition" cases, individuals are secretly detained and transferred to foreign governments known and selected because of their reliance on torture to facilitate interrogation. There have been publicized instances where entirely innocent individuals have been brutalized by mistake, and there are undoubtedly other cases of which nothing is known. When released, these individuals' efforts to receive compensation in civil suits have been shockingly dismissed by American courts because the government insists that its conduct is shielded from any scrutiny whatsoever by the State Secrets Act.[6]

There are many more facets to this troubling portrayal of official lawlessness. Perhaps, the most consequential facet from the perspective of human wellbeing was the manipulation of intelligence and the discouragement of debate in the buildup to the Iraq War.[7] Many Americans (and many more Iraqis) have perished or been wounded in this illegal war, which was not undertaken in good faith, and yet neither the Congress, the opposition party, nor the mainstream media are willing, even now, to censure the president or demand the removal from office of the officials responsible for misleading the public and leading the country into a such a war that has become a quagmire that now seems more entrapping than Vietnam. It is against this background of events and policies that this historically grounded commitment of "engagement" is mounted.

Engaging the Humanities

Ever since I encountered the following sentences initiating an essay written by Theodor Adorno, a German political philosopher of left persuasion, I have been haunted by a sense of my own lack of scholarly seriousness: "The premier demand upon all education is that Auschwitz not happen again. Its priority before any other requirement is such that I believe I need not and should not justify it. . . . To justify it would be monstrous in the face of the monstrosity that took place." [8] In a sense, Adorno's injunction seems at first too strong, and even an overbearing intrusion on intellectual autonomy, yet it certainly encourages a necessary process of reflection that any moral agent should welcome. It reminds me of a comment made in the course of a public lecture by the famous cultural historian, Norman O. Brown: "In psychoanalysis only the exaggerations are valuable."

In thinking further, I began to wonder whether such a highlighting of Auschwitz in this extraordinary way was not one more exhibition of Eurocentrism, inviting a certain moral complacency and even political acquiescence in the rendering of evil over the horizon of the Western collective self. I began to consider whether it would not be as appropriate, or even more appropriate as an ongoing reality, to insist that the primary task of education is to end the ongoing ordeal of the Palestinian people or to challenge Israeli or American claims of non-accountability under international law. Or, perhaps more historically, whether it might not be more useful here in America to begin Adorno's essay with a different sentence: "A primary demand of all education in America is to make sure that Hiroshima does not happen again." Or alternatively, "that the dispossession of the Indians is redressed to the extent possible." Or, "that long overdue amends be made for the many decades of Afro-American slavery." Unhappily, reference to Hiroshima is not just a matter of overcoming historical denial as our leaders have been recently declaring that tactical nuclear weapons remain an option if a military attack is launched in the months ahead against Iran to destroy its alleged nuclear weapons program. In fact, a few years ago, the British Foreign Secretary, Jack Straw, was reportedly sacked by Tony Blair after the White House complained that Straw had responded in public to a question by saying that the talk of using nuclear weapons against Iran was, in his words, "nutty."

I take from Adorno's provocation the challenging idea that education needs, first and foremost, to be guided by a moral compass that is directed at comprehending *past* evil with the purpose of preventing *future* evil. Beyond this, especially for Americans in the early twenty-first century, a further imperative is that the moral compass not be pointed exclusively at the North Star of Eurocentric experiences, which is properly viewed as the Holocaust. After the horrors of Vietnam, the trauma of 9/11, the wars against Afghanistan and Iraq, and the prospect of yet another war, against Iran, being coolly incubated behind closed doors in Washington, it seems crucial also to understand the extent to which American power inflicts suffering, invites resistance, and produces irreconcilable cycles of violent conflict with *others* who stand outside the Eurocentric cosmodrama. Whether or not we invoke the language of "clash" or "dialogue," the moral compass of our educational mission needs to pull out the poisonous roots of Eurocentric violence.[9] This is not meant to be a geographical observation as past crimes against African Americans and native Americans, despite the locus of their occurrence, are equally attributable to a Eurocentric calculus combining racism, greed, and vanity.

A second point of reference relates to the nature of appropriate inquiry. Tu Weiming, a leading Confucian scholar and critic of the Enlightenment project in the West as consisting of the application of calculative or instrumental reason to the qualitative problems of human existence, implicitly calls for a presentation of societal reality by an enlarged conception of reason as including artistic and spiritual reality.[10] Toni Morrison in *Beloved*, Primo Levi in *Survival in Auschwitz*, and Elie Wiesel in *Night* teach us more about the radical evils of racism in America or genocide in Germany than do a thousand texts written to convey, by social scientific methodology or legalistic argument, the statistical magnitude of these primordial assaults on humanity. To comprehend radical evil, immersion in the complexities of the experience transmits the relevant reality far better than does a realistic account written by a sociologist, political scientist, or jurist.

Even the philosophical journalism of Hannah Arendt on the Eichmann trial of 1962 has left more of a mark on our perceptions of Nazi criminality, especially her central observation of "the banality of evil" than have the several dozen scholarly accounts of the Nuremberg tribunal.[11] At the same time, jurists and specialists may be able to present the facts, and efforts at societal redress and recovery, in a manner that supplements, and deepens, fictionalized accounts or imaginative memoirs. Reading the Nuremberg Judgment or the final decision of the Tokyo War Crimes Tribunal is an encounter with facticity that touches the tissue of radical evil, although in a morally flawed, one-sided manner, exempting the crimes of the victors from scrutiny. Arendt's account of the Eichmann trial in Israel deepens our reflective response to this exposure to the Holocaust, leading readers to a series of broader questions that extend beyond the specific policies and events associated with the Nazi experience.

Orhan Pamuk, the fine Turkish Nobel novelist, has recently stressed the importance of truth-telling for a writer whose imaginative powers are enhanced by an atmosphere of unrestricted freedom of expression. But Pamuk also clarifies the difficulty of making the sort of clear political judgments that seem to be a necessary predicate of action. He writes:

> I always have difficulty expressing my political judgments in a clear, emphatic, and strong way—I feel pretentious, as if I'm saying things that are not quite true. This is because I know I cannot reduce my thoughts about life to the music of a single voice and a single point of view—I am, after all, a novelist, the kind of novelist who makes it his business to identify with all of his characters, especially the bad ones. Living as I do in a world where, in a very short time, someone

who has been a victim of tyranny and oppression can suddenly become one of the oppressors, I know that holding strong beliefs is itself a difficult enterprise. I also believe that most of us entertain these contradictory thoughts simultaneously, in a spirit of good will and with the best of intentions.[12]

Pamuk is here suggesting the tensions that may exist in some situations between artistic understanding and political action.

In his widely read novel, *Snow*, Pamuk explores the contradictory character of the appeal of Islam to young people in the provincial Turkish city of Kars.[13] I found the novel illuminating because it related Islam so convincingly to the circumstances of contemporary Turkey, especially to the continuing and mystifyingly profound struggle over whether women should be allowed to wear headscarves in Turkish public places, including state institutions of learning. Pamuk's novel helps an outsider understand why this seemingly foolish effort to ban headscarves is such a preoccupation for secular Turks, who identify modernity and their own freedoms with Kemal Ataturk's conception of the state and of modernity. The novel also shows that beneath such a symbolic expression of religious devoutness are a variety of seemingly contradictory intensities and hypocrisies associated with sexuality, jealousy, and temperament.

For Turks critical of Pamuk, of whom there are many, some consider him all along to have been a mediocre writer who has gained international fame by pandering to foreign audiences; for them, *Snow* was an occasion for particularly harsh criticism. Many Turks blamed Pamuk for abandoning his usual themes and dismissed the book as superficial and sensationalist, driven by commercial motivations. In August 2006 I recall sitting at dinner in Istanbul next to an American diplomat who was a specialist on Turkish literature, but highly secularist in his views. This man, then more than slightly intoxicated, lamented Pamuk's turn toward politics, dogmatically suggesting that Pamuk was a great writer so long as he confined his literary persona to being a fictionalizing biographer of the city of Istanbul. Supposedly, as soon as he departed from this seminal experience that had so authentically shaped his coming of age and worldview, he was out of his depth. Pamuk should be persuaded to agree upon a vow of future silence.

It is highly relevant that this diplomat did not like the ambivalence of *Snow* in relation to the status of Islam. He was an unreflective secularist of the Kemalist variety who despised the political turn in Turkey toward what they believed to be a more receptive and constructive of view of Islamic influence in Turkish national politics. This belief is itself misleading. What is being challenged is not secularism as an orientation toward governance in Turkey, but certain policies that have been engrafted upon secularism, and impose starkly discriminatory restrictions on the opportunities open to religiously observant Islamic Turkish women. It this confusion between secularism and discrimination that explains the sound and fury surrounding the headscarf issue.

Anti-headscarf militants in Turkey ardently seek a return, by a military coup if necessary, to an Ankara government run by old school secularists who adhere slavishly to an outdated version of the worldview of Kemal Ataturk. They invoke Ataturk to justify this pattern of discrimination. Ataturk still remains, after seven decades, the revered iconic founder and is treated by the Turkish armed forces as the sole guardian of a legitimate Turkish state. Old secularism insists on a version of modernity that rejected any visibility for female Muslim believers in spaces that are officially supported by the state. Such believers are supposed to stay out of such spaces, despite the denial of educational and professional opportunities available to all other Turkish citizens, including religiously observant Muslim men.

The former American diplomat mentioned earlier, who had served in Turkey under the leadership of the old secularists and continued to visit the country regularly, blended his literary tastes with some highly partisan political assessments. He objected to Pamuk, not so much because he chose to write on a political theme, but because his treatment of Islam expressed its profound appeal for Turkish youth. This religious possibility was presented by Pamuk in *Snow* as such a complex and contradictory reality that it undermined the moral clarity of either embracing or repudiating of Islam, or for that matter, the alternative Kemalist creed. The motives of all sides in the headscarf debate were probed by Pamuk, and subject to a critical presentation in a non-judgmental way through the characters and their stories. This texture of complexity posed a deliberate challenge to the banalities of the journalistic debate as it plays out in the daily Turkish press. Discussing such a book in a university course in Turkey would, I believe, if conducted in a free atmosphere, allow students to gain a sophisticated appreciation of what is at stake in the headscarf debate, and might also leave them creatively confused, possibly at odds with their parents, about what should be done at the level of policy. It would also separate issues associated with discrimination from those associated with contested conceptions of secularism.

Writers can also abandon art for politics, given the seriousness of the issues posed due either to their historic immediacy or their seeming urgency. Arundhati Roy is the author of the wonderful novel, *The God of Small Things*, which memorably addresses the human condition as it presents itself in South India.[14] In the novel Roy vividly describes the tensions that can arise when caste differences become mingled with romantic involvements. But in recent years Roy has treated politics as posing such deep challenges to her own humanity that she has temporarily abandoned fiction to become a leading global and national voice in struggles against injustice. She has sided with environmentalists and human rights activists in the long effort to prevent the Indian government from proceeding with the huge Narmada Dam Project. She has published books of essays, and collections of her public speeches, such as *War Talk*.[15] A year ago I had the pleasure of taking part with her in the World Tribunal on Iraq held in Istanbul. In her final statement at the WTI, delivered to a large audience including many media representatives, she addressed this issue of the writer as engaged:

> Yesterday, when they were making a film, they asked me, "Why did you agree? You must have so many invitations; why did you choose this one?" And I said, "You know, I feel so hurt that you are asking me this question. Because it is ours. Where else could I be? What other invitations would matter to me when we have to attend to this, this huge, enormous bloody thing?" . . . To ask us why are we doing this, why is there a World Tribunal on Iraq, is like asking someone who stops at the site of an accident where people are dying on the road: Why did you stop? Why didn't you keep walking like everybody else?[16]

With these words, Arundhati Roy is insisting on the clarity of radical evil, and the urgency of its demands on our time and energy. In contrast to Pamuk, she is refusing, at least for the historical moment, to be drawn into the murky domain of complexity and contradictory reality. In a fundamental sense there is no need to choose between these responses, nor for that matter that of the experts in international law who presented their arguments relating to issues of legality and legitimacy. Roy may not be interested in these matters, but many ordinary citizens want to know why such a tribunal was formed and what weight should be given to its legal assessments of the Iraq War and its perpetrators.

It is my position that within academic settings we can learn a great deal about both human rights and the humanities by exposing ourselves to differences of interpretation by leading intellectual figures. Let me mention one particularly prominent instance. Two of the leading French intellectuals of the period after the World War II were Jean-Paul Sartre and Albert Camus, both of whom had worked together in the French resistance to the Nazi occupation of France. These two cultural titans of the post-World War II period disagreed sharply and publicly on how to respond to the Algerian War of Independence that was being fought against colonial rule between 1954 and 1962. Sartre believed that history and morality sided with the anti-colonial movement, and he was prepared to overlook the moral complexities associated with a revolutionary struggle that resorted to attacks on innocent civilians, what we have since learned to call terrorist tactics. Camus, in contrast, who had been born poor in Algeria, remained aloof from the struggle, explaining that there was immorality on both sides, and no way to choose.[17] I have over-simplified the debate, but I think without distorting the essential dilemma: action is necessary to oppose embedded forms of political evil, but if the opposition to evil itself relies on immoral means does that invalidate the struggle? Rarely does the purity of the Gandhian option exists where one side foregoes violence, and yet finds the leverage, courage, and perseverance to prevail. These dilemmas are themselves explored best in literature, yielding no easy answers and often confronting us as citizens with tragic predicaments. There are really two kinds of challenges: that of radical evil of the sort confronted by such writers as Toni Morrison and Elie Wiesel, who seek to convey the existential horrors of racism and genocide, and the existential confusion that exists when complexity and contradictory elements make any recourse to direct action appear problematic, addressed by authors such as Orhan Pamuk and Albert Camus.

Human Rights and the Humanities After 9/11

Whether the 9/11 attacks should be viewed as transformative events remains unresolved both historically and in the American public mind. Surely, given more than seven years of response to the attacks, there are elements of the response that are deeply problematic from the perspective of human rights, and would certainly benefit from imaginative recreation by humanistic sensibilities. Images of radical evil have been globally disseminated in the course of unleashing the war on terror, and have damaged American claims to global leadership, perhaps irrevocably when coupled with such other discrediting developments as are associated with governmental failure after Hurricane Katrina, the falling dollar and rising deficit, and the steadfast embrace of Israeli militarism. But there are also some fundamental issues that do not yield one-sided answers, and are associated with acknowledging the ambiguity embedded in the still ill-defined conflict that has constituted the global war on terror. Two texts have been extremely helpful to me in clarifying the basic post-9/11 situation: a novel by Ian McEwan entitled *Saturday* and a book of academic commentary and analysis written by David Runciman and published not long ago under the title *The Politics of Good Intentions*.[18] Both are preoccupied with the words opening Runciman's book: "Did September 11, 2001, really change the world?" and both respond, yes and no.[19] McEwan emphasizes the yes part of a response, but subtly and hesitantly, and Runciman, with a lively sense of history and circumstance, highlights the no part of an answer to his defining question. I share Runciman's view that "September 11 simply provided George W. Bush and his administration with a convenient prop on which to hang a set of military and ideological objectives that had been identified well in advance." [20] He goes on to show that the question of what changed on 9/11 is best left alone at present, possibly resolved in the future by scholarly interpretation. It does seem clear that the spin given by political leaders in Britain and the United States generated credible mobilizing short-term justifications for initiating non-defensive, dubious wars. These justifications pointed to the gravity of allegedly new constellations of risk, which needed to be addressed preventively if security was to be restored in the post-9/11 world. Runciman points out how Dick Cheney in the 2004 presidential campaign poured scorn on Bush's challenger, John Kerry, by saying: "Even in this post-9/11 period Senator Kerry doesn't appear to understand how the world has changed." [21] The book goes on to explore these issues from the perspective of Tony Blair's efforts to explain why Britain has been correct to support the Bush approach rather than align with skeptical continental Europe, or even with its own public opinion.

Ian McEwan approaches the post-9/11 reality from the perspective of the morally sensitive and socially decent ordinary citizen, a successful London neurosurgeon. The novel takes place all on a single day, February 15, 2003, on which there was a major peace demonstration in London as part of a worldwide expression of opposition to the impending Iraq War. The main character in the novel, Henry Perowne, decides to carry on with his normal schedule, shopping for dinner, playing his regular Saturday squash game against a brash and rabidly pro-war American, and avoiding the crowds gathering around the city for the demonstration. One of the high points during the day is an encounter with his daughter, Daisy, home from college, and strongly against the Iraq War. An excerpt from their conversation:

"Guess where I went on my way from the station," she says.

"Um, Hyde Park?"

"You knew! Daddy, why weren't you there? It was simply amazing."

"I don't know. Playing squash, visiting Granny, cooking the dinner, lack of certainty. That sort of thing."

"But it's completely barbaric, what they're about to do. Everyone knows that."

"It might be. So might doing nothing. I honestly don't know. Tell me how it was in the park."

"I know that if you'd been there you wouldn't have any doubts." [22]

They go on to have a far longer discussion in which Henry repeats his doubts, and Daisy becomes more and more upset with his ethos of indecision. In frustration Henry says "[i]t's all about outcomes, and no one knows what they'll be. That's why I can't imagine marching in the streets." [23] Later on Henry adds, "I am not for any war. But this one could be the lesser evil. In five years we'll know." The conversation deteriorates, "moving out of control," as Daisy prophetically alleges that her father's views on Iraq will eventually bring bombs to London, blurting out, "And when the first explosion hits London your pro-war views ... " at which Henry interrupts, saying, "[I]f you're describing my position as pro-war, then you'd have to accept yours is effectively pro-Saddam," to which Daisy responds robustly, "[W]hat fucking nonsense." [24] The conversation goes on inconclusively for several more pages, pitting the political clarity of a young activist against the worried ambivalence of a sophisticated adult who sees all sides of the argument. I believe such an exposure to the issues at stake in McEwan's novel leads to a far deeper understanding of the pre-war Iraq debate than the kind of pro-war hype that was the standard fare of the American media in the months before the invasion of Iraq, or even the more perceptive anti-war polemic. If *Saturday* is read together with Runciman's effort to discuss the originality of the situation confronting leaders after 9/11, a rather impressive overview emerges. It helps us gain perspective, acknowledging the continuities between 9/11 and earlier encounters with political violence and uncertainties, as well as taking note of the spectacular discontinuities. It is only on the basis of gaining as informed an understanding as possible that we can even hope for a serious engagement with the responsibilities of citizenship by a significant fraction of American people.

Concluding Words

I think that the relationship between education and the responsibilities of citizenship is what makes it so desirable to consider this subject-matter of human rights from a variety of angles, including especially those provided by ways of knowing associated with the humanities. It is also a matter of nurturing creative forms of cross-fertilization in search of a more satisfying and responsive pedagogy. Surely, standard one-dimensional social science benefits from some integration with the sort of multi-dimensionality that is of the essence in quality film, fiction, photo-journalism, and fine art. Of course, artistic forms of representation can often be illuminated by a knowledgeable awareness of historical, political, economic, and social context. Beyond this mastery of the circumstances, certain ethical imperatives exist: to take human suffering seriously and to comprehend to the extent possible the nature and presence of radical evil. No one questions that medical research should be biased toward improving the health of the human body, and nobody should doubt that these days the validity of teaching and scholarship that is dedicated to improving the health of the body politic.

13

Humanity in Question

Humanity as a principal organizing idea in political and ethical discourse is being used as a polemical tool, as a descriptive category, and as the embodiment in social reality of essential ethical and spiritual ideals. Ambiguity and confusion results from this multiple usage, which limits the potential contributions of the idea of humanity to what I have called "moral globalization." This chapter depicts this use and abuse of humanity, so as to clarify the situation and make the case for reserving humanity as a term designating both biological inclusivity of all persons and moral expectations of treatment of humans in accordance with international law and human rights. It considers three aspects of the current discourse on humanity: the distinctively current problems of clarifying the boundaries of humanity biologically and politically; the efforts of international law to provide a normative infrastructure that confers rights and imposes duties on all human beings; the more ambitious undertaking of establishing an aspirational future for political communities based on realizing the ethical potentialities of individuals and groups throughout the world, a dynamic associated with moral globalization.

This theme of moral globalization is based on an acceptance of the degree to which networking, information technology, organizational capacity, media arrangements, trade, investment, financial markets are assuming an increasingly global character, giving the epoch a generally reliable, if amorphous, designation of "globalization." Above all, this designation implies the compression of time, space, imagination, but also the search for niches of particularity. Often overlooked in depicting globalization are its normative dimensions associated with law, religion, ethics. The late twentieth century was notable for establishing the rudiments of a normative global architecture that was moving in the direction of an enforceable system of global law animating by a universally affirmed concept of global justice.[1] The argument set forth here is that moral globalization is a vital element in the response to a deepening crisis of global governance, and that a biological and normative framing of moral globalization by reference to humanity is integral to fashioning a coherent and widely acceptable response.

Frayed Boundaries Amid a Crisis of Global Governance

There is a seemingly bright line encompassing humanity that arises from the distinctness of the human species, a bio-constructed boundary that is not socially constructed. There existed in pre-modern Europe, in particular, an even brighter line separating humans from God, a boundary certified by belief, reason, and metaphysical contemplation. Secularism, from its inception, threatened this most fundamental of socially constructed boundaries, a threat most theatrically articulated by Nietzsche's startling cry: "God is dead!" Of course, not quite. The religious resurgence around the world demonstrates that a renewed longing for God formidably challenges the power of reason and science even in the citadels of modernity.[2]

This biological enclosure of the human is fraying at the edges as clandestine efforts to clone humans go forward, as super-robots seem able to learn, repair themselves, and even "feel emotion," and as genetic engineering and postmodern medicine exhibit an increasing capacity to implant vital organs and complex body parts.[3] The normative significance of humanity as "a humane species" is also being continually challenged by despicable crimes of depraved minds, as well as by recurrent displays of genocidal fury released and manipulated by group hatreds and fears, by extremist violence against civilian society, and by extremist state violence directed at suspected enemies. There is also the issue of cruelty to animals, and whether the radical separation of humans from other forms of life, does not give a mandate in the name of humanity to kill and torture non-humans, raising questions about the normative acceptability of humanity as a defining ethical boundary. This fraying of boundaries draws into particular question the modern sense of what it means to be human. This contemporary loss of clarity with respect to boundaries raises in profound ways the question as to whether it is useful to interpret behavior from a new standpoint, a postmodern standpoint, even contemplating the bizarre notion of the "post-human."

Modernity as a political phase of human evolution was, and still is, preoccupied with boundaries, particularly those of spatial communities that can successfully claim to be sovereign states. It is states, and only states, that can fully and formally represent "peoples," at the global level, for instance, within the United Nations. A defining characteristic of a fully legitimate state is well defined and administered boundaries, not vague frontier areas. Size and density of population are irrelevant from this legalistic perspective: Liechtenstein and China are diplomatically fully equal. This state-centric modernity, came into being in the mid-seventeenth century, conveniently associated with the Peace of Westphalia (1648) and became universally realized only in the late twentieth century, when colonialism fell and independent states covered the entire world. Statism remains the chief organizing principle of world society, at least at diplomatic levels of interaction. States, as Hobbes understood so well, needed to find a justification for the loyalty of their citizens that could provide the kind of coherence that had been earlier provided by religious unity, and it was found in nationalism, possibly the most lethal creed ever invented by humans. Statism was in part a remedy for the perceived growing dysfunction growing out of friction among antagonistic religious forces as exhibited in bloody, interminable religious wars, as well as a search for larger-scale economic units to support the rising of commerce and industry.[4]

But a statist world delivered a double-coded message with respect to humanity as the core reality. It freed peoples to some extent from what might be called metaphysical oppression as manipulated by institutionalized religion, challenging the absolutist claims of authority made by official exponents of religious truth, thereby opening the way for science, technology, material progress, and pluralism of all varieties. But at the same time, the state as the outer limit of nationalist identity and as the highest source of political authority, decisively weakened the case for *human* solidarity. The pursuit of national interest in the name of "realism" became the highest expression of ethical commitment in the external affairs of states. In such a political system war has always resisted efforts to regulate its character, remaining a robust reality, and despite its seemingly growing dysfunctionality, a discretionary political option.[5] To this day, international law and foreign economic assistance have been unable to ensure either world peace or an end to poverty. At most, such efforts to regulate and help the economically disadvantaged are mainly selfishly justified by reference to the national interest in a stable and peaceful world. In political thought, altruistic and humanitarian impulses are given status as forming a part of a "thin morality" that is contrasted with the "thick morality" of a nationalist or communitarian character.[6] Cosmopolitan and species identifications are marginalized in modernity, derided as vague, vacant, abstract, and utopian. The mainstream of serious thought argues that taking seriously justice, or even survival, claims on behalf of human community is at best a harmless pastime that ignores the entrenched statist limits of political community, and at worst a dangerous fiction that has driven political movements to totalitarian excess in the last century.[7]

Beyond this, the state provided enclaves for the commission of atrocities against those resident *within* borders of sovereign states.[8] The ideology of territorial sovereignty gave governments almost unlimited authority to inflict suffering on vulnerable or subordinate segments of their own populations. The peak exposure of this failing of the state system from the perspective of "humanity" was associated with the Nazi experience, culminating in the Holocaust. Even the liberal democracies watched and appeased so long as Hitler's wrongdoing was *internal* to Germany. The United Nations (UN) Charter carried forward this deference to the state by declaring in Article 2(7) that the UN shall not intervene in matters "essentially within the domestic jurisdiction of any state," and this was understood to include the way a government treats its own citizenry. Along similar lines, the Universal Declaration of Human Rights, which set minimum standards of behavior designed to protect all persons, was adopted in the form of a non-binding "declaration" and even then was approved by the majority of governments only because it was clear that there was no intention to implement the norms set forth. It remains true that the protection of human rights, if it occurs at all, is subject to the vagaries of geopolitics, that is, to the sympathies and antipathies, of dominant states.

In some sense, this fragmenting of humanity as an essential feature of modernity exhibits the extraordinary hold of statist and nationalist consciousness on the human imagination. Especially with the advent of nuclear weaponry, the spectral character of war in the shadow cast forward by the Hiroshima bomb, it is remarkable that a biologically grounded sense of human survival did not arise to challenge the precarious geopolitics of the Cold War era. Reliance on "deterrence" as a survival mode was a risky and contrived effort to reconcile the absolute claims of survival on behalf of particular states with the overall survival of the species and advanced civilization. Any review of the period between 1950 and 1990 discloses that political life existed at the edge of catastrophe. The fact that catastrophe was somehow averted was of course a blessing, but at the cost of suppressing the risks associated with such a form of security. Such risks result from the faulty reasoning that the avoidance of World War III demonstrated the reliability of a state-based system of security that entrusted the future of humanity to the prudence and wisdom of the leaders of the dominant state or states. Since the end of the Cold War there have been various moves to shift attention to what has been named "human security," but with less emphasis on human solidarity than on the importance of thinking about people rather than governments, and thus about issues associated with "insecurity" in daily life coming from lawlessness or various forms of deprivation.

Rooting this inquiry in immediate circumstances, the idea of humanity is dramatically repressed, and evaded, in the global strategic conflict unleashed by the 9/11 attacks on the United States. To begin with, both sides operate outside the political constraints of modernity, as neither can be considered a "state" in the normal sense, and thus their "war" is a war waged between non-state actors on a battlefield that potentially embraces the entire planet.[9] It is obvious why Al Qaeda is not a state, but rather is some sort of covert transnational network of loosely linked organizations and groupings. The United States is not a normal state either. It maintains more than 700 military facilities in foreign countries, navies in every ocean, and it is seeking to control the militarization of space. The U.S. government claims the right to act anywhere it can find its enemies, and insists that those states that do not join in its "war on terror" will be viewed as opponents, if not enemies. Beyond this, both sides make explicit their view of the adversary as "evil," without human entitlement. This is not surprising for religious extremists, but it is somewhat unexpected for a constitutional democracy that lauds human rights. President Bush, in defining the struggle, has repeatedly called the enemy "evil," and the notorious policies used to deal with Al Qaeda suspects are a manifestation of the view that such individuals do not deserve to have their human dignity respected.[10] As soon as the other is categorized as evil in the setting of violent encounter, especially if the two sides have unequal access to the technology of war, actions such as beheadings or torture can be expected, although legally and morally unacceptable, and will even be defended by their proponents as "necessary" security measures.[11]

From a modernist perspective, the war is borderless, that is, its global scope ignores borders. For a moralizing perspective, invoking humanity as representing our side in the conflict, the war is premised on a distinction between good and evil that excludes "the other" from humanity. Bush, in a major speech devoted to "victory in Iraq," adopted such a self-serving dichotomy by declaring: "the terrorists have made it clear that Iraq is the central front in their war against humanity, and so we must recognize Iraq as the central front in the war on terror."[12] In effect, the adversaries of the United States in Iraq do not belong to "humanity," but rather are to be understood as non-human, as they belong to various barbaric grouping identified only by reference to their adherence to "terror."[13] Such self-justifying rhetoric helps us to understand why those defending humanity can engage in "torture" without evident moral compunction, especially when the frustrations and boundary-lessness of the struggle make "victory" itself depend upon a kind of grotesque fiction: the elimination of all non-state political violence everywhere— what is labeled as "terrorism" by Washington, but in actuality encompasses struggles against oppressive rule, resistance against illegal occupation, and the overcoming of blocked claims of self-determination. To identify all those who resist the American occupation in Iraq—itself widely regarded as illegal and associated with tactics of state terrorism—as associated with terror is to convert the word into a self-justifying figure of speech best regarded as a form of hostile propaganda. At the same time, the implication of Bush's rhetoric is to reflect the view that the term "humanity" embodies positive values, and thus is an ethical ideal rather than a biological marker ("terrorists" being excluded).

But there is another way to look at the American governmental response to 9/11, especially in light of the Iraq War. This second way views the turmoil as less an expression of an anti-terrorist "war" than as an American project to solve the crisis of global governance by providing (or imposing) a system of security for the planet as a whole. This idea of sustaining American geopolitical preeminence infuses the neoconservative blueprint, *Repairing America's Defenses*, prepared and issued well before the 9/11 attacks, and even prior to George W. Bush assuming the presidency in 2001.[14] Given this interpretation, the Iraq War should not be understood as part of an anti-terrorist campaign, but is primarily associated with an effort to restructure world order in light of postmodern challenges and opportunities that can be best understood by reference to the complex and contradictory realities of globalization. Because

Al Qaeda and its supporters define their struggle as resisting American encroachment, the two realities merge, and Iraq has become a meeting ground for these two "global" enemies. The unprecedented degree, and the global scope, of American military dominance represents a mainly undetected convergence of geopolitics and globalization in a new configuration of world order that is widely viewed by critics and apologists alike as a postmodern type of empire.[15] As such, it represents an imperial response to the crisis of global governance, resting its authority on the capacity to impose its will by means of force. In the terminology adopted here it is also a postmodern response because it subordinates "states" and centralizes control under the administration of a "world state" that acknowledges no limits upon the exercise of its jurisdiction. The historical moment gives little encouragement to such an imperial project as offering a solution of the crisis of global governance. Despite the huge American investment in military superiority, the inability to succeed in Iraq or Afghanistan at tolerable costs emphasizes the non-viability of a global empire as a sequel to the Westphalian multipolar framework of states that relied upon war, geopolitical management by leading states, and countervailing power to sustain order and allow for change. Even without this failure of viability, the imperial solution is morally unacceptable as it denies the normative postulates implied by the designation of the peoples of the world as belonging to a shared humanity.

The current situation is complex and perplexing: a crisis of global governance exists; the Westphalian structures of world order, while resilient and persistent, are being superseded by the dynamics of globalization, including the rise of non-state actors and transnational networks; technologies of mass destruction are gradually spreading, and may be possessed by or fall into the hands of extremist and suicidal non-state actors, as well as dangerous state actors; technological frontiers are stretching the limits of the human but also consolidating a shared sense of species destiny; energy resources are exhibiting signs of dangerous scarcity; a second cycle of ecological urgency is present as a result of climate change, extreme weather conditions, and essentially unregulated pollution of the global commons; and imperial solutions for the crisis seem to be failing and would in any event be ethically unacceptable and politically illegitimate. Humanity as ethical and spiritual ideal, and as invaluable biological species, seems dangerously vulnerable, and at the same time, seems to lack a mobilizing capacity of the sort required to resolve the crisis of global governance in accordance with the precepts of moral globalization.

The Evolution and Relevance of International Law:
The State versus Humanity

International law accompanied the rise of the state and the state system as the foundation of world order. It had from the outset a normative element, reflecting both the religious antecedents of medieval Europe in its incorporation of "just war" thinking and the reaction of Grotius and others to the horrors of the religious wars, regarded as "barbaric," which led over time to the formulation of legal limits on the conduct of hostilities in wartime.[16] In a sense, humanity as an implicit normative marker exerted an influence over the centuries on how international law was understood, but it was by no means the main perception.

More influential was the dismissal by Kant of the great jurists of his time as "miserable consolers" because of their tendency to provide rationalizations for the war-making of states, however lamentable from a humanistic perspective. In this regard, international law was neither better nor worse than the states that constituted Westphalian world order. As noted, such statism exempted domestic abuse of individuals and groups from legal scrutiny, deferring to territorial sovereignty. International law served also dominant state interests, especially in relations with non-Western and subordinate societies. It gave a color of legality to colonial regimes, and provided strong states with a legal rationale for intervention in weak states, including for the enforcement of property and investment claims. In these regards, the geopolitical roles of international law overshadowed its ethical features, at least until the twentieth century.

At the same time, the pretensions of international law to provide a normative order that would constrain states within agreed limits contains within its outlook the foundations of a genuine "global law" that reflects the normative hopes of all peoples for dignity and decency. These hopes were articulated in a series of moves that adopted a discourse of "humanity." It is significant that when international law reaches beyond its Westphalian role of servicing sovereign states, it relies on this terminology. The legal rules imposing legal limits on the conduct of war are known as "international *humanitarian* law."[17] At Nuremberg, the most innovative jurisprudential step was to depict certain patterns of behavior by a government against its own people as "crimes against humanity," criminalizing thereby the worse excesses of governments against persons subject to their territorial sovereignty. This poses a fundamental challenge to the idea that states are not externally accountable for what is done internally. By criminalizing such behavior, not only is the state accountable, but those who act on its behalf, including leaders, are held individually responsible. Procedurally, also, this repudiates the notion that leaders enjoy "immunity" from criminal prosecution because of their official positions.

After World War II, these trends were further reinforced in the UN Charter and by the adoption of the Universal Declaration of Human Rights along with subsequent legal instruments. Many states cynically endorsed these ambitious normative texts because there was no perceived prospect of international enforcement. But in the decades that followed, civil society initiatives converged with some global trends to lend political weight to human rights, most prominently perhaps in the struggles against oppressive regimes in East Europe during the 1980s and in the anti-apartheid movement. NGOs became, in many respects, pressure groups acting on behalf of humanity, although their priorities and understanding of what constituted "*human rights*" reflected their specific social and geographic locations and funding sources. The important point here is that the human rights movement expressed claims that were based on the identity of "human," and not based on some fragmentary sense of privileged or denigrated identity associated with religion, race, nation.

Moving further in the same direction are ideas associated with "humanitarian intervention" and "the responsibility to protect," which impose on organized international society a duty to respond in the face of humanitarian emergency. The guiding notion here is that failures to protect the human are of extra-territorial concern, overriding notions of sovereignty. The Kosovo War of 1999 was a controversial example, involving an intervention under NATO auspices that was plausibly needed to avoid a repetition of ethnic cleansing that had occurred in Bosnia in 1995 but was not authorized by the UN Security Council.[18] It is understandable that claims of humanitarian intervention are viewed with extreme suspicion in many parts of the world, especially by non-Western societies, as a means to revive Western domination under a different banner, thereby denying weaker states the fruits of political independence.[19] The genuine defense of humanity is thus challenged by realist geopolitics that does not act coercively except in the pursuit of strategic interests, and by necessity exempts powerful and large states from threats of humanitarian intervention.[20] Arguably, Kosovo represented a convergence of a genuine humanitarian emergency with geopolitical goals associated with sustaining NATO in the aftermath of the Cold War and achieving stability in the Balkans. But acting on this basis, although appearing to spare the Albanian Kosovars in a genuine circumstance of imminent danger, did set a precedent for acting coercively outside the UN that was invoked by some of those who favored regime change in Iraq by recourse to war. Bringing humanity to bear on global policy is a tricky matter and is inevitably intertwined with geopolitical ambitions, including those of inaction, as well as contradicting in some instances the prohibition on recourse to war in circumstances other than self-defense and without a Security Council mandate.[21] The normative tension between upholding human rights in circumstances of extreme abuse collides with the struggle to prohibit reliance on war as a discretionary means for projecting power by sovereign states.

The Normative Alternative: Advancing Moral Globalization

And yet, despite these many problematic aspects, the idea of humanity plays a crucial role, perhaps more than ever, in articulating aspirational goals, encouraging the formulation of what the philosopher John Rawls called "realistic utopias," what could be reasonably hoped for with respect to societal arrangements, and hence what it is worth trying to achieve. In his *The Law of Peoples* Rawls gives a rational foundation for insisting that all peoples should be treated on the basis of their inherent dignity as specified by eight principles, which he identifies as "familiar and traditional principles of justice among free and democratic peoples."[22] But more than aspiration is at stake. For an ethically acceptable solution to the crisis of global governance depicted above, a sense of human solidarity *of global scope*, with allowance for plural identities, is indispensable.[23] Putting realistic alternatives on the horizon by reference to humanity rather than to nation-states carries the quest for moral globalization into a new domain of post-Westphalian realities. The alternative to finding a solution for global governance is either perpetual conflict as initiated by the American response to 9/11 or an entropic slide into chaos and ecological unsustainability that assuredly will produce human catastrophes of colossal magnitude never before experienced, and heightened in their impact by the technological possibilities of real-time awareness.

Affirming humanity as a valuable collective source of identity does not necessarily imply a negation of difference and otherness. It is possible to think as a communitarian, to believe that being "human" implies particularities as well as shared qualities, that is, privileging such non-species identities as those of place, nation, religion, gender, race, age. Radical communitarians are dismissive of claims of an overarching "humanity" as a bloodless abstraction that fails to induce existential bonding, and does not create affinities, but often the reverse. Solidarity is not even affirmed as a goal as a sense of "the other" is allegedly required to build a strong sense of self-esteem for the individual and collective "self."[24] At most, communitarians can join with Michael Walzer, affirming a "thin" sense of loyalty to the species, contrasting with the "thick" loyalty to country and community. This minimal acceptance of a strictly human dimension is insufficient to overcome the detrimental effects of political and psychological fragmentation and antagonism. The challenges of global governance require a stronger shared base of commonality and solidarity to enable the formation of global democratic procedures and structures.[25] In effect, it will be necessary that sentiments of solidarity create a vibrant *human* identity that supports strong institutions and networks of cooperative endeavor, but certainly not of an exclusivist or homogenizing nature that repudiate other identities. In many respects the best model for human identity that now exists is that of European regional identity, which is itself presently struggling with an exclusivist backlash, hidden beneath the ethnic and psycho-political fictions of national unity. The French riots of 2005 dramatized the extent to which the marginalized minorities from Islamic North Africa felt the whiplash of a dominating French nationalism, which itself is reacting against the ethnic pluralism of a European regional identity. Whether such anti-immigrant moods are part of post-Westphalian growing pains or represent a dysfunctional refusal to abandon the hyper-nationalism of Westphalian order as embodied in the European experience remains to be seen.[26]

In this era of globalization, regional and global levels of interaction are reshaping the global setting for political action. It is not enough for realistic utopias to aim at the attainment of Westphalian communities that adhere to global normative architecture embedded in international human rights law, as amplified by the UN Charter and international law generally. The Westphalian paradigm can fulfill the imaginative quest for moral statism, but we are living in a post-Westphalian phase of world history that also needs the horizons set by humanity if it is to contribute to a benevolent solution of the crisis of global governance. Regional sequels to Westphalia, most notably the European experiment lauded by some commentators as a partial solution, also depend on an operative orientation based on humanity to sustain a balance between persistent Westphalian and even pre-Westphalian identities and the civilizational hybridity that is accompanying an emergent globalization. Bringing humanity to bear on the political imagination in this historical phase is what is meant by moral globalization, and without such a normative bonding, the socio-economic claims of the disadvantaged and enclaves of mass suffering will not be addressed in a serious manner. Again, the French riots and the exposure of racially grounded class deprivations in the wake of Hurricane Katrina remind us that Westphalian solutions in stable, prosperous, and democratic states remain morally deficient, and are far from achieving or even aspiring to achieve realistic utopias in the Rawlsian spirit. Taking humanity as our compass provides a navigational tool needed if our species is to have any hope of yet negotiating a safe and satisfying journey through the treacherous waters of globalization.

14

The Ideal of the Citizen Pilgrim

Chapter 11 of St. Paul's Letter to the Hebrews has inspired me to reconsider what it meant or should mean to be a citizen, especially 11:10–11;16. In that passage Paul describes how faith in that which has been promised, but not yet attained or tangibly seen, guides the life of the pilgrim. Paul expresses the essential spiritual identity of such a pilgrim: "They all died in faith, not having received the promises, but having seen them afar off, and were persuaded of them, and embraced them, and confessed that they were strangers on the earth." This sense of being alien to what is, thirsting for what might be, embodies the yearning of the pilgrim. In Pauline language: "they seek a country," but not a return to "that country from whence they came out." No, "now they desire a better country, a heavenly one." Faith can be understood as the belief in the reality of that which cannot yet be experienced or demonstrated, but can be, and so must be. Faith merges with hope for that better country, embodying a spiritual understanding of human destiny as potentially transcendent in relation to presently surrounding circumstances.

The image of pilgrim/stranger is rendered in some of the widely used translations of the Bible as sojourner and wanderer. The words chosen, however variable, share an impulse to render meanings that convey a sense of journeying away from disappointments with present realities, and toward a satisfying and fulfilling future. The citizen pilgrim combines a discontent with the world as s/he finds it with a dedication to an often demanding and generally solitary and hazardous journey to the future. The difficulty associated with the seeming enormity of the challenge must unsettle, however quietly, widely prevalent and conventional contentment expressed by those false, yet reassuring, voices that dominate the public imagination of most modern societies.

The understanding of citizenship at this historical moment, particularly here in America, gives this concern a special poignancy. Since 9/11, we in this country have mainly reverted to a tribalist sense of the good citizen as the obedient patriot, mindless supporters of nationalized truth, which has allowed our elected leaders to enact their program of continuous warfare at great cost to ourselves, damage to the authority of international law and the United

Nations, and devastating consequences for all those who are in the way of the military juggernaut. Furthermore, by diverting our attention from the ticking bombs of climate change and energy scarcities, we are irresponsibly putting our own future and that of all humanity under a darkening cloud of risk and an almost preordained and heightened prospect of collective calamity.

Of course, there are other ideas associated with citizenship that complicate any attempt to put forward a preferred conception. There are several varieties of "world citizen," individuals who idealistically and sentimentally, yet sincerely, regard their identity to be best comprehended at the level of humanity, a species identity that reaches beyond nationality, and who may envision a world state as the only acceptable form of global governance. This variety of world citizen yearns for the establishment of a world government. Such a globalizing vision of the citizen treats civilizational differences as matters of secondary identity. Such a world citizen tends also to regard the rootedness of traditional or local knowledge and experience as backward-looking when the challenge is to look ahead. A kind of bland advocacy that seeks a shared and governmentally consolidated human future has a very small constituency of followers, and lacks political leverage. The prospect of world government does not generate significant support anywhere on the planet, and it is dismissed for reasons of attainability and desirability. There are certainly individuals who have a certain bloodless conviction that world government is the only the path to a sustainable future, but how to get from here to there is not addressed. Rather, the sheer rationality of world government is supposed at some point to produce enough support to make such an expectation into a viable political project. It may not end up being a walk through a thornless rose garden, but world government will, it is claimed, emerge as the only way to manage the fragility and complexity of a globalized planet.

World citizens can find other ways to frame their post-nationalist identity. Perhaps most influential are the swaggering corporate globalists, who imagine themselves to be world citizens because they are equally at home in five star Intercontinental Hotels regardless of which national flag flies above their entrance. These corporate nomads are at home anywhere in the world that market opportunities arise. Their ambition is to offer their products or services on a global market and for their corporate headquarters to be adorned with as many national flags as possible. This essentially amoral view of what it means to be a world citizen tends to be oblivious to the torments of the poor or the anguish of refugees or the tenuousness of the earth's carrying capacity. This corporate, business model of world citizenship is so beguiled by the reality of world markets that it hardly notices the absence of a genuine political community capable of encompassing humanity. Until citizenship is embedded in a community that binds at the level of emotion, it will not lead to the construction of a new identity capable of addressing challenges of planetary scope.

More recently there are those who exhibit an imperial mentality, supposing that America is or can be the world, and that since the beliefs and practices guiding this territorial community are posited as benevolent, then the efforts to control the world have the side-benefits of bringing security and prosperity to all. Such a vision is arrogant, lacking in self-irony and humility, and tends to underestimate or even ignore waves of discontent and resistance that arise as responses. It is the kind of worldview proclaimed by President George W. Bush and his entourage, who contend dogmatically that there exists one and only one way to achieve political legitimacy under present world conditions. This single narrow path requires a political entity to mimic the American way of constitutionalism with respect to the development of governance and a reliance on markets and private sector initiatives. Such an outlook unwittingly blends a grandiose view of American citizenship with a nationalist image of world citizenship that is self-servingly argued to be a boon for humanity. It should not be surprising that most of the world recoils from and actively resists this made-in-America image of the future, sensing danger, exploitation, subjugation, and encroachment, not security and peace, arising from any world order that is administered by and from Washington, DC. What neoconservative proponents propose as leading to "perpetual peace," opponents are convinced is a prescription for "perpetual war." Having struggled against colonial regimes, the peoples of the global South seem united in their unwillingness to acquiesce in any new effort by the North to impose its will upon their destiny. This unwillingness is reinforced by the several failures of this imperial geopolitics, especially the costly, unpopular war in Iraq and a falling dollar signifying imperial decline.

The citizen pilgrim departs from this world of contending ideas of "world citizen," sensing that none can produce that "heavenly country" to which s/he aspires, but not in order to escape by wishful thinking (advocate of world federalism) or self-indulgence (new age escapism). The citizen pilgrim does not pretend that the promised land is at hand (the happy corporate globalist) or to suppose that an American victory in the holy war now raging in Iraq and elsewhere will lead to the happy unification of the entire world (the global imperialist disguised as missionary for democracy). The citizen pilgrim abandons neither suffering nor hope, insisting that inner healing is as "political" as elections and tribunals, and believing that a *total* disengagement from the debates of the moment may be the necessary precondition for liberating the moral imagination, opening wide spaces in the mind and heart that are receptive to drastic change, as well as being responsive to calls for justice and relief that will inform a genuinely transformative politics.

The citizen pilgrim is not an escape artist or closet hedonist, supposing that "new age" self-attentiveness will have a transformative force. Illusions and deceptions will not help us transcend our present forms of destructive self-entrapment. If the heavenly city is ever going to be built on this earth it requires a dedication to the real, to the least of humanity, to the unseemly burdens of poverty and oppression, to the menaced landscapes and seascapes of this beautiful planet, to the anguish of tortured animals, to the darkening prospects of a sustainable environment enabling healthy and comfortable future lives, to the endless struggles of beleaguered first peoples for survival, to a life of nonviolent struggle and self-discovery lived to the extent possible with "eyes wide open," and above all an attentiveness to prophets who are brave and prescient enough to address us from the wilderness. This journey of the citizen pilgrim is without any prescribed movement or clear destination, and involves a willingness and expectation that the sojourner will endure the pain of thorns as well as the pleasure of roses.

Precisely because the patterns of reflection in our current political space seem to be horizonless, a dispiriting despair or equally disquieting salvationism has taken hold, promising nothing more than drifting toward some precipice or gratuitously finding bliss in the infantile metaphysics of rapture. In fundamental respects, there is no longer a hopeful future that can be credibly communicated from *within* the frames of present world order as constituted by the precepts of modernity. Perhaps, this condition of pessimistic closure is not entirely new. Perhaps this incapacity dampened our imaginative powers long ago, and is associated with the abandonment of a more religious interpretation of the human condition and the substitution of a secularist emphasis on reason, technology, and mortality. Perhaps the death camps of the Nazis or the Hiroshima bomb were the decisive moments of secularist closure, a solemn judgment centering on the untenability of modernity so conceived. It seems likely that this incapacity is even deeper, a byproduct of the loss of religious faith, combined with exaggerated pretensions of confidence in reason, science, technology, and in modernity itself, the tragic flaws of the Enlightenment, which seemed so liberating and empowering in many positive respects, at least for a period, but gradually lost their power to inspire and to bind people together communally. It is possible that the rejection of finitude, and of human limits, eventually placed an unsustainable burden on humanity, but there seemed no road back, and no way forward.

The citizen pilgrim may be searching, above all, for the recovery of limits; if the heavenly city is to be built on this earth that human finitude has to be taken into account. In this sense the citizen pilgrim is inevitably drawn back to religious belief, or at least to spiritual practice, but not in any sense that implies an acceptance of dogma or institutional authority. This religious renewal is carried on individually, and needs to be distinguished from the religious resurgence that is leading traditional religions in many circumstances to seek and gain political influence, and pose threats to the moderation and ethos of tolerance that were such important signifiers of modernity.

It may be then that the widespread sense that we may be nearing an ending for modernity is the chaotic prelude to a new epoch of hopefulness. Perhaps the cultural infatuation with deconstruction as a means to bury the grand narrative claims of modernity is a preparation for a new reconstructive phase of collective consciousness, with its own horizons of aspiration and a renewed consciousness of limits. The citizen pilgrim is not in despair because s/he senses this latency in the current turmoil, waiting at once patiently and impatiently, not uncomfortable with what the Western rational mind would likely repudiate as "contradictory." The Eastern rational mind seems more responsive to this simultaneous need to wait and refuse to wait.

It is this receptivity that makes the citizen pilgrim welcome collaboration and dialogues within and between civilizations, and by so doing repudiate the hypothesis of either "a clash of civilizations," or its antithesis, "a convergence of civilizations." The clash thesis is the tormented cry of self-imprisoned captives of a terminal modernity that believes that conflict and violence are encoded in our genetic structure with a fatalistic determinism that makes any search for alternatives, including creative tensions between civilizational particularity and a transcendent humanism, appear as self-deception and illusion.

The convergence antithesis misleadingly believes the common core of beliefs of the world's great religions is the foundation for a positive future, regarding religious and cultural differences as superficial and unworthy of serious attention. While clash represents submission to the constraints of the present, convergence represents escapism that is nothing more than a play of words. In contrast, the dialogic way is open to exploration and discovery, as humans are genetically enabled to shape their future by learning, adapting, reciprocating, renouncing, dreaming, and encompassing. Dialogues undertaken in such a spirit allow us to experience "the other" without a sense of strangeness and fear, dysfunctional attitudes that so often reflect the discontents of the militarized, unheavenly city that the citizen pilgrim has long ago abandoned because of its negative foreclosure of human destiny, its essential hopelessness regarding human potential with respect to community-building and creative forms of humane governance.

The perspective of the citizen pilgrim is discontinuous in spirit and outlook with that of a secular citizen of a particular sovereign state, the most familiar form of citizenship. Here, too, there are choices available that make a difference, above all, the realization that a citizen is unlike a subject, having the freedom, and occasionally the responsibility, to say no to the state, as well as to any political actor whose behavior affronts conscience and fundamental moral precepts. The idea of patriotism is deformed to the extent that it is understood to imply unconditional and unquestioning obedience to the state. The true patriot as citizen of conscience does not exempt the state from moral, political, and legal accountability, especially in matters of war and peace. The true patriot in the twenty-first century accepts the discipline of international law and respect for the authority of the United Nations as the foundations of prudence and restraint in the relations among sovereign states in a world order that lacks governmental institutions and societal cohesion. The true patriot thus confidently rejects security built on the possession of nuclear weapons, and reliance on threats to use weapons of mass destruction against an "enemy." A benevolent exercise of secular citizenship, necessary as the basis of political community and to guard against excesses by the state, is an admirable calling for persons living in the historical present. Such a citizen makes a special contribution to this country and the world in the atmosphere that has prevailed since 9/11. This attention to the immediate does not obviate the defining mission of the citizen pilgrim, but extends the time available for transformative experience to reshape the nature of political leadership by reducing the costs and risks of present arrangements in the domain of security that are overly militarized, thereby obstructing adjustments required to deal with climate change, food and health security, and the squeeze on energy resources.

The difficult fulfillment of the responsibilities of secular citizenship should not be confused with the more visionary calling of the citizen pilgrim. The latter is unwilling to accept the framing of political life within the confines of states (or even regions), and embarks on a journey toward a desired future that is boundaryless, spiritually motivated, and fulfilled, celebrating both diversity and rootedness, and undertaken with a dialectical conviction that a heavenly city can and must be built on this earth. Until this possibility comes to pass, the citizen pilgrim is condemned to live a life of lonely restlessness, enlivened by hopefulness and an abiding faith that as yet unseen and profoundly uplifting conditions for human existence, including the abiding calling of living well together, can and will be brought into existence.

Notes

1 Toward a *Necessary* Utopianism: Democratic Global Governance

1 James Howard Kunstler, *The Long Emergency* (New York: Grove Press, 2005).
2 For continuity of recent American hegemonic behavior see Neil Smith, *The Endgame of Globalization* (New York: Routledge, 2005).
3 Chalmers Johnson, *The Sorrows of Empire* (New York: Metropolitan Books, 2004); Chalmers Johnson, *Nemesis: The Last Days of the American Republic* (New York: Metropolitan Books, 2006).
4 *National Security Strategy of the United States of America* (Washington, DC: White House, 2002, 2006); Joshua Muravchik, "The Past, Present, and Future of Neoconservatism," *Commentary Magazine*, Oct. 2007.
5 Richard Falk, *On Humane Governance: Toward a New Global Politics* (Cambridge, UK: Polity, 1995).
6 Nassim Nicholas Taleb, *The Black Swan: The Impact of the Highly Improbable* (New York: Random House, 2007).
7 Wonderfully depicted by Charles Jencks, *The Architecture of the Jumping Universe, A Polemic: How Complexity Science is Changing Architecture and Culture* (New York: John Wiley, 1997).
8 Torbjørn Knutson, *The Rise and Fall of World Orders* (Manchester, UK: Manchester University Press, 1999); Richard Falk, *Predatory Globalization: A Critique* (Cambridge, UK: Polity, 1999).
9 For comprehensive treatment see Daniele Archibugi, *A World of Democracy: Cosmopolitan Perspectives* (Princeton, NJ: Princeton University Press, 2008).
10 Niall Ferguson, *Colossus: The Price of America's Empire* (New York: Penguin Press, 2004); Andrew J. Bacevich, *American Empire: The Realities and Consequences of U.S. Diplomacy* (Cambridge, MA: Harvard University Press, 2002).
11 This position is most elaborately argued by Michael Mandelbaum, *The Ideas That Conquered the World: Peace, Democracy, and Free Markets in the Twenty-first Century* (New York: Public Affairs, 2002).
12 David Harvey, *The New Imperialism* (Oxford, UK: Oxford University Press, 2003).
13 Mary Kaldor, *Human Security* (Cambridge, UK, Polity, 2007).
14 See Chapter 14 for more discussion of the citizen pilgrim idea.
15 George Andreopoulos, Zehra F. Kabasakal Arat, & Peter Juviler, eds., *Non-State Actors in the Human Rights Universe* (Bloomfield, CT: Kumarian, 2006).
16 See Derek Heater, *Citizenship: The Civic Ideal in World History, Politics and Education* (London: Longmans, 1990).
17 See note 4 above, cover letter signed by President George W. Bush.
18 On the evolution of Westphalian citizen rights see classic account of the evolution of modern citizenship in T.H. Marshall, *Class, Citizen and Social Development* (New York: Anchor, 1965);

19 See Maastricht Treaty, 1993; for general discussion see Étienne Balibar, *We, the People of Europe: Reflections on Transnational Citizenship* (Princeton, NJ: Princeton University Press, 2004).

20 Richard Falk, *The Declining World Order: America's Imperial Geopolitics* (New York: Routledge, 2004), at 3–44, 81–103.

21 See Falk, note 20 above.

22 Mario Pianta, "Democracy versus Globalization: The Growth of Parallel Summits and Movements," in Daniele Archibugi, ed., *Debating Cosmopolitics* (London, UK: Verso, 2003), at 232–256.

23 Margaret Keck & Kathryn Sikkink, *Activists Beyond Borders: Advocacy Networks in International Politics* (Ithaca, NY: Cornell University Press, 1998).

24 See Chapter 14 and Falk, note 5 above, 211–212.

25 Elizabeth Shakman Hurd, *The Politics of Secularism in International Relations* (Princeton, NJ: Princeton University Press, 2008).

26 Richard Falk & Andrew Strauss, "On the Creation of a Global People's Assembly: Legitimacy and the Power of Popular Sovereignty," *Stanford Journal of International Law* 36:191–220 (2000); Andrew Strauss, "On the First Branch of Global Governance," *Widener Law Review* XIII(2):347–359 (2007); Richard Falk & Andrew Strauss, "Toward Global Parliament," *Foreign Affairs* 80(1):212–220 (2001); Richard Falk & Andrew Strauss, "The Deeper Challenges of Global Terrorism: A Democratizing Response," in Daniele Archibugi, note 9 above, 203–231.

2 The Power of Rights and the Rights of Power:
What Future for Human Rights?

1 This dual potentiality of human rights as used for purposes of mystification by dominant political actors and for emancipatory goals by and on behalf of subjugated peoples contrasts with the trenchant critique of human rights discourse and diplomacy as exclusively instrumental and regressive. For this view see Anthony Carty's important book, *The Philosophy of International Law* (Edinburgh, Scotland: Edinburgh University Press, 2007), esp. 194–195.

2 The word "genocide" is used here to describe a set of moral and political assessments, but does not imply a legal conclusion that depends, according to the International Court of Justice, on a level of documentary evidence that is unlikely to be available in the context of Israel's occupation policy directed at Palestine. For case see *Bosnia and Herzegovina* v. Serbia and Montenegro, ICJ Reports, 26 Feb., 2007; for comment see Jillayne Seymour, "Jurisdiction and Responsibility by Necessary Implication: Genocide in Bosnia," *Cambridge Law Journal* 66(2): 249–253 (2007); for a non-legal determination that Israel's policies toward Gaza have a genocidal quality see Ilan Pappe, "Palestine 2007: Genocide in Gaza, Ethnic Cleansing in the West Bank," *The Electronic Intifada*, Jan. 11, 2007: http://electronicintifada.net/v2/printer6374.shtml; Pappe, "The Mega Prison of Palestine," *The Electronic Intifada*, March 5, 2008: http://electronicintifada.net/v2/article 9370.shtml

Israel's Deputy Defense Minister, Matan Vilnai, warned Gaza of a "shoah" if rockets from Gaza continue to imperil the security of Israeli border towns and cities; later spokespersons insisted that Mr. Vilnai was using shoah in the Hebrew sense of "disaster," not in its historical sense of denoting the Holocaust experienced by the Jews in Nazi Germany, but the association of the two meanings of shoah was unavoidable, especially given the fact that Gaza was already a disaster, and Israeli policies towards the territory were being described as genocide ever since Hamas took over political control there.

3 Whether this pattern of behavior is also genocide in a *legal* sense depends on a presently unsatisfied conditions: a determination by a duly constituted tribunal that hears allegations and defenses. Note that such condition has not inhibited the label genocide from being affixed to the Holocaust, the massacres carried out by the Khmer Rouge in Cambodia, or numerous other instances. Most of the extensive literature on genocide draws its conclusion on the basis of the facts of deliberate and systematic action taken against a particular ethnic group. Although genocide usually involves killing as its core characteristic, the siege of Gaza could satisfy most definitions if an intent to destroy the group in whole or in part is considered evidence of a genocidal intent. Perhaps the Israeli approach to Gaza is best expressed by the conceptualization of "slow genocide." See Martha L. Cottam, J. Huseby, & F.E. Lutze, "Slow Genocide," paper presented at the annual meeting of the International Society of Political Psychology in Barcelona (2006).

4 For instance, such a selective outlook *sees* with unremitting clarity violations of human rights by Communist governments in Cuba or China, while not seeing much grander violations committed by Israel or the United States.

5 For devastating critiques along these lines see Carty, note 1 above, and Anne Orford, *Reading Humanitarian Intervention: Human Rights and the Use of Force in International Law* (Cambridge, UK: Cambridge University Press, 2003).

6 See the notoriously one-sided text condemning Hamas as being responsible for rocket attacks on Israel that have caused as many as 12 civilian deaths in Israel, while Israeli use of force in Gaza has caused over 2,600 Palestinian civilian deaths in the same period. U.S. House of Representatives, H. RES. 951, March 5, 2008 passed by an incredible vote of 404–1. Any deliberate targeting of civilians is illegal and immoral, but such condemnations should be balanced by reference to the realities of harm being caused.

7 For general assessment along these lines see Richard Falk, "International Law and the Peace Process," *Hastings International and Comparative Law Review* 28(3):331–348 (2005).

8 See Article 49(6) of the Geneva Convention (No. IV) Relative to the Protection of Civilian Persons in Time of War.

9 Advisory Opinion of the International Court of Justice on the Legal Consequences of the Construction of a Wall in Occupied Palestinian Territory, including in and around East Jerusalem, ICJ Reports, July 9, 2004; the legal conclusions of the International Court of Justice, the highest judicial arm of the UN system, was supported by a vote of 14–1, including several European judges with an approach to international law respectful of sovereign rights. The General Assembly urged Israel to implement the findings of law by a vote of 150–6 (Israel, USA, Australia, Micronesia, Palau, Marshall Islands), with 10 abstentions (General Assembly Doc.: GA/10248, March 9, 2004).

10 This refusal to resolve disputes by reference to respective legal rights as fairly determined is a challenge to the whole idea central to the United Nations Charter that states should renounce force in their resolution of disputes.

11 Dennis Ross, the chief diplomatic advisor to President Bill Clinton during 2000 Camp David II negotiating sessions, influentially and exhaustively reports on his pervasive effort to avoid any proposals that Israeli public opinion would be unwilling to swallow for the sake of conflict resolution without paying the slightest attention to comparable concerns on the Palestinian side, specifically, what it was reasonable to expect the Palestinians to accept. This kind of approach to the search for a diplomatic solution was particularly outrageous given the fact that the Palestinians were mainly seeking to exercise their right of self-determination over only 22 percent of the original Palestine mandate, thereby conceding prior to negotiations that pre-1967 Israel could expect to be secure within its 78 percent of the territory

in dispute if an agreement on Israeli withdrawal from the 22 percent could be achieved in the process of establishing the state of Palestine. For Ross's presentation of Camp David II see his massive account: *The Missing Peace: The Inside Story of the Fight for Middle East Peace* (New York: Farrar, Straus, & Giroux, 2004).

12 For Said's views see his *The End of the Peace Process: Oslo and After* (New York: Pantheon, 2000).

13 This tale of Israeli forthcomingness and generosity is disarmingly told in Ross, note 11 above; even Israeli sources are more candid in distributing the blame for the failure of negotiations and acknowledge that it is not clear that the Israeli proposals would have been accepted by Knesset or Israeli public opinion. For a surprisingly objective account see Yoram Meital, *Peace in Tatters: Israel, Palestine, and the Middle East* (Boulder, CO: Lynne Rienner, 2006).

14 This issue is explored in depth by two international relations experts who had been regarded previously as members of the American foreign policy establishment, but who, with this criticism of the Israeli influence on American policy formation, have been somewhat marginalized. See John J. Mearsheimer & Stephen M. Walt, *The Israel Lobby and U.S. Foreign Policy* (New York: Farrar, Straus, & Giroux, 2007).

15 This deference is disguised to some extent by the term "nation-state", as if the nation is genuinely synonymous with the state. For many minorities, the state operates as a hostile trap rather than as a security blanket. Governments do have the exclusive authority to confer nationality for international purposes, including the issuance of passports, but this only confuses the issue of whether nationalities within a particular state are adequately represented and fairly treated. The image of "captive nations" points to the reality where minorities (and occasionally majorities, as in apartheid South Africa) are denied equality of treatment, and may be targets of exploitation and abuse.

16 The indictment of the Westphalian world order on these grounds has been most persuasively achieved by Ken Booth, "Human Wrongs in International Relations," *Journal of International Affairs* 71:103–126 (1995); for further exploration see Tim Dunne & Nicholas J. Wheeler, eds., *Human Rights in Global Politics* (Cambridge: Cambridge University Press, 1999); also, from a different perspective based on the structure of world order, not on the coercive power of the individual sovereign state see Chandra Muzaffar, ed., *Human Wrongs: Reflections on Western Global Dominance and its Impact Upon Human Rights* (Penang, Malaysia: Just World Trust, 1996).

17 For a comprehensive presentations of liberal legalist hopes associated with universal jurisdiction see Stephen Macedo, ed., *Universal Jurisdiction: National Courts and the Prosecution of Serious Crimes Under International Law* (Philadelphia, PA: University of Pennsylvania Press, 2004.

18 For examples of such formal rationalizations of hegemony as inhering *within* international law see Detlev Vagts, "Hegemonic International Law," *American Journal of International Law* 95(4):843–848 (2001) and José E. Alvarez, "Hegemonic International Law Revisited," *American Journal of International Law* 97(4):873–888 (2003). See also Nico Krisch, "International Law in Times of Hegemony: Unequal Power and the Shaping of the International Legal Order," *The European Journal of International Law* 16(3):369–408 (2005).

19 For decision see *Military and Paramilitary Activities in and against Nicaragua* (*Nicaragua* v. *USA*), International Court of Justice Reports, June 27, 1986.

20 For a critique of the official dialogue on global reform from these perspectives see Richard Falk, "Illusions of Reform: Needs, Desires, and Realities," in Kevin P. Clements & Nadia Mizner, eds., *The Center Holds: UN Reform for 21st-Century Challenges* (New Brunswick, NJ: Transaction Publishers, 2008), at 19–30.

21 See Richard Falk, *The Costs of War: International Law, the UN, and World Order After Iraq* (New York: Routledge, 2008), at 37–51.
22 This statement was made on the TV program *60 Minutes*, and followed upon a statement by the news person, Leslie Stahl: "We have heard that a half million children have died.. . . I mean, that's more children than died in Hiroshima. And . . . and you know, is the price worth it?" For full text see http://www.uwire.com/content/topops0214001001.html
23 See Jeremy Scahill, "The Real Story Behind Kosovo's Independence," *Truthout*, Feb. 23, 2008, http://www.truthout.org/docs_2006/022408Y.shtml
24 For a devastating critique see John Laughland, *Travesty: The Trial of Slobodan Milosevic and the Corruption of International Justice* (London, UK: Pluto, 2007).
25 Most completely depicted in the context of the Tokyo war crimes trials in Richard H. Minear, *Victors' Justice: The Tokyo War Crimes Tribunal* (Princeton, NJ: Princeton University Press, 1971).
26 This critique is well developed in Philippe Sands, *Lawless World* (New York, Viking, 2005) and Marjorie Cohn, *Cowboy Republic: Six Ways the Bush Gang has Defied the Law* (Sausalito, CA: PoliPoint Press, 2007).
27 Balakrishnan Rajagopal, "Counter-Hegemonic International Law: Rethinking Human Rights and Development as a Third World Strategy," *Third World Quarterly* 27(5):767–783 (2006), at 775.
28 Several recent publications are relevant and encouraging. See Anne Orfeld, note 5 above; Carty, note 1 above; Amy Bartholomew, ed., *Empire's Law: The American Imperial Project and the "War to Remake the World"* (London, UK: Pluto, 2006); Ikechi Mgbeoji, *Collective Insecurity: The Liberian Crisis, Unilateralism, and Global Order* (Vancouver, Canada: UBC Press, 2003); Susan Marks, "Empire's Law," *Indiana Journal of Global Legal Studies* 10:449–466 (2003).
29 See Upendra Baxi, "From Human Rights to the Right to be Human: Some Heresies," in Smitu Kothari & Harsh Sheth, eds., *Rethinking Human Rights* (Delhi, India: Lokayan, 1989), 181–166, at 166; more recently, Baxi has extended his analysis to the emerging circumstance of possibly being "posthuman." Baxi, *Human Rights in a Posthuman World* (Delhi, India: Oxford, 2007).
30 Kothari & Sheth, note 29 above, "On Categories and Interventions," 1–17, at 9.
31 For proceedings see Müge Gürsöy Sökman, ed., *World Tribunal on Iraq* (Northampton, MA: Olive Branch Press, 2008).

3 Orientalism and International Law

1 This de-Orientalizing is part of the effort of Richard Falk, Balakrishnan Rajagopal, & Jacqueline Stevens, eds., "Special Issue: Reshaping Justice—International Law and the Third World," *Third World Quarterly* 27(5): 707–957 (2006).
2 For three significant and sophisticated explorations along these lines see Robert Jackson, *The Global Covenant: Human Conduct in a World of States* (Oxford, UK: Oxford University Press, 2000); James N. Rosenau, *Turbulence in World Politics: A Theory of Change and Continuity* (Princeton, NJ: Princeton University Press, 1990); Daniel H. Deudney, *Bounding Power: Republican Security Theory from the Polis to the Global Village* (Princeton, NJ: Princeton University Press, 2007).
3 Edward Said, *Orientalism* (New York: Pantheon, [1978] 2003), xxix.
4 Said, note 3 above, xxix.
5 See George W. Bush, "Commencement Address at West Point," June 1, 2002; Bush, 2003 State of the Union Address," Jan. 28, 2003. Also *National Security Strategy of the United States of America* (Washington, DC: White House, 2002).
6 Anders Stephanson, *Manifest Destiny: American Expansion and the Empire of Right* (New York: Hill & Wang, 1995).

7 See Fouad Ajami, "The Sentry's Solitude," *Foreign Affairs* 80(6): 2–16 (2001); Ajami, "Two Faces, One Terror," in Micah L. Sifry & Christopher Serf, eds., *The Iraq War Reader* (New York: Simon & Schuster, 2003), 387–391; Bernard Lewis, *What Went Wrong? Western Impact and Middle Eastern Response* (New York: Oxford University Press, 2001); Lewis, "The Revolt of Islam," *The New Yorker*, Nov. 19, 2001, 50–63; Lewis, "Did you say 'American Imperialism'?" *National Review*, Dec. 17, 2001, 26–29; Lewis, "What Went Wrong?" *The Atlantic*, Jan. 2002, 43–45.

8 Declaration on the Granting of Independence to Colonial Countries, UN General Assembly Res. 1514, adopted Dec. 14, 1960; Permanent Sovereignty over Natural Resources, UN General Assembly Res. 1803, adopted Dec. 14, 1962, and 3171, adopted Dec. 17, 1973.

9 Balakrishnan Rajagopal, *International Law from Below: Development, Social Movements and Third World Resistance* (Cambridge, UK: Cambridge University Press, 2003).

10 Paul Kennedy, *The Rise and Fall of the Great Powers: Economic Change and Military Conflict 1500–2000* (New York: Random House, 1987).

11 See Richard Falk, *The Declining World Order: America's Neoimperial Geopolitics* (New York: Routledge, 2004), 3–44.

12 See Richard Falk, *The Great Terror War* (Northampton, MA: Olive Branch Press, 2003).

13 See David Held, *Democracy and the Global Order: From the Modern State to Cosmopolitan Governance* (Cambridge, UK: Cambridge University Press, 1995).

14 See Said, note 3 above, at 25.

15 For such a perspective taken by a distinguished international jurist see B.S. Chimni, *International Law and World Order: A Critique of Contemporary Approaches* (Newbury Park, CA: SAGE, 1993).

16 For example, on Rajagopal, note 9 above, and the readings in the edited special issue of *Third World Quarterly*, note 1 above.

17 As in Richard Falk, *On Humane Global Governance: Toward a New Global Politics* (Cambridge, UK: Polity).

18 As depicted in Giovanna Borradori, *Philosophy in a Time of Terror: Dialogues with Jürgen Habermas and Jacques Derrida* (Chicago: University of Chicago Press, 2003).

19 See David Kennedy, *International Legal Structures* (Baden-Baden, Germany: Nomos Verlagsgesellschaft, 1987); Kennedy, Review of *The Rights of Conquest*, *American Journal of International Law* 91:745–748 (1997).[0]

20 Kennedy, Review, note 19 above, at 748.

21 See Robert Kagan, *Of Paradise and Power: America and Europe in the New World Order* (New York: Knopf, 2003).

22 Richard Perle, "Thank God for the Death of the UN: Its Abject Failure Gave Us Only Anarchy, the World Needs Order," *The Guardian*, March 20, 2003.

23 As argued by Ken Booth, "Human Wrongs and International Relations," *Journal of International Affairs* 71:103–126 (1995).

24 Brilliantly analyzed in Upendra Baxi, *The Future of Human Rights* (New Delhi, India: Oxford University Press, 2002) and Baxi, *Critical Essays* (Bombay, India: Tripathi, 1988); also Rajagopal, note 9 above.

25 "The Legality of Nuclear Weapons," Advisory Opinion, International Court of Justice, 1996.

26 Samuel P. Huntington, "The Clash of Civilizations?" *Foreign Affairs* 72(1):22–49 (1992); and Huntington, *The Clash of Civilizations and the Remaking of World Order* (New York: Simon & Schuster, 1996).

27 Thomas Friedman, *The Lexus and the Olive Tree: Understanding Globalization* (New York: Farrar, Straus, & Giroux, 1999); and Lewis, *What Went Wrong?* note 7 above.

28 Roxanne Euben, *Enemy in the Mirror: Islamic Fundamentalism and the Limits of Western Rationalism* (Princeton, NJ: Princeton University Press, 1999).

29 For discussion of the UN-administered sanctions regime see Richard Falk, *Costs of War: International Law, the UN, and World Order after Iraq* (New York: Routledge, 2008).

30 Bob Woodward, *Plan of Attack* (New York: Simon & Schuster, 2004).

31 For perceptive discussion, see Susan Sontag, "Regarding the Torture of Others: Notes on What Has Been Done—and Why—to Prisoners, by Americans," *New York Times Magazine*, May 23, 2004.

32 David Frum & Richard Perle, *An End to Evil: How to Win the War on Terror* (New York: Random House, 2003).

33 Falk, note 11 above, at 122–126.

34 For a range of views on this claim of judicial universality, see Stephen Macedo, *Universal Jurisdiction: National Courts and the Prosecution of Serious Crimes under International Law* (Philadelphia: University of Pennsylvania Press, 2004).

35 As quoted in Reuters news article online, "U.S. Pushes World Court Immunity Amid Iraq Scandal," May 14, 2004.

36 For some viewpoints that were contending for influence see*Restoring America's Defenses* (Washington, DC: Project for a New American Century, 2000); National Security Strategy, note 5 above; Frum & Perle, note 31 above; Zbigniew Brzezinski, *The Choice: Global Dominance or Global Leadership* (New York: Basic Books, 2004); Jim Garrison, *America as Empire: Global Leader or Rogue Power?* (San Francisco: Barrett-Koehler, 2004); Walter Russell Mead, *Power, Terror, Peace, and War: America's Grand Strategy in a World at Risk* (New York: Knopf, 2004); Michael Ignatieff, *The Lesser Evil: Political Ethics in an Age of Terror* (Princeton, NJ: Princeton University Press, 2004).

4 Toward Global Democracy

1 For a major depiction of the evolution of democratic forms of governance as applicable to different social and political arrangements see David Held, *Democracy and the Global Order: From the Modern State to Cosmopolitan Governance* (Stanford, CA: Stanford University Press, 1995).

2 *Our Global Neighborhood*, Report of The Commission on Global Governance (New York: Oxford, 1995); and see James N. Rosenau & E.-O. Czempiel, eds., *Governance without Government: Order and Change in World Politics* (Cambridge: Cambridge University Press, 1992).

3 For classic critique of world government as a solution to the crisis of global governance see Inis L. Claude, Jr., *Swords into Plowshares: The Problems and Progress of International Organization*, 4th edn. (New York: Random House, 1971).

4 For exposition and critique see Richard Falk, *The Declining World Order: America's Neo-Imperial Geopolitics* (New York: Routledge, 2004).

5 Richard Falk, *Predatory Globalization: A Critique* (Cambridge, UK: Polity, 1999). On climate change see the Stern Review, published as Nicholas Stern, *The Economics of Climate Change* (Cambridge, UK: Cambridge University Press, 2007); UN Intergovernmental Panel on Climate Change, *IPCC Fourth Assessment Report: Climate Change 2007*.

6 Influentially depicted in Hedley Bull, *The Anarchical Society: A Study of Order in World Politics* (London, UK: Macmillan, 2nd edn., 1977); see also F.H. Hinsley, *Power and the Pursuit of Peace* (Cambridge, UK: Cambridge University Press, 1963); for a conservative reading of global governance from the perspective of resolving tensions between the increasing demands for international cooperation arising from the different dimensions of globalization and the requirements of constitutional

government in the United States see John Yoo, *The Powers of War and Peace: The Constitution and Foreign Affairs after 9/1* (Chicago: University of Chicago Press, 2005), 293–303.

7 For fuller discussion of "the Grotian moment," and its surrounding conceptual context see Burns H. Weston, Richard Falk, Hilary Charlesworth, & A. Strauss, eds., *International Law and World Order* (St. Paul, MN: West Publishing Co., 4th edn., 2006), 1265–1286.

8 For a striking account of the rise of regions and erosion of state sovereignty, see Terrence Paupp, *Crumbling Walls, Rising Regions*, unpublished ms., 2008.

9 For an early argument along these lines see Richard Falk, *This Endangered Planet: Prospects and Proposals for Human Survival* (New York: Random House, 1972); a recent response in a generally similar spirit is James Gustave Speth, *The Bridge at the Edge of the World: Capitalism, the Environment, and Crossing from Crisis to Sustainability* (New Haven, CT: Yale University Press, 2008); see also "Fighting Climate Change: Human Solidarity in a Divided World" *Human Development Report, 2007/2008* (New York: Palgrave Macmillan, 2007).

10 For a valuable exploration along these lines see Burns H. Weston, "Climate Change and Intergenerational Justice: Foundational Reflections," *Vermont Journal of Environmental Law* 9(3) (2008).

11 For optimistic assessments of the European experiment in regional governance see Mark Leonard, *Why Europe Will Rule the 21st Century* (London: Fourth Estate, 2005), Jeremy Rifkin, *The European Union: How Europe's Vision of the Future is Quietly Eclipsing the American Dream* (New York: Jeremy Tarcher/Penguin, 2004). See John B. Headley, *The Europeanization of the World: On the Origins of Human Rights and Democracy* (Princeton, NJ: Princeton University Press, 2008); James J. Sheehan, *Where Have All the Soldiers Gone? The Transformation of Modern Europe* (Boston: Houghton Mifflin, 2008).

12 See Timothy Garton Ash, "Kosovo Has Earned a Place," *The Guardian Weekly*, Feb. 23–March 1, 2007, 4; but see Ash, "The Kosovo Precedent," *Los Angeles Times*, Feb. 21, 2008, A21.

13 See John Ikenberry for an important study of this dynamic, *After Victory: Institutions, Strategic Retreat, and the Rebuilding of Order after Major Wars* (Princeton, NJ: Princeton University Press, 2001).

14 For useful account see D. Sidjanski, *The Federal Future of Europe: From the European Community to the European Union* (Ann Arbor: University of Michigan Press, 2000).

15 See Ian Buruma, *Murder in Amsterdam: The Death of Theo van Gogh and the Limits of Tolerance* (New York: Penguin, 2006).

16 As argued in Robert Kagan, *Of Paradise and Power: America and Europe in the new world order* (New York, Vintage, 2004).

17 For one critical look among many, see Chalmers Johnson, *Nemesis: The Last Days of the American Republic* (New York: Metropolitan Books, 2006).

18 Most impressively considered in Paupp, note 8 above.

19 See report issued prior to the Bush presidency and before 9/11, *Repairing America's Defenses* Report of Project for a New American Century (PNAC), Washington, DC, 2000; for a sense of the neoconservative tenor of the Bush presidency see James Mann, *Rise of the Vulcans: The History of Bush's War Cabinet* (New York, Viking, 2004).

20 *National Security Strategy of the United States of America* (Washington, DC: White House, 2002, updated version, 2006); for a more popular presentation of the same approach see David Frum & Richard Perle, *An End to Evil: How to Win the War on Terror* (New York: Random House, 2003).

21 There is much recent literature on all sides of this issue; among important contributions are Andrew Bacevich, *American Empire: The Realities and Consequences of*

U.S. Diplomacy (Cambridge, MA: Harvard University Press, 2002); Michael Hardt & Antonio Negri, *Empire* (Cambridge, MA: Harvard University Press, 2000); Rashid Khalidi, *Resurrecting Empire: Western Footprints and America's Perilous Path in the Middle East* (Boston, MA: Beacon Press, 2004); and Niall Ferguson, *Colossus: The Price of America's Empire* (New York: Penguin, 2004).

22 For the neoconservative argument spelled out see David Frum & Richard Perle, note 20 above.

23 On the case for continuity see Neil Smith, *The Endgame of Geopolitics* (NewYork: Routledge, 2005).

24 See Nico Krisch, "International Law in Times of Hegemony: Unequal Power and the Shaping of the International Legal Order," *European Journal of International Law* 16(3):369–408 (2005); see also José E. Alvarez, "Hegemonic International Law Revisited," *American Journal of International Law* 97(4):873–888 (2003).

25 Daniele Archibugi & David Held, eds., *Cosmopolitan Democracy: An Agenda for a New World Order* (Cambridge, UK: Polity, 1995); more comprehensively, Daniele Archibugi, ed., *Debating Cosmopolitics* (London, UK: Verso, 2003).

26 For an early effort to depict "humane global governance" see Richard Falk, *On Humane Global Governance: Toward a New World Politics* (Cambridge, UK: Polity, 1995).

27 Not since Grenville Clark & Louis Sohn, *World Peace Through World Law* (Cambridge, MA: Harvard University Press, 3rd edn., 1966), has there been a comprehensive ambitious proposal for world government set forth.

28 See M. Kaldor, *Global Civil Society: An Answer to War* (Cambridge, UK: Polity, 2003).

29 See S. Macedo, ed., *Universal Jurisdiction: National Courts and the Prosecution of Serious Crimes Under International Law* (Philadelphia: University of Pennsylvania Press), 2004; N. Roht-Arriaza, *The Pinochet Effect: Transitional Justice in the Age of Human Rights* (Philadelphia, PA: University of Pennsylvania Press, 2005).

30 Susan Marks, "Empire's Law," *Indiana Journal of Global Legal Studies* 10:449–466 (2002).

31 Among our several publications advocating the establishment of a global peoples assembly see Richard Falk & Andrew Strauss, "On the Creation of a Global People's Assembly: Legitimacy and the Power of Popular Sovereignty," *Stanford Journal of International Law* 36(2):191–219 (2000); "Toward a Global Parliament," *Foreign Affairs* 80(1):212–220 (2001).

32 For an argument supportive of "utopian" advocacy see Chapter 1, this volume.

33 For complete tribunal proceedings see Müge Gürsöy Sökman, ed., *World Tribunal on Iraq: Making the Case Against War* (Northampton, MA: Olive Branch Press, 2008).

5 Citizenship and Globalization

1 See Manuel Castells, *The Information Age: Economy, Society and Culture* (Oxford: Blackwell, 3 vols., 1996–98) for a most elaborate specification.

2 The right of self-determination was supposed to be exercised in a manner that did not result in the dismemberment of existing states. See UN GA Res. 2625; but the break-up of the Soviet Union, and especially of the former Yugoslavia, has abandoned this limitation. What was significant was not only the claims of state-shattering political independence by the former federal units in these two countries, but the readiness of the international community to abandon its own doctrine of statist unity for the sake of geopolitical expediency, that is, welcoming these particular instances of break-up. Such doctrinal opportunism inevitably weakens the inhibition on the assertion of other comparable claims.

Albanian Kosovar insistence on full political independence is difficult to oppose on principled grounds, and has been established over Serb opposition in early 2008.

3 See the various lines of exploration in Wolfgang Danspeckgruber, with Arthur Watts, ed., *Self-Determination and Self-Administration: A Sourcebook* (Boulder, CO: Lynne Rienner, 1997).

4 One of the early authors to argue along these lines was Hedley Bull, *The Anarchic Society: A Study of Order in World Politics* (New York: Columbia University Press, 1977).

5 See Chapter 7, this volume.

6 See Elazar Barkan, *The Guilt of Nations: Restitution, and Negotiating Historic Injustices* (New York: Norton, 2000) on this broad theme.

7 See Andrew Linklater, "Citizenship and Sovereignty in the Post-Westphalian European State," in Daniele Archibugi, David Held, & Martin Köhler, eds., *Re-Imagining Political Community: Studies in Cosmopolitan Democracy* (Cambridge, UK: Polity, 1998), 113–137; also Andrew Linklater, *The Transformation of Political Community* (Cambridge, UK: Polity, 1998).

8 See Ulrich Beck, *World Risk Society* (Cambridge, UK: Polity, 1999).

9 See Robert H. Jackson, *Quasi-States: Sovereignty, International Relations and the Third World* (Cambridge, UK: Cambridge University Press, 1990), on the failures of the post-colonial process to achieve transition to Westphalian states.

10 The state responds, characteristically, with a technological fix by way of warfare without casualties.

11 Ken Booth, "Human Wrongs and International Relations," *International Affairs* 71(1):103–126 (Jan. 1995); this perspective is more fully developed in Tim Dunne and Nicholas J. Wheeler, eds., *Human Rights in Global Politics* (Cambridge, UK: Cambridge University Press, 1999).

12 See Nicholas J. Wheeler, *Saving Strangers* (Oxford: Oxford University Press, 2000).

13 The exceptional challenges that do occur arise from issues related to Eurocentrism and geopolitical policy imperatives, as in the NATO War over Kosovo.

14 Freedom House, an American NGO, and the UN Development Programme (UNDP), each put out an annual report featuring indicators of political and economic progress by the countries of the world

15 The experiences of the 1990s relating to Somalia, Bosnia, and Rwanda have been crucial.

16 This view that I favor contrasts with what I understand Martin Shaw to be advocating in his stimulating book, *Theory of the Global State: Globality and the Unfinished Revolution* (Cambridge: Cambridge University Press, 2000). Shaw's stress is a pragmatic one that builds on current trends, especially on the democratizing projects of transnational social movements and their links to Western power, and culminates with the development of a system of global governance that inhibits war, see esp. 259–270.

17 For discussion of these two faces of religion in a global setting see Richard Falk, *Religion and Humane Global Governance* (New York: Palgrave, 2001).

18 Balakrishnan Rajagopal, "Counter-Hegemonic International Law: Rethinking Human Rights and Development as a Third World Strategy," *Third World Quarterly* 27(5):767–784 (2006).

19 For a depiction of this technological horizon by a celebrated computer scientist and business executive see Bill Joy, "Why the Future Doesn't Need Us," *Wired* 8(4):238–262 (2000).

20 See Joy, note 19 above, and Ray Kurzweil, *The Singularity Is Near: When Humans Transcend Biology* (New York: Viking, 2005).

6 The Holocaust and the Emergence of International Human Rights

1 Stephen Krasner has convincingly shown that such claims of unconditional sovereignty have always been exaggerated and "conditional," although their conditionality did not relate to international standards of human rights. See Stephen Krasner, *Sovereignty: Organized Hypocrisy* (Princeton, NJ: Princeton University Press, 1999).

2 See United Nations Declaration on the Rights of Indigenous Peoples adopted by a vote of 143–4 (U.S., New Zealand, Canada, Australia) with 11 (abstentions) in the UN General Assembly, A/61/L.67, September 7, 2007. This is a particularly notable challenge, suggesting that the human rights texts agreed upon as a result of negotiations between governments did not adequately incorporate or represent the cultural outlook or values of indigenous communities, and thus required a completely separate formulation. There are an estimated 350 million people who regard themselves as "indigenous," spread around the world, but lacking in representation in almost every global arena because none of their communities qualify as sovereign states.

3 There was much discussion of these issues, especially prompted by these two controversial experiences, along with severe criticism associated with the inaction of the international community in relation to the Rwanda genocide of 1994 and the Srebrenica massacre in 1995. See Linda Melvern, *A People Betrayed: The Role of the West in Rwanda's Genocide* (London: Zed, 2000); Melvern, *Conspiracy to Murder: The Rwanda Genocide* (London: Verso, 2004); and for the Bosnia experience see David Rieff, *Slaughterhouse: Bosnia and the Future of the West* (New York: Simon Schuster, 1996).

4 Elazar Barkan, *The Guilt of Nations* (New York: Norton, 2000), ix and xv, where the Swiss reimbursement and compensation initiative is singled out as a defining moment that separated the past from the future on such matters. See also Richard Falk, *Human Rights Horizons: The Promise of Justice in a Globalizing World* (New York Routledge, 2000), esp. 13–36, 189–216.

5 Ken Booth, "Human Wrongs and International Relations," *International Affairs* 71(2): 103–126 (1995).

6 It was this legalism that prompted a re-thinking of positivist jurisprudence that had prevailed in German legal education during the pre-Nazi era, and provided judges, citizens, and bureaucrats with excuses for unquestioning compliance with the most horrific of German laws and governmental practices. One way of countering this deference to "law" was to encourage an ethos of what Habermas has labeled "constitutional patriotism," that is, privileging the values embedded in the German Constitution above those that might be decreed by the institutions of government from time to time.

7 See the book bearing this title devoted to the Nanking Massacre of 1937: Iris Chang, *The Rape of Nanking: The Forgotten Holocaust of World War II* (New York: Basic Books, 1997).

8 An alternative rationale, less historically grounded in the Nazi experience, would take its cue from the treaty formalization of the international crime of genocide. These two rationales substantially converge as the Holocaust continues to be viewed as the paradigmatic instance of genocide.

9 On the relevance of normative factors to effective global leadership see Torbjørn L. Knutsen, *The Rise and Fall of World Orders* (Manchester, UK: Manchester University Press, 1999), 234–303.

10 See Noam Chomsky & Edward S. Herman, *The Political Economy of Human Rights* (Boston, MA: South End Press, 2 vols., 1979).

11 John Ikenberry, *After Victory: Institutions, Strategic Restraint, and the Rebuilding of Order after Major Wars* (Princeton, NJ: Princeton University Press, 2001).

12 See Charles W. Kegley, Jr. & Gregory A. Raymond, *Exorcising the Ghost of Westphalia: Building World Order in the New Millennium* (Upper Saddle River, NJ: Prentice Hall, 2002).

13 But see David J. Bederman, *International Law Frameworks* (New York: Foundation Press, 2006), at 99 on the allegedly new paradigm of international law premised on "human dignity," as well as "sovereignty," which emerged after World War II.

14 Woodrow Wilson indulged the vain hope that geopolitics could be transcended, or at least regulated to the margins, by the establishment of the League of Nations and through commitments to collective security and international law.

15 George F. Kennan, *American Diplomacy 1900–1950* (New York, Mentor, 1951), 82–83.

16 Convenient text of PPS 23 in Thomas H. Etzold and John Lewis Gaddis, eds., *Containment: Documents on American Policy and Strategy 1945–1950* (New York: Columbia University Press, 1978), 226–228, at 227.

17 Etzold & Gaddis, note 16 above, at 385–442, at 387.

18 See the formulation of these objections in the Asian context in Richard H. Minear, *Victors' Justice: The Tokyo War Crimes Trial* (Princeton, NJ: Princeton University Press, 1971).

19 Telford Taylor, *Nuremberg and Vietnam: An American Tragedy* (Chicago: Quadrangle Books, 1970); also see Telford Taylor, *The Anatomy of the Nuremberg Trials* (New York: Knopf, 1992).

20 Barkan, note 4 above, 342–343; this question is posed in relation to a very well conceptualized discussion of restitution in a chapter aptly titled "Toward a Theory of Restitution," at 308–349.

21 See the argument of Richard Falk, *On Humane Global Governance: Toward a New World Politics* (Cambridge, UK: Polity, 1995).

22 This distinction and its world order implications are explored in Richard Falk, *Predatory Globalization: A Critique* (Cambridge, UK: Polity Press, 1999).

7 The Pinochet Moment: Whither Universal Jurisdiction?

1 Howard Ball, *Prosecuting War Crimes and Genocide: The Twentieth-Century Experience* (Lawrence: University Press of Kansas, 1999), 232.

2 *El Mundo*, quoted by Ball, note 1 above, 232.

3 Tunku Varadarajan, WSJ, II/14/2000, A43.

4 As Jordan Paust points out in his chapter in Stephen Macedo, ed., *Universal Jurisdiction: National Courts and the Prosecution of Serious Crimes under International Law* (Philadelphia, PA: University of Pennsylvania Press, 2004), other allegedly criminal heads of state had been previously indicted in domestic courts, but with far less publicity and with less emphasis on crimes of state that seemed to qualify as Crimes Against Humanity. Legal proceedings in foreign domestic courts against Noriega (Panama), Marcos (Philippines), and Stroessner (Paraguay), are examples.

5 See Daniele Archibugi & David Held, eds., *Cosmopolitan Democracy* (Cambridge, UK: Polity, 1995); also Martha Nussbaum's lead essay in Joshua Cohen, ed., *For Love of Country: Debating the Limits of Patriotism* (Boston, MA: Beacon, 1996).

6 The Milosevic indictment and prosecution will remain controversial because it is intertwined with both the NATO War of 1999 relating to Kosovo and to the overall status of Serbian nationalist claims. For such a critical account see John Laughland, *Travesty: The Trial of Slobodan Milosevic and the Corruption of International Justice* (London, UK: Pluto, 2007).

7 In the absence of a Security Council referral, the prosecutor can only initiate a proceeding if either the state where the crime occurred or of the nationality of the accused is itself a party or gives its consent to ICC jurisdiction. This seemingly

crippling constraint was established to placate the sovereignty-oriented insistence of several states, especially the United States and France.

8 Book Review, *Amer. J. Int'l L.* 94(2), 2000, 416–418, at 417.

9 For assessment see Richard Falk, *Human Rights Horizons: The Pursuit of Justice in a Globalizing World* (New York: Routledge, 2000), esp. 1–56.

10 At the same time, the Chilean picture remained clouded for several years. The Chilean military establishment exerted considerable pressure on the Lagos administration to avoid prosecutions of Pinochet and other officials associated with Pinochet-era policies. There was a complex series of legal developments in Chile after Pinochet's return in March 2000. These developments included due process objections to the mode of interrogation in Britain, as well as continuing objections to Pinochet's prosecution based on his ill-health. As indicated above, the Supreme Court finally resolved the fitness issue in Pinochet's favor, ending the prospect of further litigation and any substantive decision. For a journalistic account of these Chilean maneuverings see Mark Mulligan, "Appeal against Pinochet Charges Upheld," *Financial Times*, 21 December 2000, 3.

11 See *When Tyrants Tremble: The Pinochet Case*, Human Rights Watch, Vol. 11, No. 1 (Oct. 1999), 2.

12 For an argument to this effect see Gregory Weeks, "Waiting for Cincinnatus: The Role of Pinochet in Post-Authoritarian Chile," *Third World Quarterly* 21(5):725–738.

13 HRW, note 11 above, 3

14 For an important clarification see José Zalaquett's Introduction to the Report of the Chilean National Commission on Truth and Reconciliation of 1993 in Henry Steiner & Philip Alston, eds., *International Human Rights in Context* (Oxford University Press, 2nd edn., 2000), 1221–1224.

15 A summary account of Chilean cross-currents with respect to Pinochet during the presidency of Ricardo Lagos is contained in Clifford Krauss, "In Chile, Democracy Depends on a Delicate Balance," *New York Times*, Dec. 31, 2000, §4, 5. Krauss calls attention to the Chilean use of the word "convivencia," or living together, as a way of expressing a search for some middle ground between pro- and anti-Pinochet tendencies in Chile.

16 See the strong argument for maximal flexibility in the application of legal standards in Pinochet-type situations put forward in Max Boot, "When 'Justice' and 'Peace' Don't Mix," *Wall Street Journal*, Oct. 2, 2000, A34.

17 This presentation of the Spanish phase of the Pinochet proceedings relies heavily on María del Carmen Márquez Carrasco & Joaquín Alcaide Fernández, "In re Pinochet," 93 *Amer. J. Int'l L.* 690 (1999).

18 The Criminal Division of the National Court indicated that more than 500 Spanish subjects had disappeared or were killed in Argentina, and another 50 in Chile. Id. at 691. It not clear why the events in Argentina should have been included in an inquiry legally concerned only with Chile.

19 For evaluation of the Spanish proceedings see Id. at 694–96; for parallel consideration of investigation, indictment, and extradition requests in the French Tribunal de grande instance (Paris) see Brigette Stern, "In re Pinochet," 93 *Amer. J. Int'l L.* 696 (1999); for Belgian proceedings, which included allegations of crimes against humanity, that took place in the Belgian Tribunal of First Instance of Brussels, see Luc Reydams, "In re Pinochet," 93 *Amer. J. Int'l L.* 700 (1999). Only in Spain did the proceedings commence *before* the detention of Pinochet

20 See footnote 2 of Luc Reydams' report on the Belgian experience in 1998, 93 *Amer. J. Int'l L.* 703 (1999) for summary and references.

21 It may be that a mutation on the general moral climate of world politics occurred in this interim. Such a ruptured continuity has been noted, with particular reference to reparations and restitutions claims being acted upon around the world. Elazar

Barkan considers this pattern, noting that "on or about March 5, 1997, world morality—not to say, human nature—changed. The reason was unexpected: In response to accusations of profiting from Jewish suffering during World War II, Switzerland announced its intention to sell substantial amounts of its gold to create a humanitarian fund of five billion dollars." Barkan, *The Guilt of Nations: Restitution and Negotiating Historical Injustices* (New York: Norton, 2000), xv. I would argue that issues of restitution are cut from the same moral climate as the sort of questions of criminal accountability raised by the claims against Pinochet.

22 The French experience is summarized by Bridgette Stern, "In re Pinochet," 93 *Amer. J. Int'l L.* 696 (1999).

23 Id. at 699.

24 Interestingly, in 1998 the Belgian Parliament amended the 1993 statute, qualifying crimes against humanity and genocide as international law crimes under Belgian law. See footnote 7, Id. at 701.

25 Id. at 703

26 Ibid.

27 Cf. footnote 11, Id. at 703, for citations and reference to Antonio Cassese's reliance on Scelle's ideas within the contemporary setting.

28 See overview of the British litigation provided by Christine M. Chinkin, "In re Pinochet," 93 *Amer. J. Int'l L.* 703.

29 *R. v. Bow Street Metropolitan Stipendiary Magistrate and Others, ex parte Pinochet Ugarte*, [1998] 3 WLR 1456; it should be noted that the House of Lords, which is formally the senior chamber of the British Parliament, contains the highest court in the United Kingdom, consisting of twelve Law Lords appointed for life, and known as life peers. The panel of judges that hears a particular case is designated by the presiding law lord, who during the Pinochet proceedings was Lord Browne-Wilkinson.

30 Lord Hoffman was a director of AI's charity division, and his wife was a member of the AI administrative staff.

31 *R. v. Bow Street Stipendiary Magistrate and Others, ex parte Pinochet Ugarte* (No. 2), {1999}2 WLR 272.

32 See HRW, note 11 above, 21: stressing "self-amnesty," Pinochet's senatorial immunity, and the jurisdiction of military tribunals.

33 For details see Chinkin, note 28 above, at 705, fn 11.

34 38 *International Legal Materials*, 581, 583 (1999).

35 As quoted in HRW, note 11 above, at 17.

36 Id., at 588; more fully explained in Lord Hope's opinion, at 613–615.

37 Id. at 591.

38 Id. at 594.

39 Id. at 595–609.

40 Id. at 595–609.

41 *Attorney-General of Israel* v. *Eichmann* (1962) 36 *Inetrnational Law Reports*, 5; also noted was the American extradition case of *Demjanjuk* v. *Petrovsky* (1985) 603 F. Supp. 1468, aff'd 776 F. 2d 571.

42 Id. at 648.

43 Id. at 649.

44 Isolated offense by political leaders would not pass the test. Ibid.

45 Id. at 650.

46 Id. at 652.

47 Civil charges against heads of state for official wrongdoing have been previously accepted, and without much international fanfare. For instance, in various proceedings in American courts against the former Filipino leader, Ferdinand Marcos. See *Republic of the Philippines* v. *Marcos*, 806 F.2d 344 (2d Cir. 1986). See

also on drug charges used to convict Noriega for acts committed while he was head of state, *United States v. Noriega*, 746 F. Supp 1506 (S.D. Fla. 1990) and 117 F.3d 1212 (11th Cir., 1997).

48 A new important challenge to the ethos of accountability arose as a result of Milosevic's fall from power in the FRY, and Kostunica's initial pledge of non-cooperation with the ICTY in The Hague. For an argument that this is an unacceptable retreat from accountability see Michael Ignatieff, "The Right Trial for Milosevic," *New York Times*, Oct. 10, 2000, A27. In the end, Belgrade facilitated the arrest of Milosevic and his transfer to The Hague for prosecution, succumbing to pressures relating to much-needed economic assistance that would not be forthcoming unless Milosevic was made available as a criminal defendant to face international charges.

8 Genocide at the World Court: The Case Against Serbia

1 *Bosnian Genocide Case*, ICJ Reports, Feb. 26, 2007; see also the European Court of Human Rights case, *Jorgic v. Germany*, judgment, July 12, 2007. FRY was the official name of former Yugoslavia at the time the legal dispute was referred to the World Court. For most purposes, the FRY by the time of this litigation was reduced to "Serbia," which had previously been but one of the constituent republics of a unified federal state.

2 Article IX of the Genocide Convention gives parties the right to refer legal disputes arising under the treaty to the ICJ. Bosnia took advantage of this provision to bring the issue to The Hague, and the FRY accepted its obligation to participate in the legal proceedings.

3 For a sharp criticism of the ICTY interrupted proceeding against Milosevic see John Laughland, *Travesty: The Trial of Slobodan Milosevic and the Corruption of International Justice* (London, UK: Pluto, 2007). For a positive assessment see Michael Scharf and William A. Schabas, *Slobodan Milosevic on Trial: A Companion* (New York: Continuum).

4 Balakrishnan Rajagopal, "Counter-Hegemonic International Law: Rethinking Human Rights and Development as a Third World Strategy," *Third World Quarterly* 27(5):767–783 (2006); for general background, see Detlev Vagts, "Hegemonic International Law," *American Journal of International Law* 95(4):843–848 (2001); some international law scholarship that claims sensitivity to realist dimensions of international life is also implicitly endorsing hegemonic international law. Perhaps the conceptually most impressive example of this is to be found in some of the writing of Thomas Franck. See Franck on World Court and on UN: *Judging the World Court* (New York: Priority Publishers, 1986), *Nation against Nation: What Happened to the UN Dream and What the U.S. Can Do About It* (New York: Oxford University Press, 1985).

5 See *Military and Paramilitary Activities in and against Nicaragua* (*Nicaragua v. United States*), ICJ Reports, June 27, 1986.

6 *Legality of the Threat of Nuclear Weapons*, Advisory Opinion, ICJ Reports, July 9, 2004.

7 See *Legal Consequences of the Threat of the Construction of a Wall in the Occupied Palestinians Territories*, Advisory Opinion, ICJ Reports, July 9, 2004.

8 As was widely reported at the time, great effort was made in these cases by the United States to avoid the assertion of jurisdictional authority by the ICJ.

9 See assessment along these lines in *Kosovo Report*, Independent International Commission on Kosovo (Oxford: Oxford University Press, 2000).

10 See Noam Chomsky, *The New Military Humanism* (Monrie, ME: Common Courage Press).

Notes

9 A Descending Spiral

1   The full title is *The Lesser Evil: Political Ethics in an Age of Terror* (Princeton, NJ: Princeton University Press, 2004); a similar title appears in an outstanding volume, Giovanna Borradori, *Philosophy in a Time of Terror: Dialogues with Jürgen Habermas and Jacques Derrida* (Chicago: University of Chicago Press, 2003).

2   Such a perspective is given its most expansive expression by Norman Podhoretz, in an article insisting that the American response to September 11 be treated as World War IV. See Norman Podhoretz, "World War IV: How It Started, What It Means, and Why We Have to Win," *Commentary* Sept. 2004.

3   It is useful to recall the evolution of the term "terrorism," which had its origins in the use of state terrorism in the Thermidor stage of the French Revolution, perhaps most memorably described by Crane Brinton in his influential book *The Anatomy of Revolution* (New York: Vintage, 1957, originally published in 1952). It has been a successful statist campaign to engineer this shift in word usage, restricting the word "terrorism" to anti-state violence, and extending its usage even to political violence that occurs in the course of a legitimate political struggle against oppressive rule and is directed at military and governmental targets.

4   I have tried to reconstruct a more satisfactory pattern of usage for the terminology of terrorism, considering its usage in some form as unavoidable. See Richard Falk, *Revolutionaries and Functionaries: The Dual Face of Terrorism* (New York: E.P. Dutton, 1988), esp. 1–39; Falk, *The Great Terror War* (Northampton, MA: Olive Branch Press, 2003).

5   An argument cogently presented by Zbigniew Brzezinski in *The Choice: Global Domination or Global Leadership* (New York: Basic Books, 2004), esp. 24–36.

6   This failure to restrict the objective of the U.S. response to September 11 has been a consistent feature of official statements, starting with President Bush's Address to a Joint Session of Congress on September 20, 2001. It became realized at a global level as the U.S. government kept extending its militarist responses, first verbally by its designation of states as forming an "axis of evil" and then by initiating a non-defensive war against a member of the axis, Iraq, without any prior authorization by the United Nations Security Council.

7   The emergence of a consensus among international law specialists as to the illegality of the Iraq invasion and subsequent occupation was evident at a plenary panel of the 2004 Annual Meeting of the American Society of International Law. See "Iraq, One Year Later," Proceedings of the 98th Annual Meeting, March 31–April 3, 2004, Washington, DC, 261–273.

8   Such a discussion is imaginatively present in the Borradori volume, cited in note 1 above.

9   There is a vast literature on this theme of empire. Among the most notable works are the following: Michael Hardt & Antonio Negri, *Empire* (Cambridge, MA: Harvard University Press, 2000); Alain Joxe, *Empire of Disorder* (Cambridge, MA: MIT Press/Semiotext(e), 2002); Andrew J. Bacevich, *American Empire: The Realities and Consequences of U.S. Diplomacy* (Cambridge, MA: Harvard University Press, 2002); David Harvey, *The New Imperialism* (Oxford, UK: Oxford University Press, 2003); Michael Mann, *The Incoherent Empire* (London, UK: Verso, 2003).

10 For background on state terrorism in an Asian setting, but also useful for its conceptual understanding, see Mark Selden & Alvin Y. So, eds., *War and State Terrorism: The United States, Japan, and Asia-Pacific in the Long Twentieth Century* (Lanham, MD: Rowman & Littlefield, 2004); on a more general level, see the older but still useful collection of essays: Alexander George, ed., *Western State Terrorism* (London, UK: Routledge, 1991).

11 With some hesitation I have earlier made the argument that labeling the 1990s as the era of globalization was justified. Richard Falk, *Predatory Globalization: A Critique* (Cambridge, UK: Polity, 1999).

12 For consideration of what I have called "the normative revolution" of the 1990s, with its emphasis on a global justice agenda that accented the role of human rights see Richard Falk, *The Declining World Order: America's Neo-Imperial Foreign Policy* (New York: Routledge, 2004), 107–136.

13 For the most comprehensive critique along these lines see Noam Chomsky & Edward T. Herman, *The Political Economy of Human Rights* (Boston, MA: South End Press, 2 vols., 1979)

14 I have argued along these lines in Richard Falk, "What Future for the UN Charter System of War Prevention? Reflections on the Iraq War," in Irwin Abrams & Wang Gungwu, eds., *The Iraq War and Its Consequences: Thoughts of Nobel Peace Laureates and Eminent Scholars* (Singapore: World Scientific, 2003) 195–214.

15 To the extent that a humanitarian emergency existed in Iraq, it was the result of the devastating bombing of the Iraqi civilian infrastructure during the 1991 Gulf War, reinforced by the twelve years of punitive sanctions between 1991 and the onset of the Iraq War in 2003.

16 *The Kosovo Report: Conflict, International Response, Lessons Learned*, Report of the Independent International Commission on Kosovo (Oxford, UK: Oxford University Press, 2002), 185–198, drawing a distinction between "legality" and "legitimacy," and drawing the precarious conclusion that the Kosovo War was illegal, yet legitimate. This conditional endorsement was further limited by a framework of principles restricting the claim of legitimacy within principled boundaries. It should be mentioned that I was a member of the Commission, and participated in the drafting of the report.

17 See tract by David Frum & Richard Perle, *An End to Evil: How to Win the War on Terror* (New York: Random House, 2003).

18 A statement made on a number of public occasions in 2004 by Professor Ahmet Devutoglu, chief advisor to the Prime Minister and Foreign Minister of Turkey.

19 See *The Great Terror War*, note 4 above, 61–72.

20 Of course, despite this statist opposition to violent penetrations of territorial sovereignty, states had frequently—and none more than the United States—supported anti-state exile movements engaged in transnational violence against established governments. Consider, for instance, support over the years for anti-Castro exiles in Florida and elsewhere, culminating in CIA involvement in the Bay of Pigs failed invasion of April 1961, or the extensive help given to the Contras who were seeking to disrupt by political violence the Sandinista government of Nicaragua, and more recently the help given to Iraqi exile groups committed to the overthrow of the Saddam Hussein regime in Iraq.

21 For a short trenchant analysis along these lines see Garry Wills, "Iraq: A Just War," *New York Review of Books*, Nov. 18, 2004, 32–35, esp. 32–33.

22 A series of books critical of the Bush foreign policy have argued for the restoration of American leadership in a manner that endorses the economistic and multilateralist approaches of the 1990s by the United States. This restoration involves a resumption of the global empire project, but with more reliance on market forces, a renewed sense of legitimacy, and a reliance on persuasive forms of diplomacy. Useful texts in this regard are Brzezinski, note 3 above, Bacevich, note 9 above, and Amitai Etzioni, *From Empire to Community: A New Approach to International Relations* (New York: Palgrave, 2004).

23 Among the most compelling insider books on these failures to follow the trail of intelligence signposts are Richard A. Clarke, *Against All Enemies: Inside America's*

War on Terror (New York: Free Press, 2004); Anonymous, *Imperial Hubris: Why the West Is Losing the War on Terror* (Dulles, VA: Brassey's, 2004); a focus on the intelligence component of security is a feature in *The 9/11 Commission Report*, Final Report of the National Commission on Terrorist Attacks upon the United States (New York: Norton, 2004). See also the scathing attack on the 9/11 Commission and its refusal to examine more fully and accurately the context of the attacks by David Ray Griffin, *The 9/11 Commission Report: Omissions and Distortions* (Northampton, MA: Olive Branch Press, 2004).

24 See Podhoretz, note 2 above, who is also dismissive of reliance on law enforcement without providing any convincing grounds for substituting recourse to global war if indeed the goal is the avoidance of mega-terrorism in the future.

25 See Clarke and Anonymous, both cited in note 23 above, as well as the 9/11 Commission Report and surrounding discussion.

26 See Falk, note 12 above, ch. 1.

27 Robert Kagan, *Of Paradise and Power: America and Europe in the New World Order* (New York: Knopf, 2003).

10 Encroaching on the Rule of Law: Counter-Terrorist Justifications

1 For an attempt in this direction see Richard Falk, "Demystifying Iraq?" *The New Centennial Review* 5(1):43–62 (2005).

2 For useful discussion of this observation see Pierce O'Donnell, *In Time of War: Hitler's Terrorist Attack on America* (New York: New Press, 2005); on the American tendency to absolutize its goals in wartime see the influential study by Robert W. Tucker, *The Just War: A Study in Contemporary American Doctrine* (Baltimore, MD: Johns Hopkins University Press, 1960).

3 See Richard Falk, "Toward Regional War in the Middle East?" *International Journal of Contemporary Iraqi Studies*, 1(1):77–92 (2007).

4 For good statement as to this continuity see Julie Mertus, "Human Rights and Civil Society in a New Age of American Exceptionalism," in Richard A. Wilson, ed., *Human Rights in an "Age of Terrorism"* (New York: Cambridge University Press, 2005), 317–335, at 320.

5 This story is narrated in a persuasive manner by Alfred W. McCoy in his important book *A Question of Torture: CIA Interrogation from the Cold War to the War on Terror* (New York: Metropolitan Books, 2006).

6 For a depiction of this dynamic in the setting of the Vietnam War see Richard Falk, Robert Jay Lifton, & Gabriel Kolko, eds., *Crimes of War* (New York: Random House, 1971).

7 *Repairing America's Defenses*, Report of the Project for a New American Century (PNAC), Sept. 2000, offers strong criticisms of Clinton's economistic approach to world order, and provides a blueprint for a much more militarist foreign policy. The report was signed by many core members of the Bush entourage of advisors, and is notable for three reasons: its stress on the importance of regime change in Iraq; its failure to relate American strategic priorities to counter-terrorism; and its recognition that its recommendations could not be operationalized without a change in the political climate that would mobilize the American people for war.

8 This acknowledgement in the PNAC (note 7 above), together with the many failures to heed warnings about a terrorist attack on American targets, as well as the mystifying oversights in the face of the attack itself, have fueled suspicions about some level of official complicity with respect to the 9/11 events, at least a willingness to allow something to happen that might have been prevented. The most responsible and comprehensive critique of the official version of 9/11 can be found in two books written by a highly respected philosopher of religion,

David Ray Griffin, *The New Pearl Harbor: Disturbing Questions about the Bush Administration and 9/11* (Northampton, MA: Olive Branch Press, 2004), *The 9/11 Commission Report: Omissions and Distortions* (Northampton, MA: Olive Branch Press, 2005).

9   See H.C.L. Merillat, ed., *Legal Advisors and Foreign Affairs* (Dobbs Ferry, NY: Oceana, 1964); John Norton Moore, Frederick S. Tipson, & Robert F. Turner, eds., *National Security Law* (Durham, NC: Carolina Academic Press, 1990). Perhaps, the most penetrating exploration of this issue is to be found in the jurisprudential approach of Myres S. McDougal. See McDougal and Associates, *Studies in World Public Order* (New Haven, CT: Yale University Press, 1960).

10   See Jack L. Goldsmith & Eric A. Posner, *The Limits of International Law* (New York: Oxford University Press, 2005) for a highly intellectualized argument for the subordination of international law, which means generally subordinating the rule of law to the extent that it is structured by reference to international standards; on highly unprecedented arguments favoring presidential unaccountability in wartime see John Yoo, *The Powers of War and Peace: The Constitution and Foreign Affairs after 9/11* (Chicago: University of Chicago Press, 2005). For a useful defense of legality as the basis for foreign policy see Philippe Sands, *Lawless World: America and the Making and Breaking of Global Rules* (London, UK: Penguin, 2005) and Amy Bartholomew, ed., *Empire's Law: The American Imperial Project and the "War to Remake the World"* (London, UK: Pluto 2006); for a critique of Yoo see David Cole, "All Power to the President—The Case of John Yoo," *New York Review of Books*, Nov. 17, 2005, pp. 8–12. For the resistance of some government lawyers to the neoconservative assault on legality see Lisa Hajjar, "An Army of Lawyers: From Disgruntled JAGs to Civil Libertarians, Legal Professionals Have Come Together Against Torture," *The Nation*, Dec. 26, 2005, pp. 41–42; also see Richard B. Bilder & Detlev F. Vagts, "Speaking Law to Power: Lawyers and Torture," in Karen J. Greenberg, ed., *The Torture Debate in America* (New York: Cambridge University Press, 2006), pp. 151–161.

11   See the useful range of interpretations in Michael Ignatieff, ed., *American Exceptionalism and Human Rights* (Princeton, NJ: Princeton University Press, 2005); for a neoconservative approach to this issue of a distinctive American role that is less law-oriented than that of Western European liberal democracies see Robert Kagan, *Of Paradise and Power: America and Europe in the New World Order* (New York: Knopf, 2003).

12   I originally shared this sense of plausibility, justifying recourse to war against the Taliban regime in power in Afghanistan as the appropriate response to the sort of continuing threat that seemed to be posed by Al Qaeda. See Richard Falk, *The Great Terror War* (Northampton, MA: Olive Branch Press, 2003).

13   This strategic posture was initially depicted by President Bush in his address to the graduating class at West Point on June 1, 2002; it was authoritatively set forth in *National Security Strategy of the United States of America* (Washington, DC: White House, Sept. 2002), Section V, and has been restated in the sequel document, *National Security Strategy of the United States of America* (Washington, DC: White House, March 16, 2006), pp.18–24.

14   Israel's attack on the Iraqi nuclear reactor at Osirak in 1981 was premised on such a preventive rationale, but not as associated with a terrorist threat. The attack exhibited an overall unwillingness to allow any neighbor to become a potential challenger to Israeli military dominance in the region.

15   See various legal memoranda by government lawyers, especially Jay S. Bybee, Alberto Gonzales, and William J. Haynes, II, main documents listed note 1 in Bilder & Vagts, note 6 above; for the main official texts see Joshua Dratel & Karen J. Greenberg, eds., *The Torture Papers* (New York: Cambridge University Press,

2005); also, Karen J. Greenberg, note 10 above. The most authoritative political defense of U.S. government practices is given by President Bush, "President Discusses Creation of Military Commissions to Try Suspected Terrorists," White House, Sept. 6, 2006.

16 See the exhaustive assessment of this position by David Lubin, "Liberalism, Torture, and the Ticking Bomb," in Greenberg, note 10 above, pp. 35–83; for a notorious scholarly argument favoring "legalized" torture see Alan M. Dershowitz, *Why Terrorism Works* (New Haven, CY: Yale University Press, 2002). Also Kim Lane Scheppele, "Hypothetical Torture in the "War on Terrorism,"" *Journal of National Security Law* 1(2):285–340 (2005).

17 John Major & Kim Campbell, "Terrorism in Democracies," IXXI breakfast conversations, London School of Economics, Dec. 1, 2005.

18 Condoleezza Rice made this same argument in a widely quoted talk given in Cairo, June 20, 2005, but it did not result in any visible change in policy. Her essential message was as follows: "For 60 years, my country, the United States, pursued stability at the expense of democracy in this region here in the Middle East—and we achieved neither. Now, we are taking a different course. We are supporting the democratic aspirations of all peoples." "Remarks at the American University of Cairo," <www.state.gov/secretary/rm/2005/48328.htm>

19 Indeed the 2006 Quadrennial Defense Review highlights its extensive review of American defense planning by reference to what it describes as "the long war" for which it posits no benchmarks for an eventual outcome. *Quadrennial Defense Review Report*, Feb. 6, 2006, esp. section entitled "Fighting the Long War," pp. 9–11.

20 See useful study focused on the World War II experience by Pierce O'Donnell, note 2 above.

21 See *Korematsu v. United States* 320 U.S. 214 (1944); also *Hirabayashi v. U.S.* 320 U.S. 81(194-). See O'Donnell, note 2 above,

22 O'Donnell, note 2 above, 271

23 See *Hamdi v. Rumsfeld*, 296 F.3rd 278 (2002); further upheld in *Hamdi v. Rumsfeld*, 542 U.S. 507 (2004); *also Jose Padilla v. Donald Rumsfeld*, 243 F. Supp. 2d 42 (2003).

24 *Hamdan v. Rumsfeld*, 548 US 557 (2006) decided by a 5–3 vote of the Supreme Court that Common Article 3 of the Geneva Conventions of the Law of War (1949) were applicable, and this result was reinforced by *Boumediene v. Bush*, 553 U.S. ___ (2008) by a 5–4 vote.

25 See on this Hajjar, note 10 above.

26 See Memorandum of William H. Taft IV, The Legal Advisor of the Department of State, "President"s Decision about the Applicability of Geneva Conventions to al Qaeda and Taliban," in Greenberg, note 10 above, March 22, 2002, pp. 283–316; a conservative rationale is to be found in Lee A. Casey & David B. Rivkin, Jr., "Rethinking the Geneva Conventions," in Greenberg, note 10 above, pp. 203–213.

27 For a relevant overview of tendencies toward "new wars" and their implications for domestic political order see Mary Kaldor, *New and Old Wars: Organized Violence in a Global Era* (Cambridge, UK: Polity, 1999).

28 There is a growing important literature on this, see especially the views presented in Greenberg, note 10 above; also, the volume prepared by Human Rights Watch: Kenneth Roth & Minky Worden, eds., *Torture: Does It Make Us Safer? Is It Ever OK?* (New York: New Press and Human Rights Watch, 2005); see also the special issue of *The Nation* entitled "The Torture Complex," Dec. 26, 2005, pp. 11–42.

29 "President Discusses Creation of Military Commissions to Try Suspected Terrorists," White House, Sept. 6, 2006.

30 See Lubin, note 14 above, in Greenberg, note 10 above.

31 This argument is developed in its most nuanced form by Michael Ignatieff, *The Lesser Evil: Political Ethics in an Age of Terror* (Princeton, NJ: Princeton University Press, 2005); for a shorter statement of this viewpoint, chastened and less deferential to the rationales put forward by the U.S. government, made in the aftermath of the Abu Ghraib disclosures, see Michael Ignatieff, "Moral Prohibition at a Price," in Roth & Worden, note 28 above, pp. 18–27; a broader exchange of views can be found in Sanford Levinson, ed., *Torture: A Collection* (New York: Oxford University Press, 2004).

32 John Bolton has been the most outspoken neoconservative voice on the proper view of international law (and the authority of the United Nations). In his own words, "It is a big mistake for us to grant any validity to international law even when it may seem in our short-term interest to do so—because, over the long-term, the goal of those who think international law really means anything are those who want to constrict the United States." For this and related assertions see "John Bolton: An Unforgivable Choice as UN Ambassador," Council on Hemispheric Affairs, March 10, 2005, <www.coha.org>. Jack Goldsmith and especially John Yoo have been the most influential academic supporters of the approaches to legal issues taken by the Bush presidency.

33 See Yoo, note 10 above; for critique of these views see Cole, note 10 above.

34 See Arthur M.Schlesinger, Jr., *The Imperial Presidency* (Boston, MA: Houghton-Mifflin, 1973); J. William Fulbright, *The Arrogance of Power* (New York: Random House, 1967).

35 See Peter Dale Scott, "New Multimillion-Dollar Contract to Construct Detentions Camps," Pacific New Service, Jan. 30, 2006.

36 UN Report, E/CN.4/2006/120, Feb. 15, 2006.

37 Pub. L. No. 107-40, 115 Stat. 224.

38 For text of Geneva Convention relative to the Treatment of Prisoners of War, of August 12, 1949, see *The Geneva Conventions of August 12 1949* (Geneva: International Committee of the Red Cross, undated), pp. 75–134, at 75–78. Article 5 is particularly pertinent as it confers prisoner of war status on any person detained as a combatant until such time "as their status has been determined by a competent tribunal."

39 See 10 U.S. Code §§821, 836 (2001); and Public Law No. 10740, 115 Statute 224 (2001).

11 Humanitarian Intervention

1 See Samuel Huntington, *The Dilemma of American Ideals and Institutions* (Washington, D.C.: AEI, 1981).

2 See William Blum, *Rogue State: A Guide to the World's Only Superpower* (Monroe, ME: Common Courage Press, 2000).

3 See Elazar Barkan, *Guilt of Nations: Restitution and Negotiating Historical Injustices* (New York: Norton, 2000); Martha Minow, *Between Vengeance and Forgiveness: Facing History after Genocide and Mass Violence* (Boston, MA: Beacon Press, 1998); Gary Jonathan Bass, *Stay the Hand of Vengeance: The Politics of War Crimes Trials* (Princeton, NJ: Princeton University Press, 2000); Richard Falk, *Human Rights Horizons: Pursuit of Justice in a Globalizing World* (New York: Routledge, 2000).

4 For various understandings of the law and politics of humanitarian intervention see Nicholas J. Wheeler, *Saving Strangers: Humanitarian Intervention in International Society* (Oxford: Oxford University Press, 2000); Julie Mertus, *Bait and Switch: Human Rights and U.S. Foreign Policy* (Washington, DC:Foreign Policy in Focus, 2004); Sean Murphy, *Humanitarian Intervention: The UN in an Evolving World Order* (Philadelphia: University of Pennsylvania Press, 1996); David Rieff, *Slaughterhouse: Bosnia and the Failure of the West* (New York: Simon & Schuster, 1995).

5   It is important to appreciate that in these settings the credibility and weight of humanitarian *motivations* were less significant than humanitarian *consequences*.

6   See Michael J. Glennon, *Limits of Law, Prerogatives of Power: Interventionism after Kosovo* (New York: Palgrave, 2001).

7   See Independent International Commission on Kosovo, *The Kosovo Report* (Oxford: Oxford University Press, 2000).

8   Indeed the latter stages of the Iraq debate follow on from Kosovo, with the continuing indication that the Bush administration feels empowered to act without UN authorization by relying on a coalition of the willing.

9   For theoretical support see Glennon, note 6 above, and A. Mark Weisbrud, *Use of Force: The Practice of States Since World War II* (University Park, PA: Pennsylvania State University Press, 1997).

10 *The Millennium Development Goals Report* (New York: United Nations, 2005), 46.

11 For instance, Tanzania invading Uganda, India in East Pakistan, Vietnam in Cambodia.

12 *Global Civil Society Yearbook 2001* (Oxford, UK: Oxford University Press, 2001), 109–143, at 140.

13 Of course, there is a definitional ambiguity here: "freedom fighters" and mercenaries were active in the Balkan Wars and sub-Saharan Africa, and can be considered either as a kind of civil society initiative or as a form of state sponsorship depending on the facts.

14 Richard Falk, *The Declining World Order: America's Imperial Foreign Geopolitics* (New York: Routledge, 2004).

15 For text see George W. Bush, Second Inaugural Ceremony, White House website, Jan. 20, 2005; on some occasions Bush was described as following a right-wing Wilsonian foreign policy, but however described it was the most pronounced departure from a realist approach since Woodrow Wilson.

16 See Falk, *The Great Terror War* (Northampton, MA: Olive Branch Press, 2003).

17 See *Repairing America's Defenses*, Report of the Project for a New American Century (PNAC), Washington, DC, Sept. 2000.

18 Such an assessment does not excuse the American failure to take more care to avoid civilian casualties or to fail to commit itself more fully to post-conflict reconstruction, nor does it enter the debate about such ulterior motives as securing the pipeline planned for northern Afghanistan under American auspices.

19 Tony Blair's speech to the Labour Party conference in Glasgow, Scotland on Feb. 15, 2003, reprinted in abridged version, *Los Angeles Times*, Feb. 23, 2003, Opinion, M6.

20 For comprehensive assessment of these issues see Falk, *The Costs of War International Law, the UN, and World Order after Iraq* (New York: Routledge, 2008).

21 Kaldor, "In Place of War, Open Up Iraq," Open Democracy, Feb. 13, 2003, <http://www.opendemocracy.net/conflict-iraqwarquestions/article_974.jsp>

22 Kaldor, in note 21 above.

23 See *The Responsibility to Protect*, International Commission on Intervention and State Sovereignty (Ottawa, Canada: International Development Centre, 2001).

24 See Nicholas Wheeler, *Saving Strangers: Humanitarian Intervention in International Society* (Oxford: Oxford University Press, 2000).

12 Crimes, Lies, and Law: Human Rights in Adversity

1   The U.S. government is meant here in a comprehensive sense as encompassing Congress and the judiciary, mainstream opposition political parties, and corporatized portions of the private sector linked closely to public funding and official policies, especially those companies comprising the military/industrial/homeland security complex.

2 A useful compendium of the torture debate, including apologists, can be found in Sanford Levinson, ed., *Torture: A Collection* (New York: Oxford University Press, 2004); also Mark Danner, *Torture and Truth: America, Abu Ghraib, and the War on Terror* (New York: New York Review of Books, 2004). See George W. Bush, "President Discusses Creation of Military Commissions to Try Suspected Terrorists" (White House website, Sept. 6, 2006), where he advocates Congressional legislation establishing military commissions to prosecute detainees at Guantanamo accused of terrorist crimes.

3 For somewhat differing insider accounts of the way lawyers in the Bush administration behaved after 9/11 see John Yoo, *War by Other Means: An Insider's Account of the War on Terror* (New York: Atlantic Monthly, 2006); Jack Goldsmith, *The Terror Presidency: Law and Judgment Inside the Bush Administration* (New York: Norton, 2007); for critique of effects see David Cole & Jules Lobel, *Less Safe, Less Free: Why America is Losing the War on Terror* (New York: The New Press, 2007).

4 See Brian Urquhart, "One Angry Man," *New York Review of Books*, March 6, 2008, pp. 12–15, reviewing the insider's anti-international law polemic of John Bolton, *Surrender Is Not an Option: Defending America at the United Nations and Abroad* (New York: Threshold, 2007).

5 But not consistently so; see e.g. the *Hamdan v. Rumsfeld* 548 U.S. 557 (2006) case, reinforced subsequently in *Boumediene v. George W. Bush*, 553 U.S. ___ (2008).

6 See, for instance, the appalling treatment of Maher Arar on false suspicions of terrorism, resulting in his detention and transfer to Syria, where he was tortured despite being completely innocent of any wrongdoing. The Arar experience is briefly discussed in Cole & Lobel, note 3 above, at 25–28.

7 For a full treatment of issues associated with the Iraq War see Richard Falk, *The Costs of War: International Law, the UN, and World Order after Iraq* (New York: Routledge, 2008).

8 "Education after Auschwitz," in Theodor Adorno, *Critical Models: Inventions and Catchwords* (New York, Columbia University Press, 1998), at 200; see also Ira Katznelson, *Desolation and Enlightenment: Political Knowledge after Total War, Totalitarianism, and the Holocaust* (New York: Columbia University Press, 2003).

9 See here especially Sven Lindquist, "*Exterminate All the Brutes*" (New York: New Press, 1996).

10 See Tu Weiming, "Confucianism and Civilization," in Majid Tehranian & David W. Chappell, *Dialogue of Civilizations: A New Peace Agenda for a New Millennium* (London: I.B. Taurus, 2002), 83–90.

11 See Hannah Arendt, *Eichmann in Jerusalem: A Report on the Banality of Evil* (New York: Viking, rev. ed., 1964).

12 "Freedom to Write," *New York Review of Books*, May 25, 2006, at 6.

13 Orhan Pamuk, *Snow* (New York: Knopf, 2004).

14 Arundhati Roy, *The God of Small Things* (New York: Random House, 1997).

15 Arundhati Roy, *War Talk* (Cambridge, MA: South End Press, 2003).

16 See Müge Gürsöy Sökmen, ed., *World Tribunal on Iraq: Making the Case Against War* (Northampton, MA: Olive Branch Press, 2008) at 490.

17 For their views see Peter Royle *Sartre–Camus Controversy.: A Literary and Philosophical Critique* (Ottawa, Canada: Ottawa University Press).

18 It may be relevant that both books consider 9/11 from within the setting of Blair's Britain. Ian McEwan, *Saturday* (New York: Doubleday, 2005) and David Runciman, *The Politics of Good Intentions: History, Fear and Hypocrisy in the New World Order* (Princeton, NJ: Princeton University Press, 2006)

19 Runciman, note 18 above, 1.

20 Id. at 2.

21 Id. at 3.

22 McEwan, note 18 above, 190.
23 Id. at 192.
24 Id. at 195.

13 Humanity in Question

 1 For inquiries see Elazar Barkan, *The Guilt of Nations: Restitution and Negotiating Historical Injustices* (New York: Norton, 2000); Darrel Moellenddorf, *Cosmopolitan Justice* (Boulder, CO: Westview Press, 2002); Luis Cabrera, *Political Theory of Justice: A Cosmopolitan Case for the World State* (London, UK: Routledge, 2004); Richard Falk, The Declining World Order: America's Imperial Geopolitics (New York: Routledge, 2004).
 2 See Richard Falk, *Religion and Humane Global Governance* (New York: Palgrave, 2001).
 3 Bill Joy, "Why the Future Doesn't Need Us" *Wired* 8(4):238–262 (2000).
 4 Hugo Grotius, *Law of War and Peace* (first pub. 1623) (Francis W. Kelsey, trans. New York: Classic Books, 1962); See Benedict Anderson, *Imagined Communities*, 2nd rev edn (London: Verso, 1991).
 5 See Jonathan Schell, *Unconquerable World: Power, Nonviolence, and the Will of the People* (New York: Metropolitan Books, 2003) on potential catastrophic dysfunction of war; also, Schell, *The Fate of Nations* (New York: Knopf, 1982).
 6 Michael Walzer, *Thick and Thin: Moral Argument at Home and Abroad* (Notre Dame, IN: Notre Dame University Press, 1994).
 7 Russell Jacoby, *Future Imperfect: Utopian Thought for an Anti-Utopian Age* (New York: Columbia University Press, 2005).
 8 Best diagnosed by Ken Booth, "Human Wrongs in International Relations," *Journal of International Affairs* 71:103–126 (1995).
 9 Some of the conceptual issues are discerned by Mary Kaldor, *New and Old Wars* (Cambridge, UK: Polity, 2006) ; also Falk, *The Great Terror War* (Northampton, MA: Olive Branch Press, 2003).
10 See Bush's West Point Commencement speech, June 1, 2002, White House website.
11 See John Yoo, *War by Other Means: An Insider's Account of the War on Terror* (New York: Atlantic Monthly, 2006); also Jonah Goldberg, "How We Should Judge Torture," *LA Times*, Dec. 8, 2005.
12 "President Outlines Strategy for Victory in Iraq," US Naval Academy, Nov. 30, 2005, White House website; at other times, the adversary is declared to be waging war against "civilization," which is used interchangeably with "humanity."
13 There are many reports that Bush's formulations are underpinned by a personal sense of religious destiny that guides his actions, taking precedence over considerations of prudence or political calculation. See for example Seymour M. Hersh, "Up in the Air: Where is the Iraq War Headed Next?" *The New Yorker*, Dec. 5, 2005, 42–54, at 44.
14 See *Repairing America's Defenses*, Report of the Project for a New American Century (PNAC), Washington, DC, Sept. 2000; a vision reiterated in *National Security Strategy of the United States of America* (Washington, DC: White House, 2002, updated 2006).
15 See Andrew J. Bacevich, *American Empire: The Realities and Consequences of U.S. Diplomacy* (Cambridge, MA: Harvard University Press, 2002); Chalmers Johnson, *The Sorrows of Empire: Militarism, Secrecy, and the end of the Republic* (New York: Metropolitan Books, 2004); David Harvey, *The New Imperialism* (Oxford, UK: Oxford University Press, 2005); Derek Gregory, *The Colonial Present: Afghanistan, Palestine, and Iraq* (Malden, MA: Blackwell, 2004); Phyllis Bennis, *Challenging Empire: How People, Governments and the UN Defy U.S. Power* (Northampton, MA: Olive Branch Press, 2006).

16 Grotius, note 4 above, Prolegomena.
17 Geneva Conventions on the Law of War (1949) and the Additional Protocols to the Geneva Conventions on the Law of War (1977).
18 For detailed inquiry see Independent International Commission on Kosovo *The Kosovo Report* (Oxford, UK: Oxford University Press, 2000)
19 See Anne Orfeld, *Reading Humanitarian Intervention: Human Rights and the Use of Force in International Law* (Cambridge, UK: Cambridge University Press, 2003).
20 China in relation to Tibet, Russia in relation to Chechnya
21 Rwanda 1994 as example
22 John Rawls, *Law of Peoples* (Cambridge, MA: Harvard University Press, 2001), 37.
23 For sophisticated depiction see Giles Gunn, *Beyond Solidarity: Pragmatism and Difference in a Globalized World* (Chicago: University of Chicago Press, 2001).
24 See Anne Norton, *Reflections on Political Identity* (Baltimore, MD: Johns Hopkins Press, 1988)
25 See Daniele Archibugi, David Held, and others, *Cosmopolitan Democracy: An Agenda for a New World Order* (Oxford, UK: Polity, 1995)
26 The American experience was one of multinational nationalism almost from its origins, and thus the myth of national unity is not ethnically grounded to nearly the same extent as in Europe.

Acknowledgements

I have relied to varying degrees on prior publications and conference or lecture presentations in the preparation of this volume. I take this opportunity to acknowledge this background.

Chapter 1 is derived from a chapter that is scheduled to appear in a volume edited by Chiba Shinn under the title *Toward a Grand Theory of Peace*, to be published by Edward Elgar at the end of 2008.

Chapter 2 is published in altered form with the permission of Eva Erman, the editor of a new journal, *Ethics and Global Politics*, where it will appear in 2008. The poem "Dreams" by Gunther Eich, from *Poetry*, April 2007, translated from German by Michael Hofmann, is reprinted with premission. All rights are reserved by Suhrkamp Verlag Frankfurt am Main.

Chapter 3 is based on an article published in the *Arab World Geographer*, 7 (1–2): 22–37, in 2004.

Chapter 4 is based on a paper initially presented at the European Centre of Culture, Delphi, Greece at a conference in 2005 celebrating the 2000th anniversary of the birth of democracy in ancient Greece.

Chapter 6 is based on a paper initially presented at a conference on comparative genocide held at UCLA in 2001.

Chapter 7 is an extensively revised version of a chapter in a volume, edited by Stephen Macedo, *Universal Jurisdiction: National Courts and the Prosecution of Serious Crimes under International Law*, published by the University of Pennsylvania Press in 2004.

Chapter 9 is an extensively revised version of a chapter in a volume, edited by Robert A. Wilson, *Human Rights in the 'War on Terror'*, published by Cambridge University Press in 2005.

Chapter 10 is an extensively revised version of a chapter in a volume, edited by Alison Brysk and Gerson Shafir, *National Insecurity and Human Rights: Democracies Debate Counterterrorism*, published by the University of California Press in 2007.

Chapter 11 is an extensively revised version of a chapter in a volume, edited by Julie Mertus and Jeffrey W. Helsing, *Human Rights and Conflict: Exploring the Links Between Rights, Law, and Peacebuilding*, published by United States Institute of Peace Press in 2006.

Chapter 14 is loosely based on an article that appeared in *Kosmos*, 6(1):31–32 (2005).

Index